POSTCARD HISTORY SERIES

Tarpon Springs

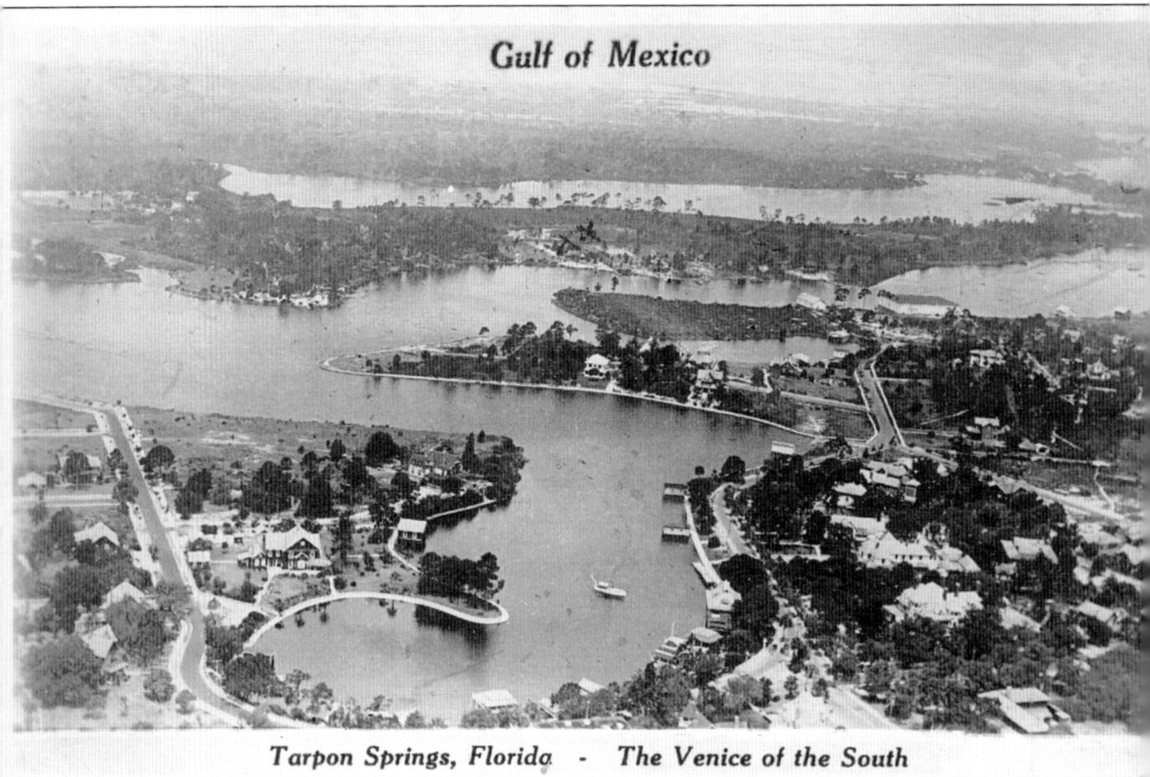

It is easy for one to see the quantity of water in the Tarpon Springs area. From the bayous to the river to the Gulf, water is part of the life of this city. It is what earned Tarpon Springs the nickname, the "Venice of the South." (Courtesy of Sam H. Mack.)

On the Front Cover: Sen. Ebenezer B. Hawkins's house is seen across Spring Bayou. In this c. 1920s postcard image, a fountain in operation and one of the many boathouses can be seen in the foreground. (Courtesy of Tarpon Springs Area Historical Society.)

On the Back Cover: The men posing for this photograph on a gaff rig hook sponging boat show it being used as a diving boat. The hard-helmet diver is in gear seated by the bow ladder. In 1911, Anthony Avgerinos was commissioned from Greece to support the industry. He was the first hard-helmet maker to add three windows—one on each side and one on the top. He also engineered the air hose to vent into the window and defog the glass. (Courtesy of Irene Giannaras Garner.)

POSTCARD HISTORY SERIES

Tarpon Springs

Carol Mountain

ARCADIA PUBLISHING

ISBN 978-0-7385-9118-6

Published by Arcadia Publishing
Charleston, South Carolina

Printed in the United States of America

Library of Congress Control Number: 2011934977

For all general information contact Arcadia Publishing at:
Telephone 843-853-2070
Fax 843-853-0044
E-mail sales@arcadiapublishing.com
For customer service and orders:
Toll-Free 1-888-313-2665

Visit us on the Internet at www.arcadiapublishing.com

This book is dedicated to those who went before us, leaving footprints on pathways for us to follow. It is dedicated to all who are in the present, walking along and creating their own footprints. And this book is dedicated to the future, to those who will create history anew by walking in paths that we cannot even imagine.

Contents

Acknowledgments

This book would not have been possible without the support and assistance of my best friends—those I already had, as well as those I made during the writing process. Edward Hoffman Sr. awakened a love of history through his most interesting accounts of the Tarpon Springs area. Hampton Dunn, another great man, had written local history books and collected postcards that proved an invaluable resource. I would like to thank and acknowledge the following people and institutions that have offered their collections of postcards for this book: Sam H. Mack; Jackie Payne; Hammond Salley; Irene Giannaras Garner; Pauline Pavlis Phillips; Shelly Rocktoff; Heritage Village Archives and Library; Tampa Bay History Center; Tarpon Springs Area Historical Society; and Hampton Dunn Collection of Florida Postcards, Special and Digital Collections, Tampa Library, University of South Florida. Unless otherwise noted, all postcards appear courtesy of the author. Several friends offered support in other ways, and I appreciate their ability and willingness to help: R.C. and Carolyn Gause; my sister, Elaine Shannon; Yasmin Pianese; Karyn Zervos; and Julie Keffalas. I would also like to thank Salvatore Miranda and the Tarpon Springs Public Library; Irene Jacobs and the Tarpon Springs City Clerk's Office; and Sharon Sawyer and the Tarpon Springs Area Historical Society.

Two special people in particular worked tirelessly. A special thank-you to my ultimate friend and supporter Lisa Sibley, whose beautiful photographic images are inspirational; she worked diligently to prepare each image used in this book. And lastly, thanks to my loving husband, Skip Mountain. Always there, always supportive, always encouraging, ready to help in whatever way possible—he is my inspiration.

Introduction

Water is the symbol of life, and life began in Tarpon Springs, centered on the water. Spanish explorers came up the Anclote River from the Gulf of Mexico to visit the Indian wells to restock their vessels with freshwater. Wealthy northerners came down the Atlantic coastline to build winter homes surrounding the bayous. Spongers came from Greece to harvest the abundant beds offshore. African Americans originally settled close to the river, which employed them through the fisheries and the lumber mills necessary to build the homes, businesses, and churches in town. The Greek Orthodox religion rejoices with the largest Epiphany festivities outside of Greece annually with a celebration of diving for the cross. This town's heritage is tied to the wealth of the water.

This story begins with the ultimate land deal of the 19th century. Florida needed to be rescued from an impending bankruptcy. The governor of Florida at the time, William D. Bloxham, advised his friend Hamilton Disston of a real deal: land at 25¢ an acre. Disston was a wealthy man and invested in Florida's future—specifically four million acres of it, in 1881. While saving Florida from financial ruin, Disston raised the ire of the common man. Many settlers had homesteaded their acreage, and now that there was a new owner of these previously state-owned lands, it became incumbent on them to purchase back their own lands. Naturally, because Disston was a shrewd investor, he was not selling the homesteaders back their land at the price he had bought the land for—he wanted five times more. And unless they wanted to lose everything they had worked for, they were obliged to pay his price.

A portion of Disston's four million acres was swamplands, which he was obligated to improve under his contract with Florida's Internal Improvement Fund. Vestiges of his dredging and filling, intended to create channels of waterfront property, remain today. However, much of the area that he chose in central Florida was good, dry land. Some of the land was in Hillsborough County that, back then, included Pinellas County. In 1882, he deeded over about 9,500 acres to the Lake Butler Villa Company. At that time, Lake Tarpon was called Lake Butler. Anson P.K. Safford, the president of the company, was previously the governor of the Arizona Territory. Safford gave generously in Arizona and would also do so in Florida. Having little formal schooling himself, he was a proponent of a free school system and would be credited with founding the Arizona public school system. In Tarpon Springs, he gave much to the community, including land for many churches. In 1883, he brought his family with him, including his third wife, Soledad (Bonillas) Safford, his daughter Margarita, and his adopted daughter and son, Gladys and Leandro. A governess, known as "Auntie Sage," was with them. Anson's sister, Dr. Mary J. Safford, Florida's first female physician and the first doctor in Tarpon Springs, also accompanied the family on their relocation. Their house, originally a one-story home, was on the corner of Spring and Grand Boulevards at one time. Soledad (Bonillas) Safford had it moved off of the water, further back on the property after Anson passed away. She sold the more valuable land, and the Clemson mansion was built there. The governor's house is now on Parkin Court. After Anson P.K. Safford died, his widow, Soledad, married William W. Parkin. Once again a widow, she married Salvador F. Martin. Anson, Mary, Soledad, and her second husband, William, are buried in the family plot at Cycadia Cemetery in Tarpon Springs.

Tarpon Springs was surveyed and plotted by John W. Walton in 1883. Tarpon Avenue went from the downtown area out to Lake Butler. It was thought that people would want to purchase land on the freshwater lake, but in actuality it was a rough road. Most people decided to settle closer to the bayous.

Walter and Amelia Meres came to town in the early 1880s. They managed the Tropical Hotel, later named the Ferns. Amelia, or "Mother Meres," as she became known, was a kind-hearted woman who took care of her hotel guests just like they were family. She had a green thumb and provided flowers for all the events and funeral services in town. Their son Ernest Meres, along with John Cheney, would found the Sponge Exchange in 1907.

The year 1887 was very important for Tarpon Springs. The residents voted to incorporate into a city, the Orange Belt Railroad chugged along Safford Avenue, and the federal government put a lighthouse on Anclote Key. Tarpon Springs was the first city to incorporate in what is now Pinellas County. In 1900, according to the US Census Bureau, Tarpon Springs had 541 people. In 1910, the city enjoyed a population of 2,212—a tremendous growth due in part to Greek spongers immigrating into the city. The coming of the railroad enabled commodities to be transported and established supporting industries such as the hotel and dining commerce, the hack trade, local real estate speculators, shopping, and the quick, convenient, and somewhat comfortable means of travel. It served as a major link to the outside world, providing the capability to travel and communicate. The train depot was a place for people to gather and learn and discuss the happenings outside of their community. Built in 1909, the depot was segregated with separate waiting rooms and entrances. It now serves as the home for the Tarpon Springs Area Historical Society and their Depot Museum. The railroad corridor (Safford Avenue) has since been replaced by the Pinellas Trail, which runs a total of 50 miles long. Recognized as one of the best trail systems in the United States, it has been inducted into the Rail-Trail Hall of Fame. What once transported and connected people through travel by train remains a pathway to link people. The Anclote Key Lighthouse provided a beacon to the seafaring travelers and the incoming shipping, fishing, and sponge-diving boats. With its lighthouse keeper, assistant, and their families living on the island, it became a friendly destination for picnics and outings. Robert E. Meyer was the first lighthouse keeper to live on the island, and he did so for 35 years. His ancestors established the settlement at Anclote on the north side of the river, west of Tarpon Springs. The lighthouse was decommissioned and fell into a state of ruin, but with a core of dedicated volunteers and activists is now once again lit. It still is a destination for social gatherings.

The Pinellas Peninsula was neglected by its county of Hillsborough. Taxes were sent in, but it seemed that the improvements were primarily aiding the city of Tampa. A campaign began to break away and establish the county of Pinellas, which officially happened January 1, 1912. Now, good hard roads were built linking cities on the peninsula. Granville Edwin Noblit Sr. became known as the "daddy of Pinellas County" and the father of good roads. This was because of his unyielding dedication in creating the county and his ability to see the need for roads. He believed roads, along with the railroads and waterways, were what would make Florida the winter playground of the nation. And he was right.

The city of Tarpon Springs became the major sponging industry heart of the world. John Cheyney joined forces with John Cocoris, and the two radically changed the method of sponging in the Gulf of Mexico. Previously, a two-man crew would go out in a smaller boat; one would row while the other used a long pole with a hook on the end to harvest sponge from the floor of the Gulf, where they were growing attached to a hard surface. This limited the depth at which the sponges could be gathered to approximately 15 to 40 feet. Hard-helmet diving was in use in Greece. A diver was outfitted in a dive suit complete with a helmet and air supplied by a mechanical pump. Cocoris had experience in this and, with Cheyney's backing, they brought over Greek divers to pluck the abundant growth of sponge in the Gulf waters. The hardworking, dedicated men developed the industry, and Tarpon Springs became known as the Sponge Capital of the World. Along with the divers came their families, customs, religion, and food. One cannot visit the city without feeling the warmth and impact of these people.

Postcards have been in use since the mid-1800s, offering a glimpse of what the past held as it was unfolding. Their messages convey events in everyday life, and their images provide documentation of structures, events, prevailing viewpoints, and social formation.

This book offers a view of the history of this dynamic city. Tarpon Springs, for all of its changes, has remained a genuine relic. Its story is revealed in the following pages, based upon the picturesque postcard images available. Enjoy this documentary of the rare gem known as Tarpon Springs.

One

We Have Just Arrived

The earliest known settlers in the area surrounding Tarpon Springs were a tough group of pioneers. They had to travel through primitive, heavily forested areas of uncharted territory. It was possible to take the railroad to Cedar Key and then travel by boat to the Pinellas Peninsula. Then pathways, which developed into rough sandy roads, were the way to reach inland areas. An alternate way to come into what would be known as Tarpon Springs was by water. In the late 19th century, frontier settlers arrived this way, building their cabins by the bayous. However, the first settlement was upriver at Anclote where the two Meyer brothers brought their families. This settlement grew to include the essentials of a town such as a post office, school, and general store. But even despite that, Tarpon Springs became the location of the city, primarily due to the railroad's arrival. In 1876, a father and his daughter, A.W. Ormand and Mary, arrived by boat and built their cabin up river on a bayou. Joshua Boyer arrived from Nassau, visited with the Ormands, and decided to stay. The rest, one might say, is history.

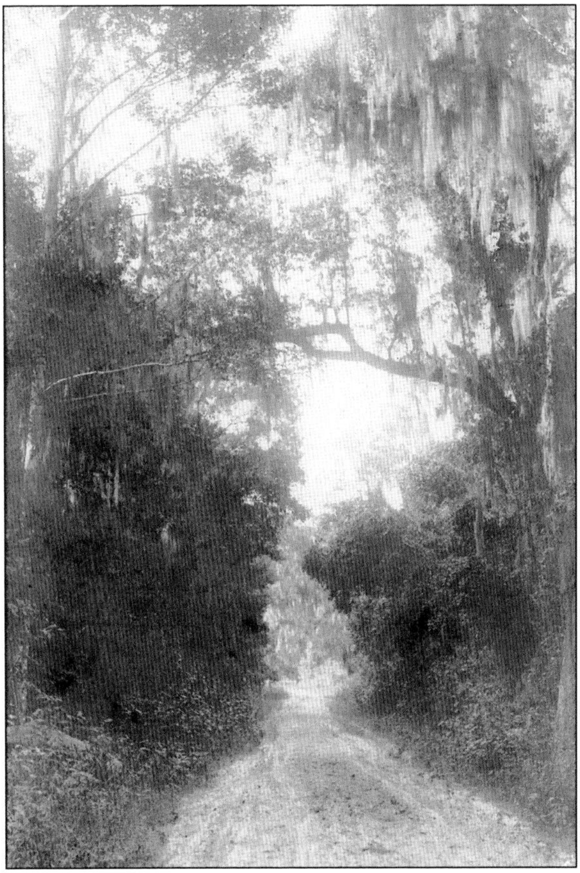

When driving into the town of Tarpon Springs from either north or south on Alternate 19, it is difficult for one to image a time when the busy thoroughfare was a scenic one-lane sand road with a forested overhang. This postcard, photographed by C.C. Allen of St. Petersburg, documents the entrance to the city when travel by horse and buggy was commonplace. (Courtesy of Tarpon Springs Area Historical Society.)

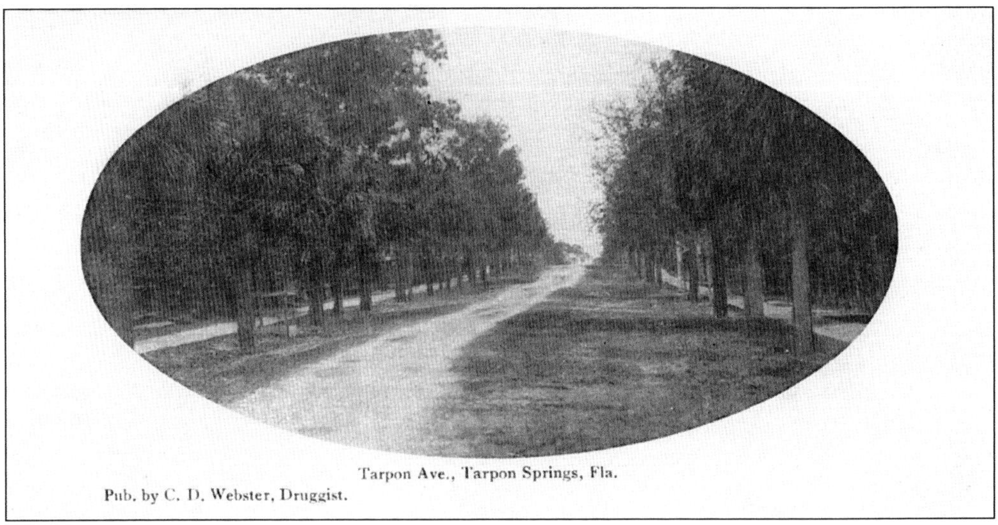

Looking down the east–west main street of Tarpon Avenue, a sand road is visible. The early wooden board sidewalks are in place and the road is lined with palm trees and an occasional oak. This card was printed for Charles Dix Webster, a paymaster in the Union army. He was one of Tarpon's earliest residents and the town druggist. Founded in 1886, his business was named the Old Reliable Drugstore. (Courtesy of Tarpon Springs Area Historical Society.)

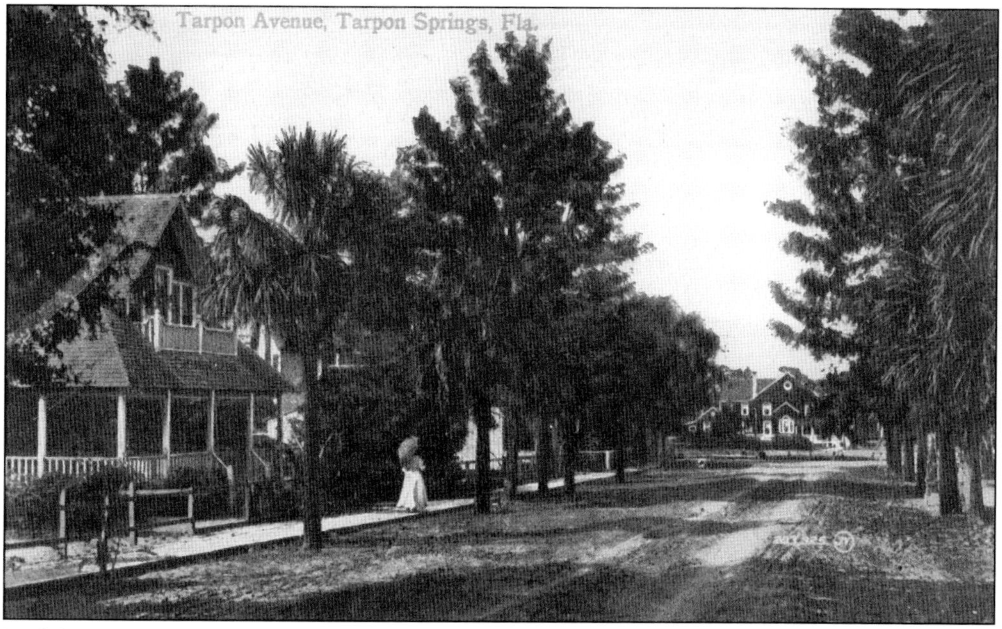

In this c. 1909 postcard, the lady with the parasol is headed west on Tarpon Avenue, strolling toward Spring Bayou. This first block off the water served as the main downtown area prior to the arrival of the railroad, after which the business district located closer to the train depot, the preferred travel and shipping destination. The home visible at the end of the street is directly across Spring Bayou. (Courtesy of Jackie Payne.)

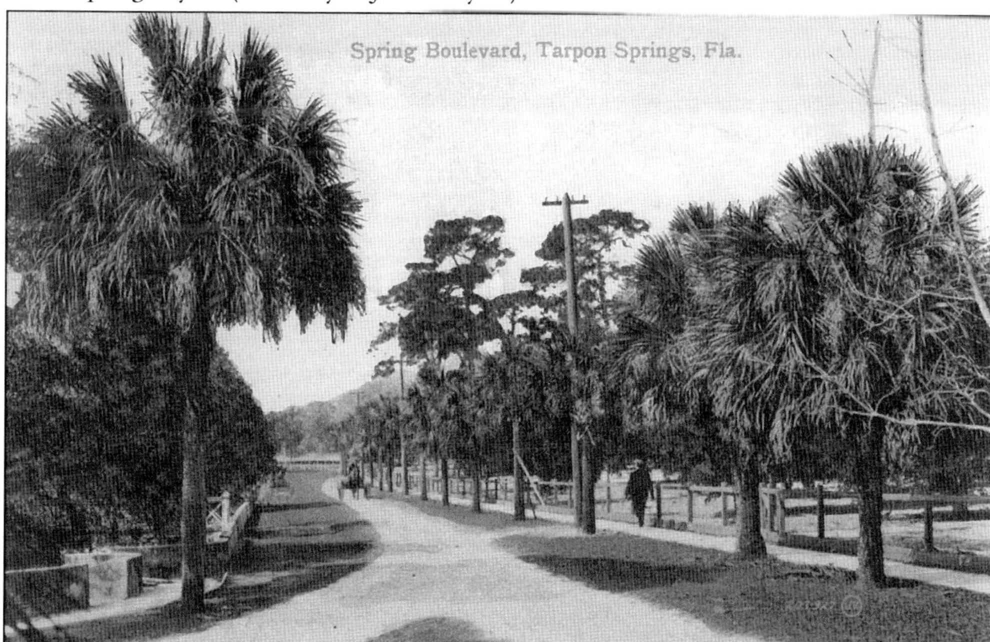

The three-way intersection in the road could be the corner of what is now the junction of Spring Boulevard, Orange Street, and Grand Boulevard. Visitors to the area may find it difficult to follow directions to their destinations, since many of the roads follow the waterway's curves. (Courtesy of Jackie Payne.)

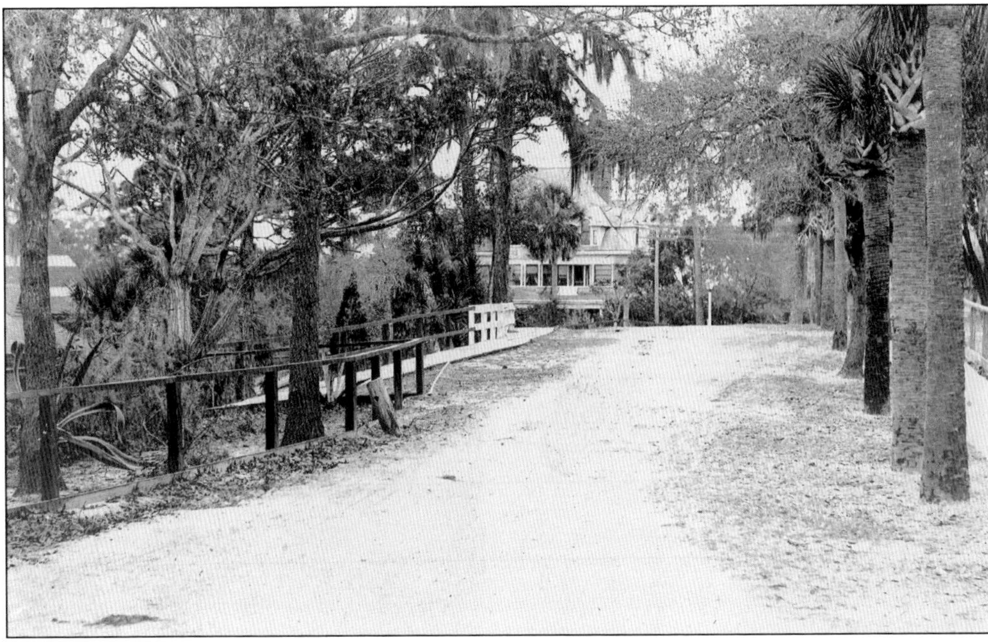

Facing the opposite direction of the three-way junction on the previous page, this street is heading north. The home in the background was that of George Clemson, a wealthy New Yorker who made his fortune in hacksaw blades. Built in 1902 at a cost of $70,000, this house was the biggest home on the bayou and still remains an impressive home. Note the wood hand railings along the walkway. (Courtesy of Tarpon Springs Area Historical Society.)

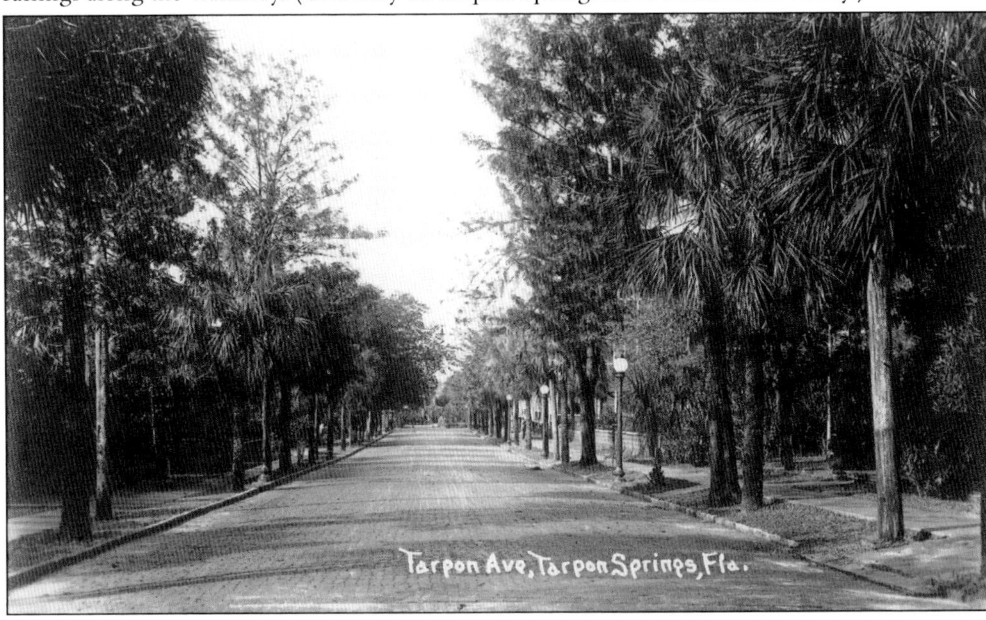

In this postcard looking west down Tarpon Avenue, the sand street has been replaced with paving bricks. Many of the streets in Tarpon Springs remain brick, a historical reminder of days gone by. The light posts have been replaced with fiberglass versions that are similar in style. The old-fashioned round globes are now of the acorn type. The Tarpon Inn is barely visible on the right behind the concrete block fence. (Courtesy of Jackie Payne.)

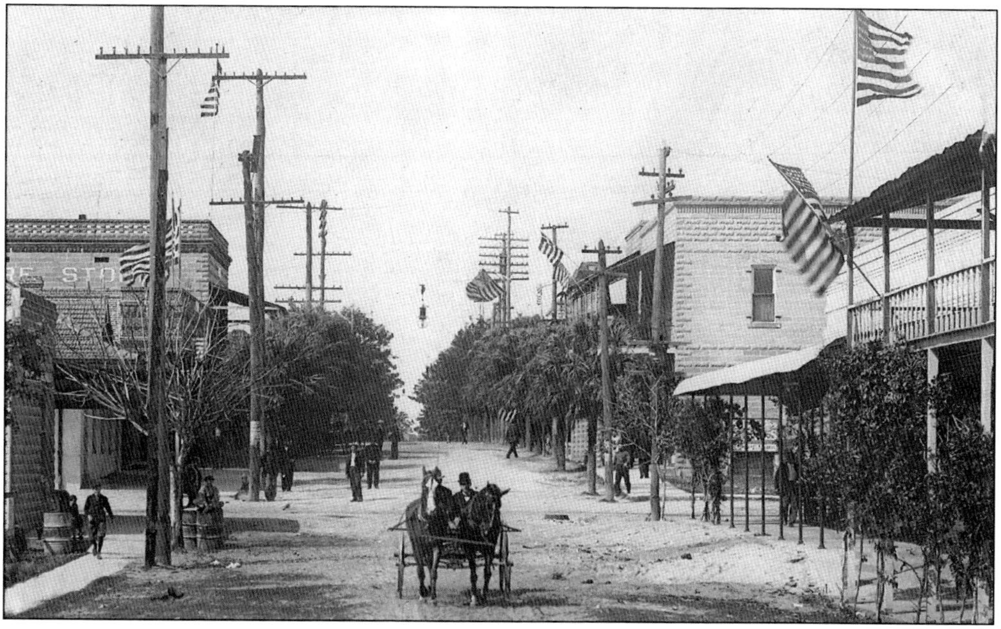

Patriotism runs high in 1908 as town physician Dr. A.P. Albaugh drives his team and buggy down flag-decorated Tarpon Avenue. He was one of the founding members of the Pinellas County Medical Association and served on the city council. The first physician to arrive was Dr. Mary Safford, Florida's first female physician, in 1883. (Courtesy of Tarpon Springs Area Historical Society.)

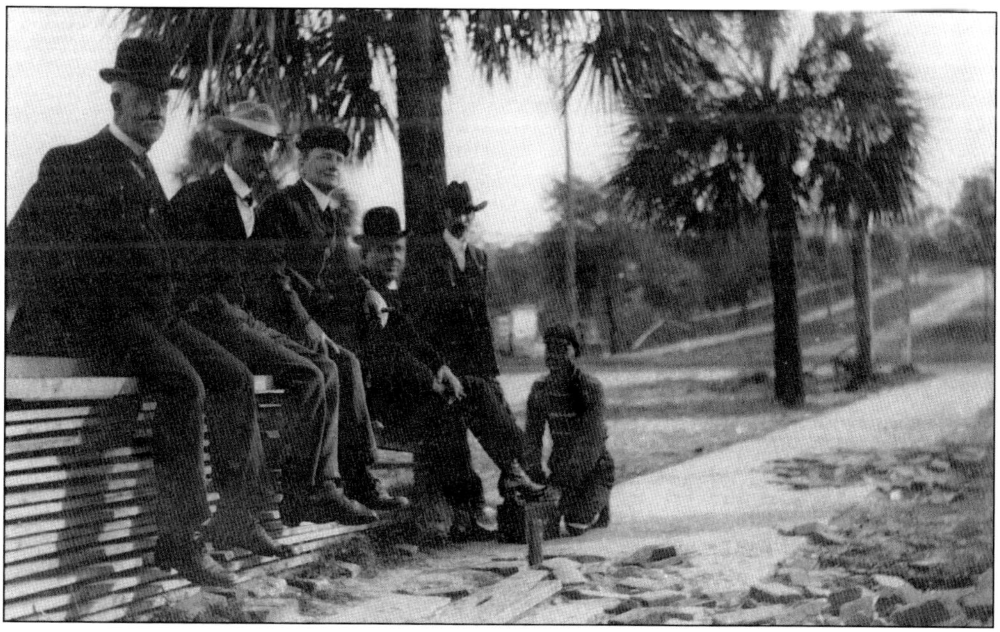

A stack of lumber provides a convenient seat for four of these men. Dirt from dug-up sidewalk pavers probably covered their shoes, but this boot polisher was making them shine like new. Ernest Meres, who founded the Tarpon Springs Sponge Exchange along with John Cheyney, is seated second from left. Dr. William Morgan stands at the right. The others are unidentified. (Courtesy of Hammond Salley.)

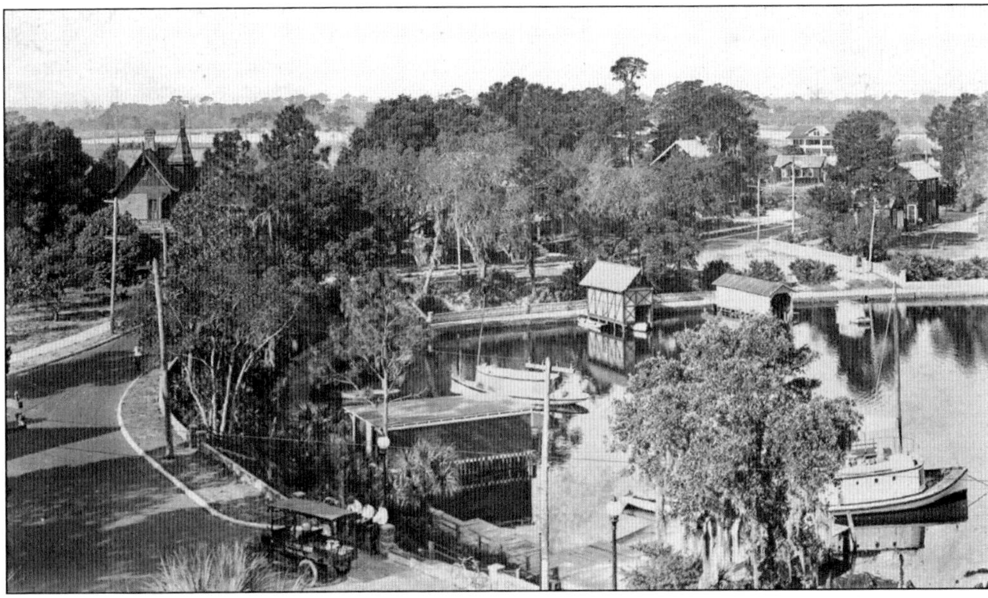

In this postcard of Spring Bayou, other bayous can be seen above and through treetops. A work truck has stopped, allowing three men in white shirts to visit as they sit on a concrete retaining wall. Concrete was chosen for its durability to make the walkways, retaining walls, and seawalls. The original wooden sidewalks and railings lining the bayou were in need of repair by 1896. (Courtesy of Tarpon Springs Area Historical Society.)

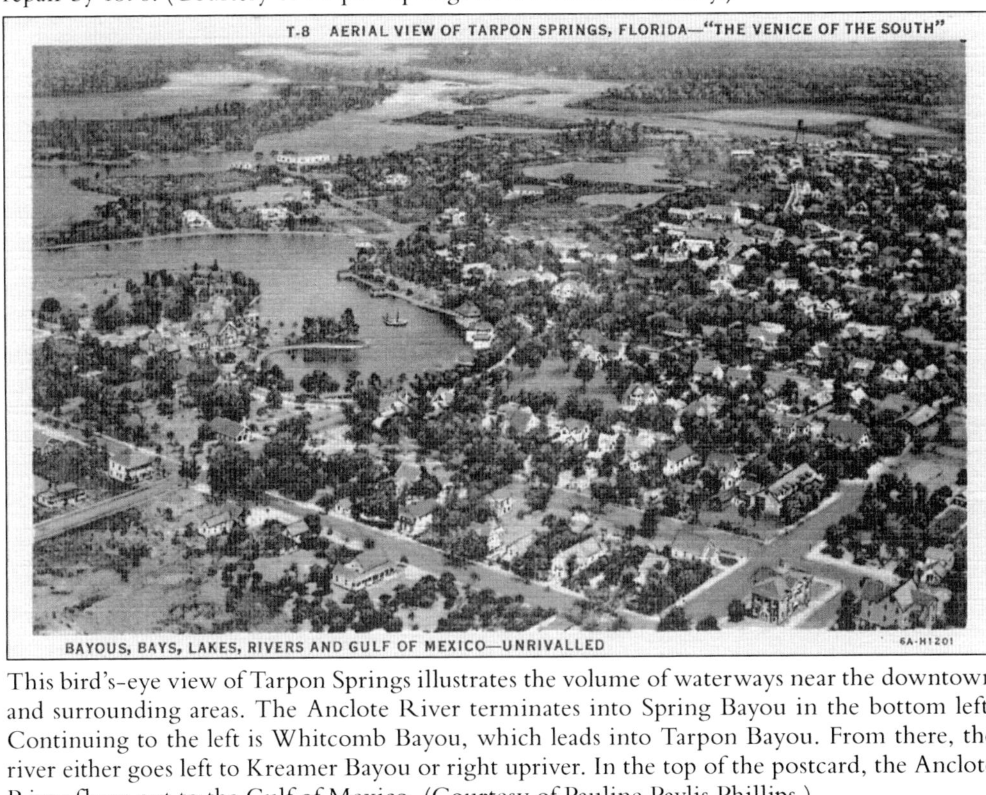

This bird's-eye view of Tarpon Springs illustrates the volume of waterways near the downtown and surrounding areas. The Anclote River terminates into Spring Bayou in the bottom left. Continuing to the left is Whitcomb Bayou, which leads into Tarpon Bayou. From there, the river either goes left to Kreamer Bayou or right upriver. In the top of the postcard, the Anclote River flows out to the Gulf of Mexico. (Courtesy of Pauline Pavlis Phillips.)

This postcard, postmarked in 1913, identifies Spring Boulevard as Tarpon Springs Boulevard. Boathouses rim the bayou. Balmy breezes sift through aesthetically spaced palm trees, which may have been planted to beautify and provide a meager amount of shade for pedestrians. (Courtesy of Hampton Dunn Collection of Florida Postcards, Special and Digital Collections, Tampa Library, University of South Florida.)

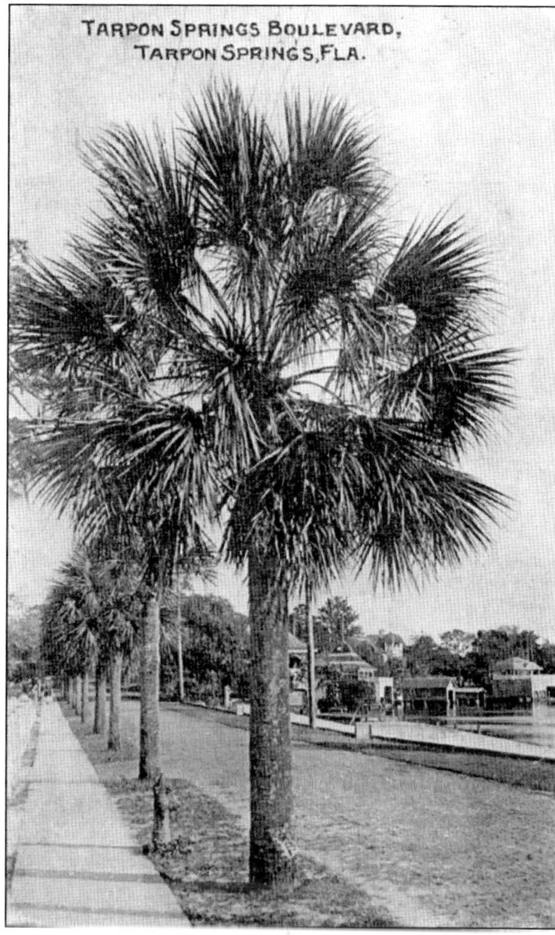

Governor Safford donated land for many churches and built the first small schoolhouse, which was replaced by this one. On February 12, 1887, a very important meeting took place in this schoolhouse. A vote was taken to incorporate Tarpon Springs as a city of what was then Hillsborough County. Anson P.K. Safford was elected as one of the five aldermen. He was known as one of the founders of the city and was previously the territorial governor of Arizona and the founder of the Arizona public school system. (Courtesy of Jackie Payne.)

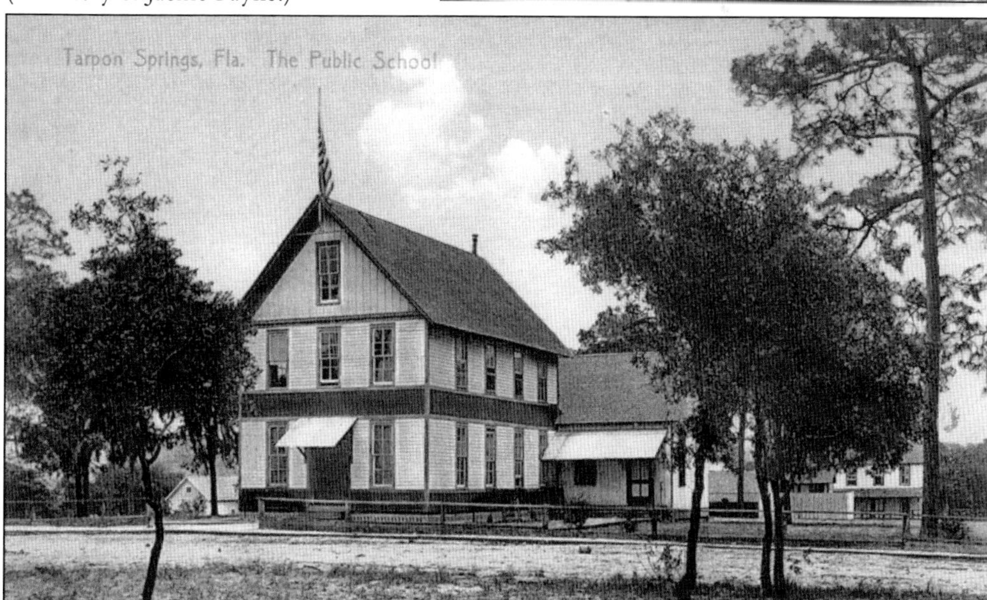

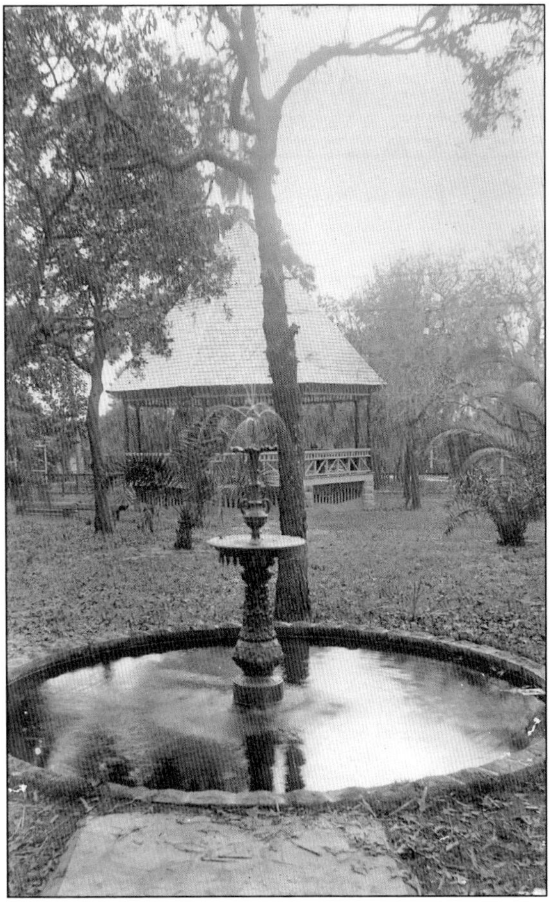

This early view of the southeast corner of Tarpon and Pinellas Avenues is a city parking lot that holds a beautiful history. Residents would meet at the downtown park to enjoy the refreshing sounds of the fountain and the melodious orchestrations from the band shell, which replaced the gazebo. Bohumir Kryl's band played free daily concerts during the winter months of the 1920s. (Courtesy of Hammond Salley.)

Amelia (Petzold) "Mother Meres" and her husband, Walter, ran the first lodging houses in the city. Honored posthumously in 1926, this urn, inscribed with "Mother Meres," was placed in her former garden. She donated her property at the southeast corner of Tarpon and Pinellas Avenues to the city for the park, pictured here. A self-taught gardener and a trained florist, she provided arrangements for all of the city's events. (Courtesy of Sam H. Mack.)

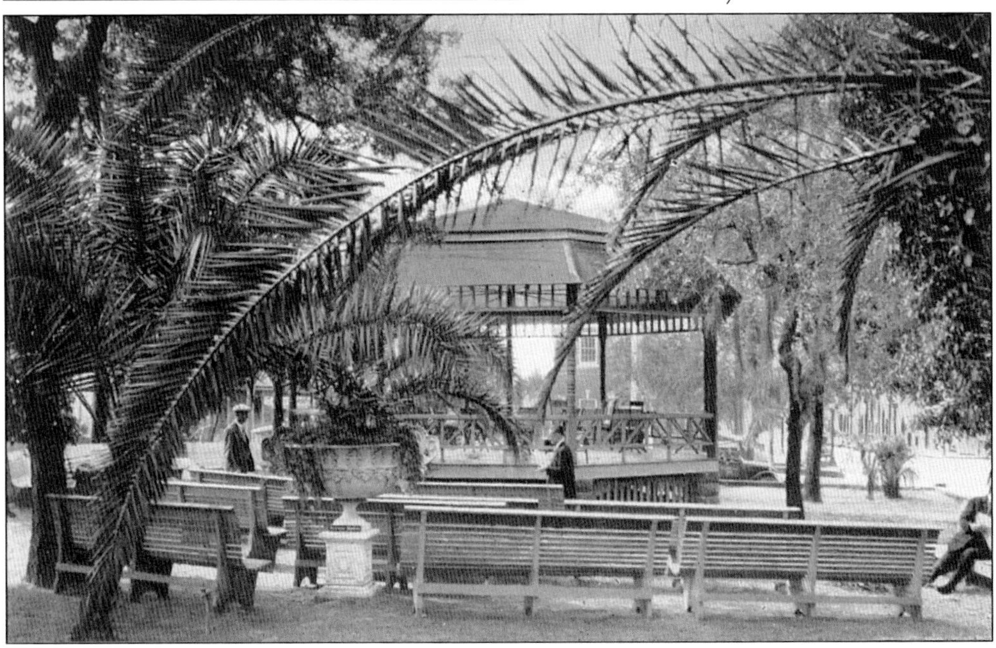

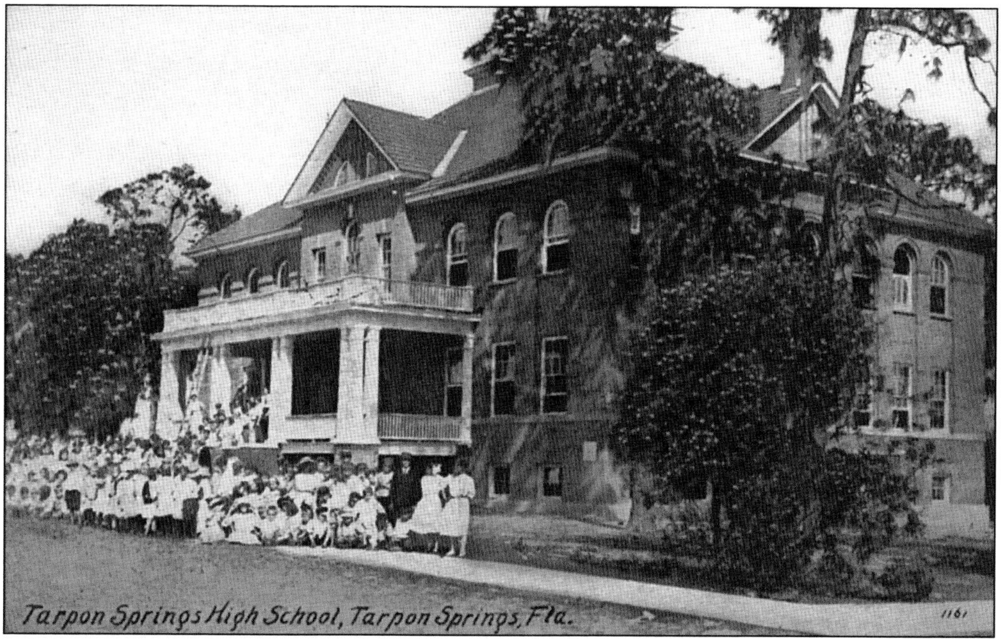

A two-story wood schoolhouse originally stood between Pinellas Avenue and Hibiscus Street north of Cypress Street. It was replaced by this building, which is identified in the postcard as Tarpon Springs High School though it probably served as an all-grade school in its early years. Later, it would be used as the elementary school; it no longer exists. Similar in style, the high school, constructed in 1927 and located on East Pine Street, is now used as the city hall. On October 11, 1990, it was added to the US National Register of Historic Places. (Courtesy of Sam H. Mack.)

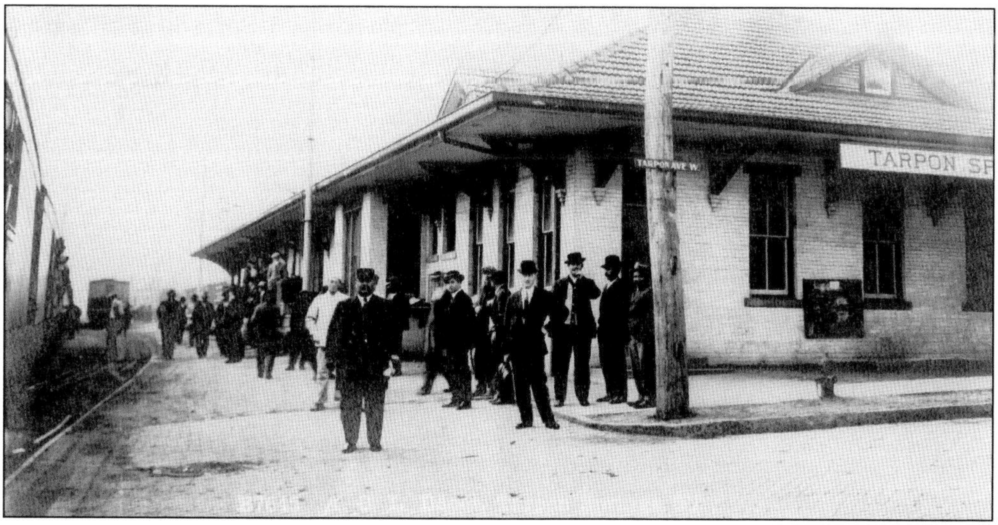

Tarpon Springs welcomed the arrival of Peter A. Demen's narrow-gauge Orange Belt Railroad in 1887. With a transfer in Sanford from the Atlantic Coast Line, passengers from New York could reach Tarpon Springs in 36 hours. This train depot, located at the corner of Tarpon Avenue and Safford Avenue, is made of brick with a clay tile roof. It replaced the original wooden depot, located a block south on Safford Avenue and Court Street, which burned to the ground in a 1908 fire. (Courtesy of Heritage Village.)

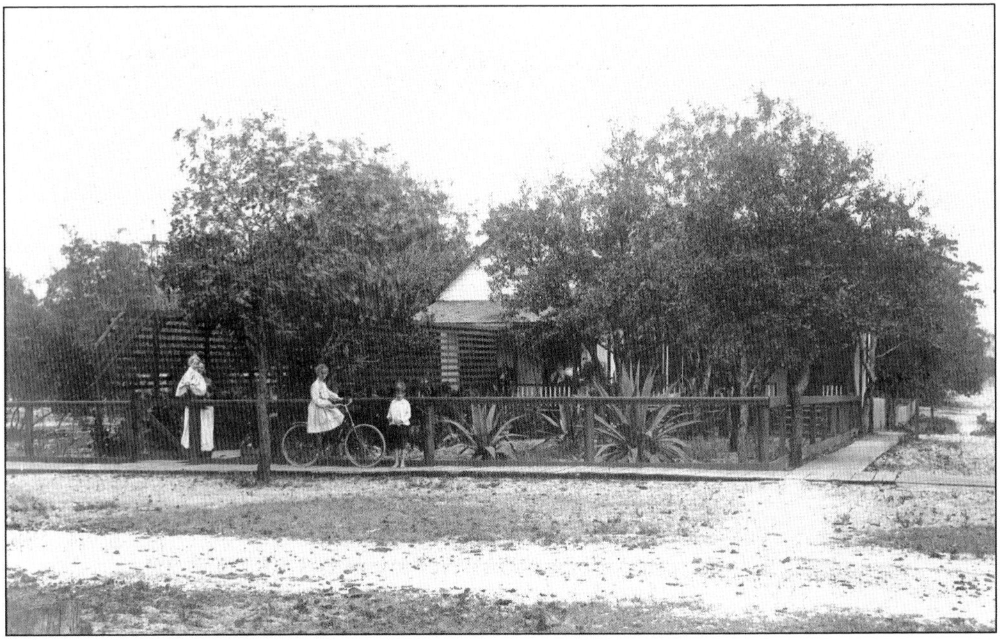

A century plant in the front yard of this house is taller than Amelia Petzold Meres. Emily is being held by Mother Meres, her grandmother. Granddaughter Katherine is riding her bicycle on the wood plank sidewalk, while grandson Walter looks on. One of the first ordinances passed after Tarpon Springs was incorporated dealt with keeping larger livestock off of city streets. Perhaps that was the purpose of the wood-and-wire fence. (Courtesy of Hammond Salley.)

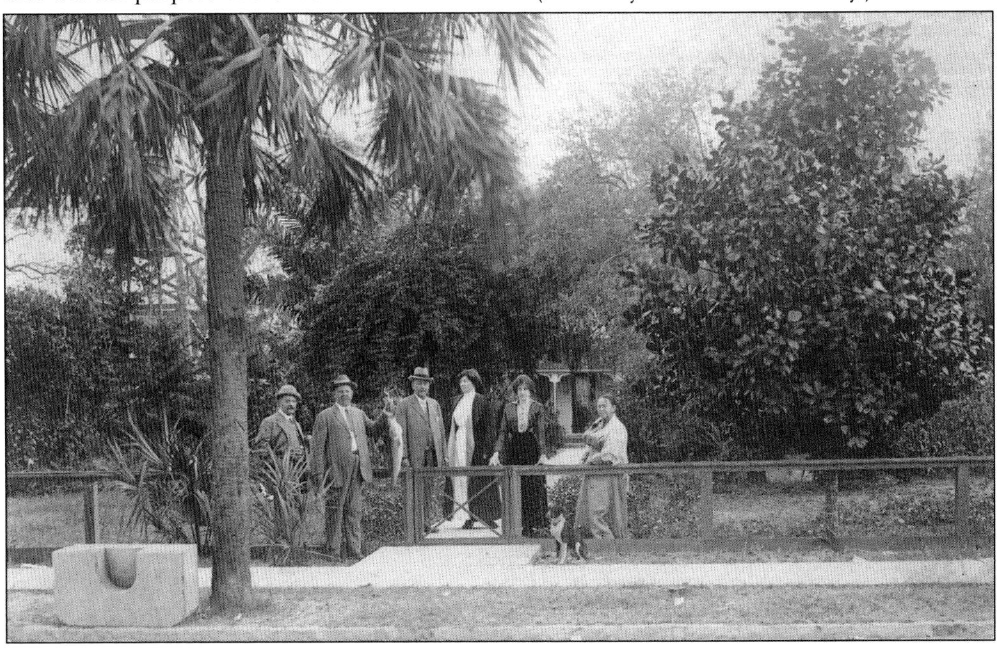

This postcard was taken later than the one above, as evidenced by the concrete sidewalk. Here, Mother Meres, right, is visiting with unidentified people in front of her house. Two gentlemen on the left appear to be returning with supper. A windmill can be seen behind the trees to the left of the palm. (Courtesy of Hammond Salley.)

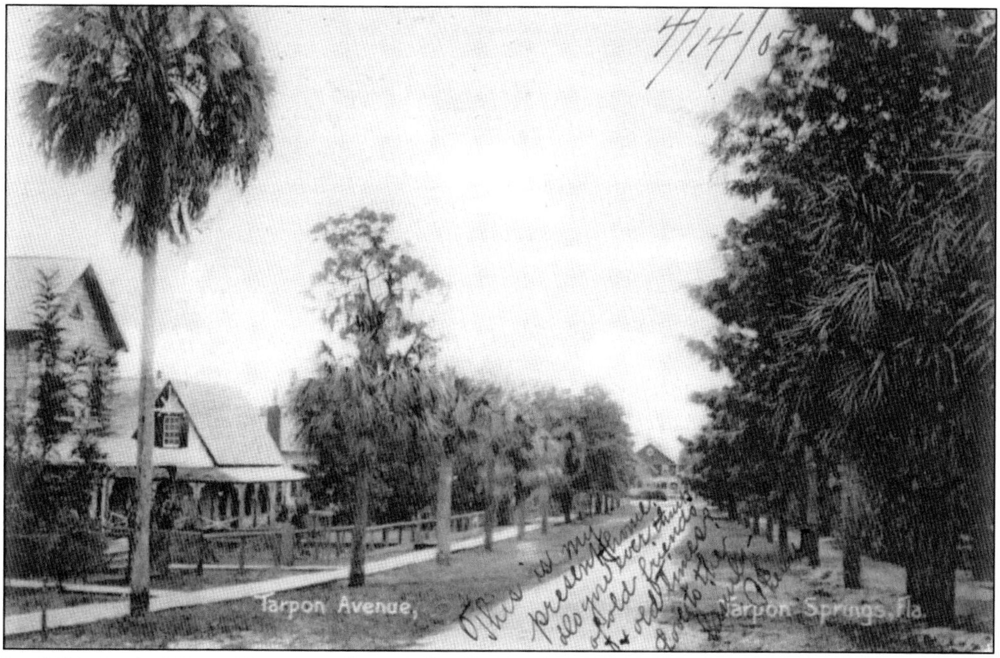

In 1907, the US Postal Service allowed divided back postcards so that the address and message could be written on the same side of the card, leaving the front to be used entirely as an image; however, this card was published prior to this change. The message written on the front reads, "This is my present home. Do you ever think of old friends and old times? Love to the family, Avery." (Courtesy of Sam H. Mack.)

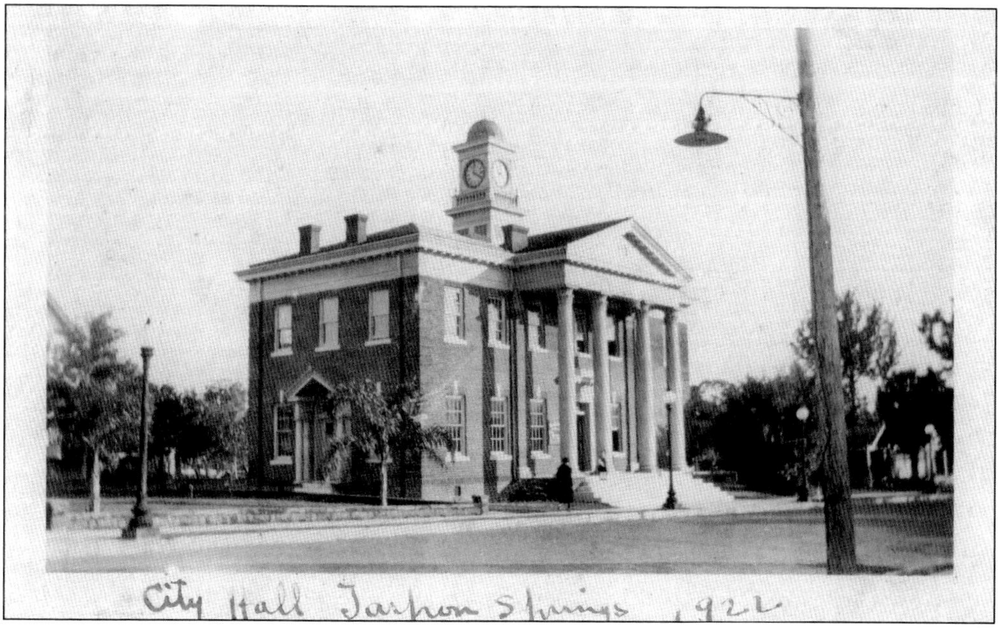

This building on South Pinellas Avenue, constructed in 1915 in the Classical Revival style, functioned as city hall. In this 1922 postcard, the police station was located on the near side of the building and the fire department operated on the far or south side. Now the building serves as the Tarpon Springs Cultural Center. (Courtesy of Tarpon Springs Area Historical Society.)

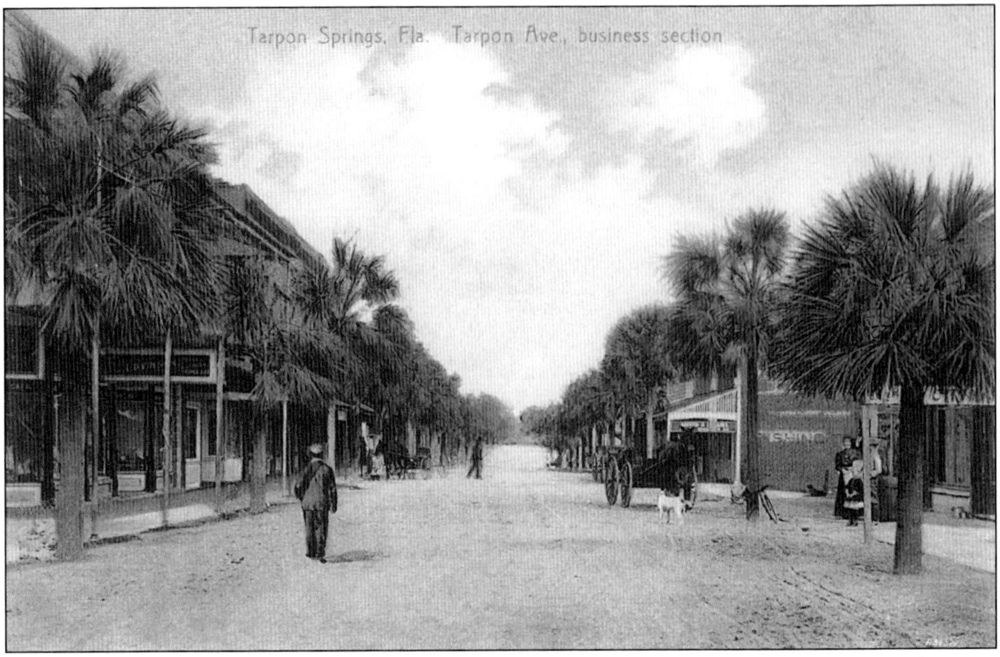

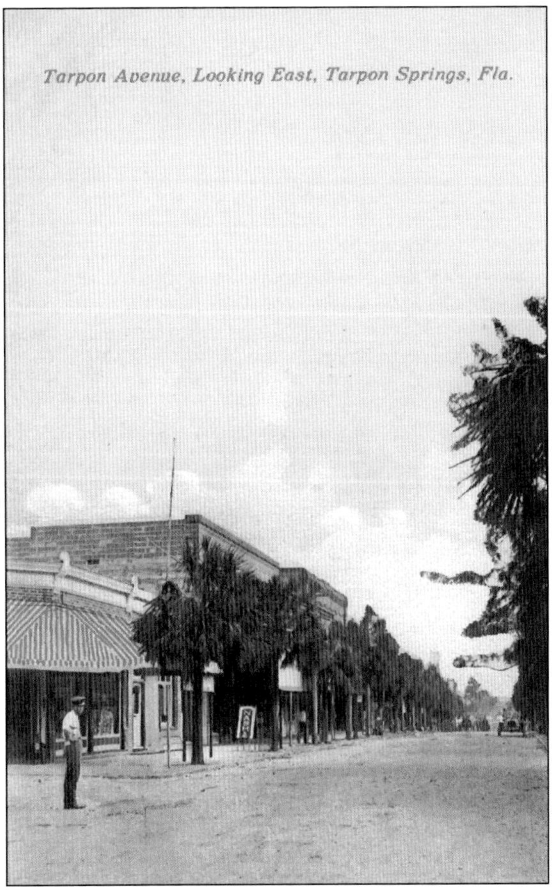

These two views of downtown face east on Tarpon Avenue. In the earlier image above, the storefront on the left with a black overhang is L.D. (Levin Denton) Vinson's Department Store. His brother James was first to arrive around 1884. L.D. joined him in business in 1890, then took over after James returned to Tallahassee. The store also sold coffins, and L.D. became a certified embalmer in 1894. Vinson Funeral Home, located further east on Tarpon Avenue, is still a family business. Pioneer C.L. Webster was buried at Cycadia Cemetery before the cemetery in Tarpon Springs was officially established. Viola Beekman donated the land in 1887. Rose Cemetery, the oldest African American cemetery in Pinellas County, is located east of Cycadia Cemetery across the street on Jasmine Avenue. It was established in the early 1900s as a segregated cemetery. Although its earliest marked burial is 1904, it is generally believed that there are older gravesites. (Above, courtesy of Jackie Payne; below, courtesy of Sam H. Mack.)

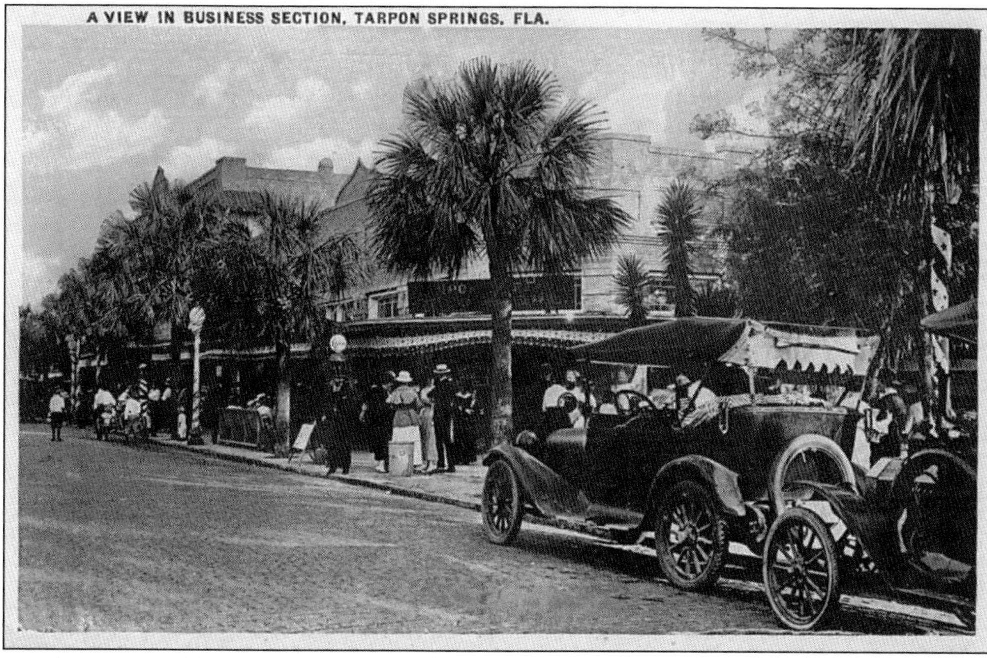

Looking east on Tarpon Avenue, the sidewalk bustles with activity in the c. 1920s postcard above. Just past the automobile is Tarpon Springs Drug Store. Later, this was known as Baynard Drug Company, below, where a soda jerk would fix milkshakes and sundaes from scratch and make sodas with syrup from a pump dispenser and carbonated water. The building was later torn down and became part of the city parking lot where Mother Meres's garden and home were previously located. In 1906, a special election was to be held to vote on an agreement allowing George Fernald and his associates to furnish electric lights. He, along with Ernest Meres and Bert Lauden, operated the ice factory and electric plant. (Courtesy of Jackie Payne.)

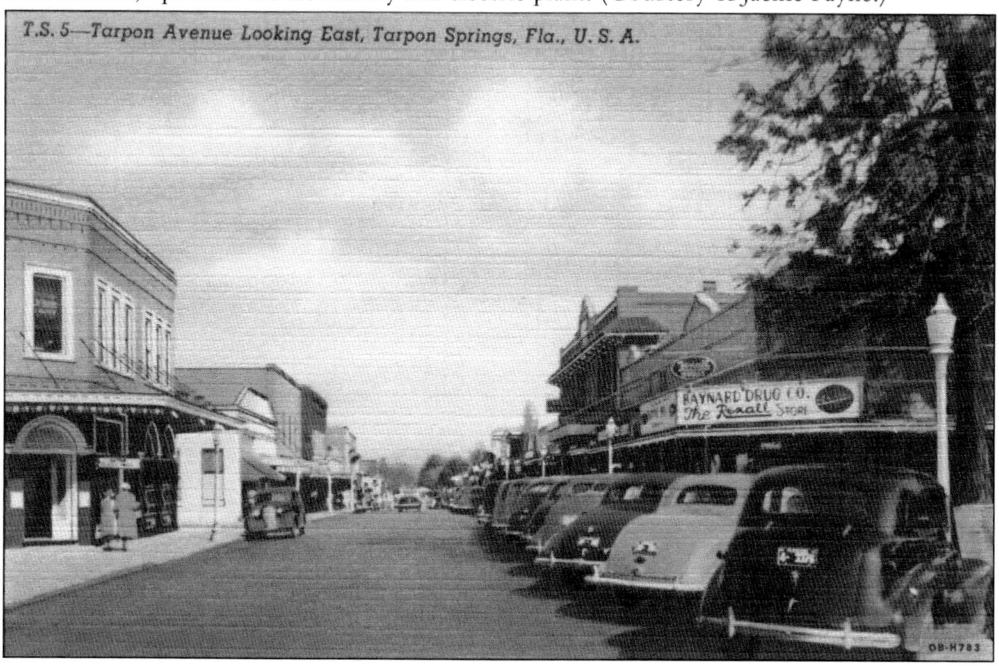

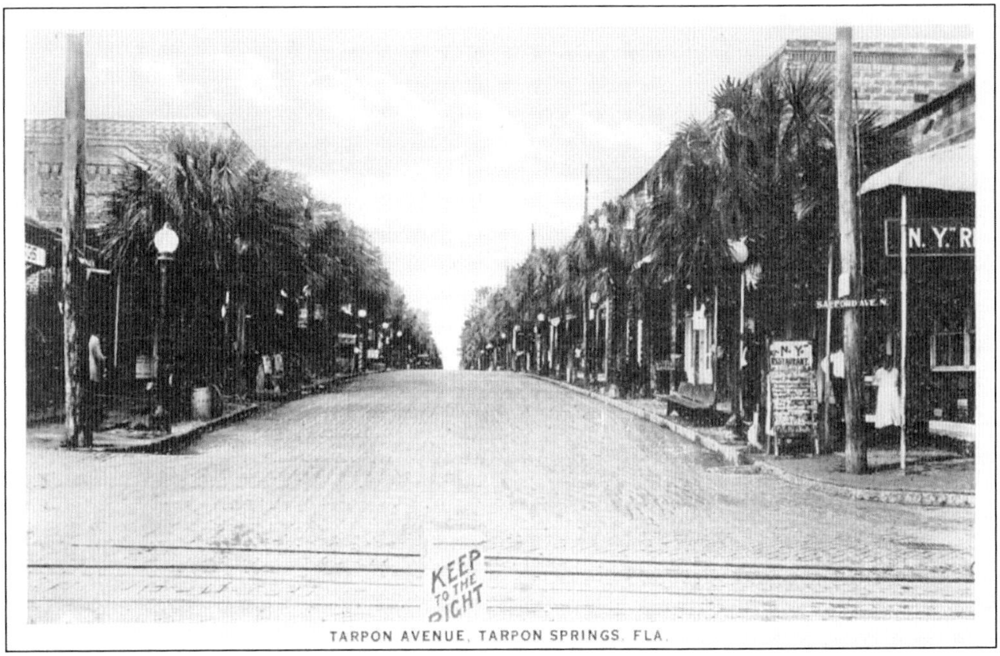

This photograph of Tarpon Avenue's business district must have been taken before or after the day's activities, due to the noticeable lack of people and traffic. Several postcard publishers used this same photograph and deleted out detracting items such as the Safford Avenue North sign and electric post next to the "N.Y. Restaurant" signboard, all or parts of the electric poles, and the railroad tracks at the bottom along with the "Keep to the Right" sign. The card above shows the truest version except for the clouds, which the artist took liberty of adding. (Above, courtesy of Tampa Bay History Center; below, courtesy of Sam H. Mack.)

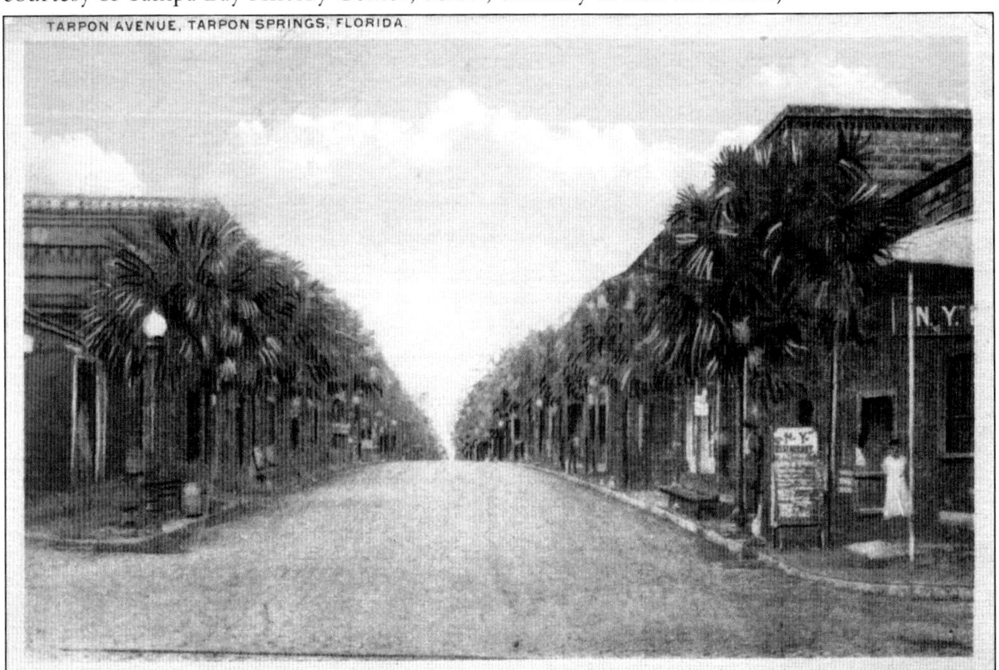

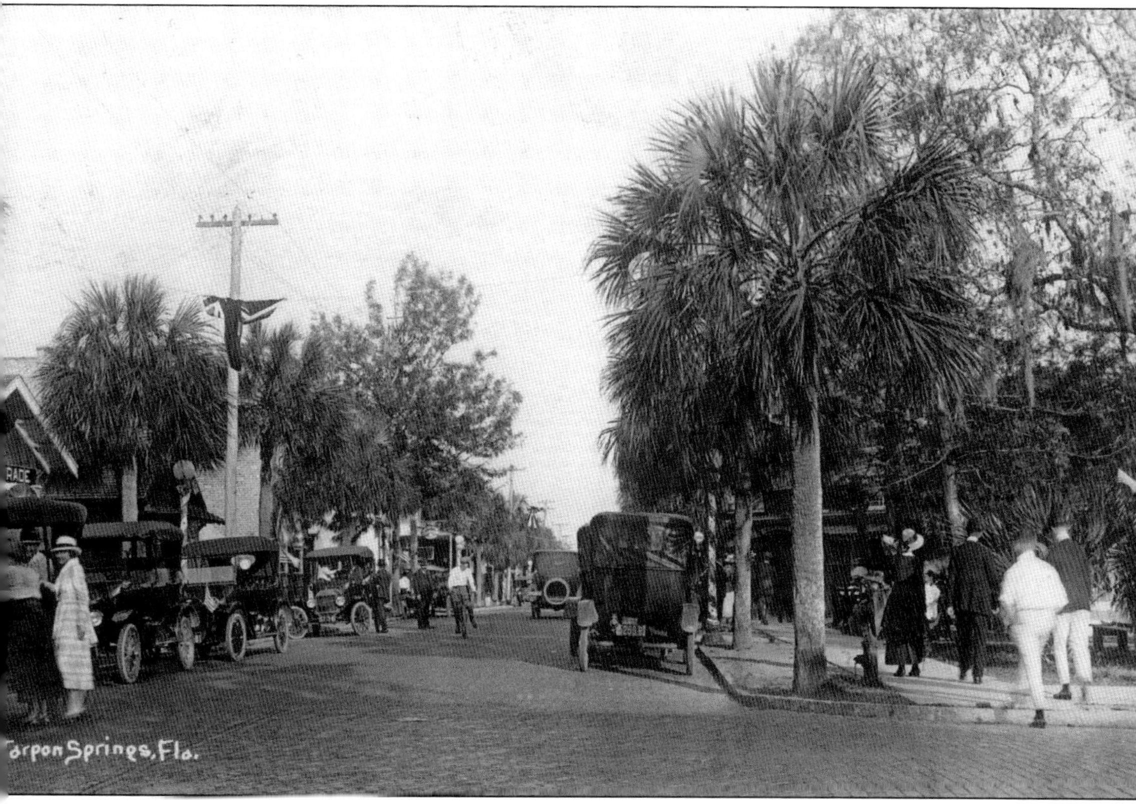

In what must be a celebratory occasion, the corner of Tarpon Avenue and Citron Street, which later became Pinellas Avenue, is shown as a bustling downtown. Flags are flying as people crowd the sidewalks and automobile-lined streets. The Board of Trade building, constructed in 1915, can be seen to the far left. The importance of tourism was identified early in Tarpon Springs. The message on the back of this card reads, "All here in auto—38 miles away—for dinner, and to see the sponge fisheries and fleet. Love ride on brick road, oranges on trees." (Courtesy of Sam H. Mack.)

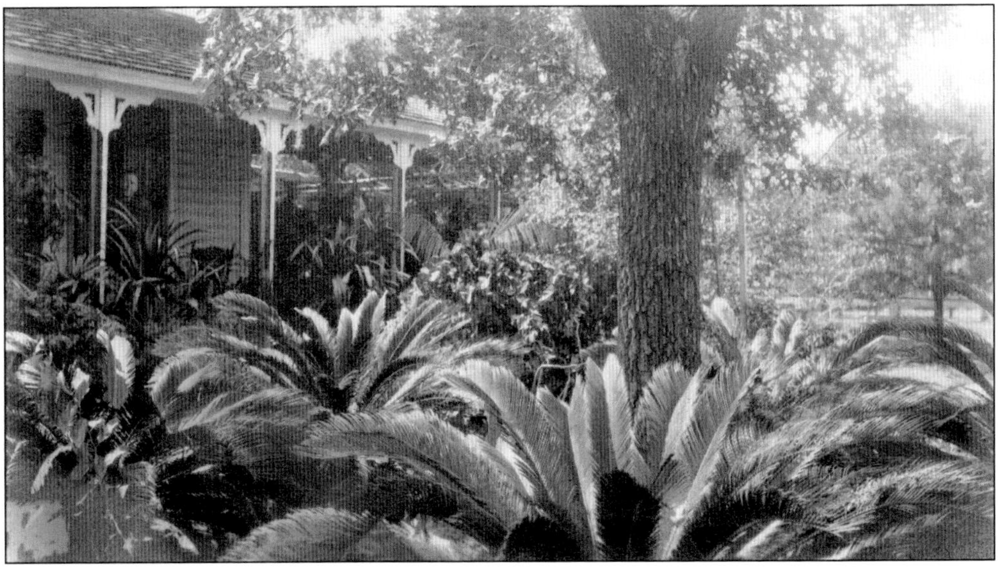

These cycad palms were planted by Amelia Petzold Meres in her front yard. Mother Meres also planted cycads along the entrance to Cycadia Cemetery and cared for it with Viola (Keeney) Beekman. The cycads were lost in a freeze but replaced with oleanders, seen lining the original entrance on the west side of the cemetery off of Tarpon Springs Road. (Courtesy of Hammond Salley.)

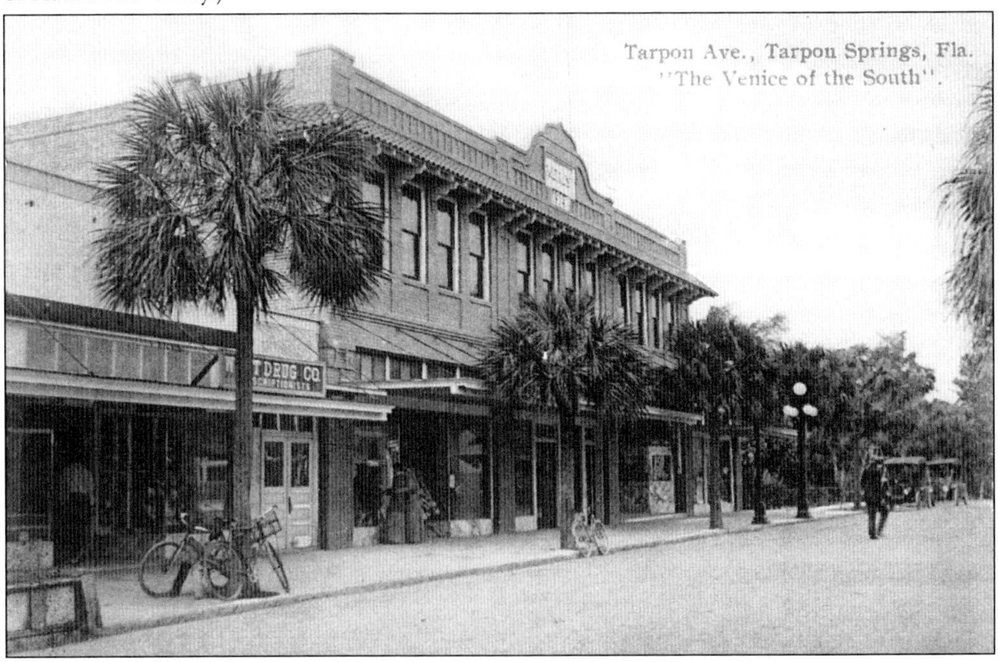

The Meres Building on the south side of Tarpon Avenue was constructed in 1914. Mother Meres's son Ernest was the head of Meres Sponge and Trading Company, a major buyer of sponges. The structure served as an office building, as well as one of the city's first movie houses, the Royal Theatre. Will Rogers, the legendary star of Broadway and movies, popular broadcaster and radio commentator, writer, and master at using a lariat, performed at this venue. (Courtesy of Sam H. Mack.)

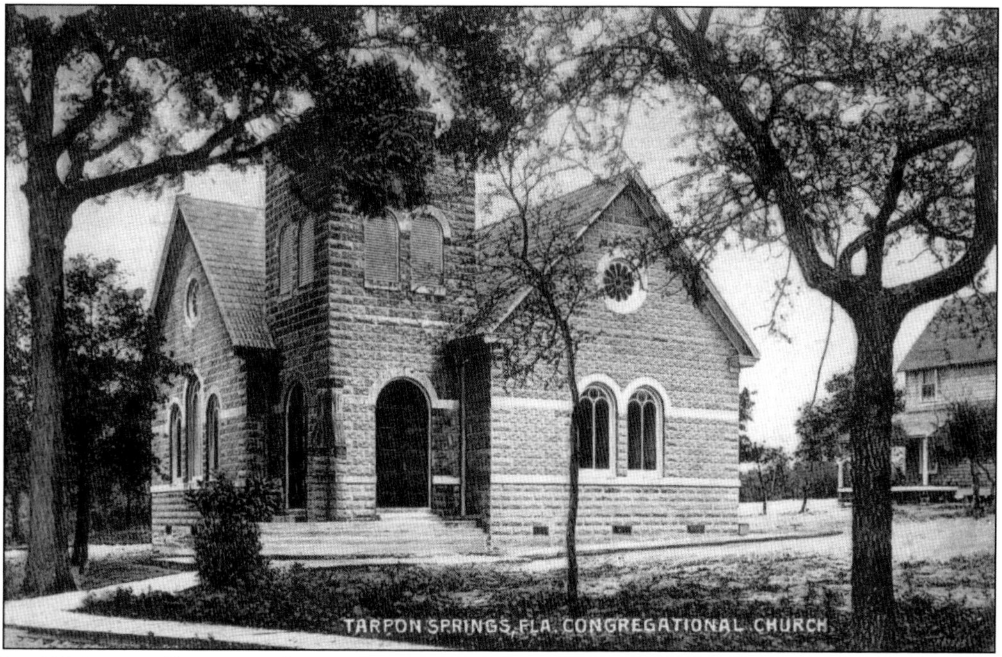

In 1885, a small group of 14 came together in a hall over a store to worship and form a congregation of Universalists. Anson P.K. Safford, one of the founding members, donated land for the first church in Tarpon Springs. Located on Tarpon Avenue between Safford Avenue and Ring Street, it was built within a year. When destroyed by a 1908 fire, this church was erected at the corner of Grand Boulevard and Read Street. Many denominations were afforded use of the space until their own places of worship could be constructed. The church is now known as the Unitarian Universalist Church of Tarpon Springs. (Courtesy of Sam H. Mack.)

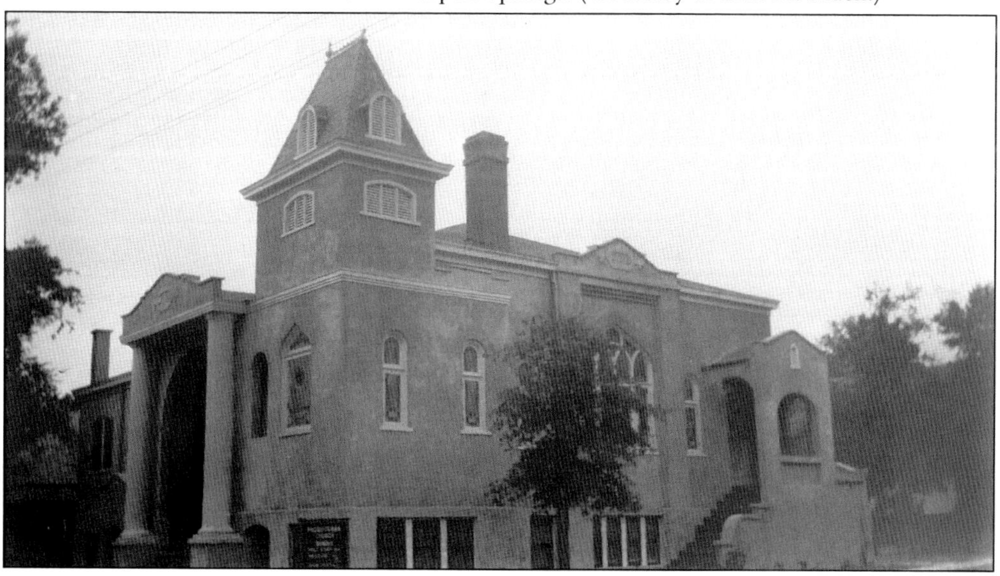

The next congregation to organize was the First Presbyterian Church, currently known as the Church on the Bayou Presbyterian Church. It was organized in 1886. This former Presbyterian church building on Grand Boulevard and Center Street underwent extensive remodeling and is now a private residence. (Courtesy of Tarpon Springs Area Historical Society.)

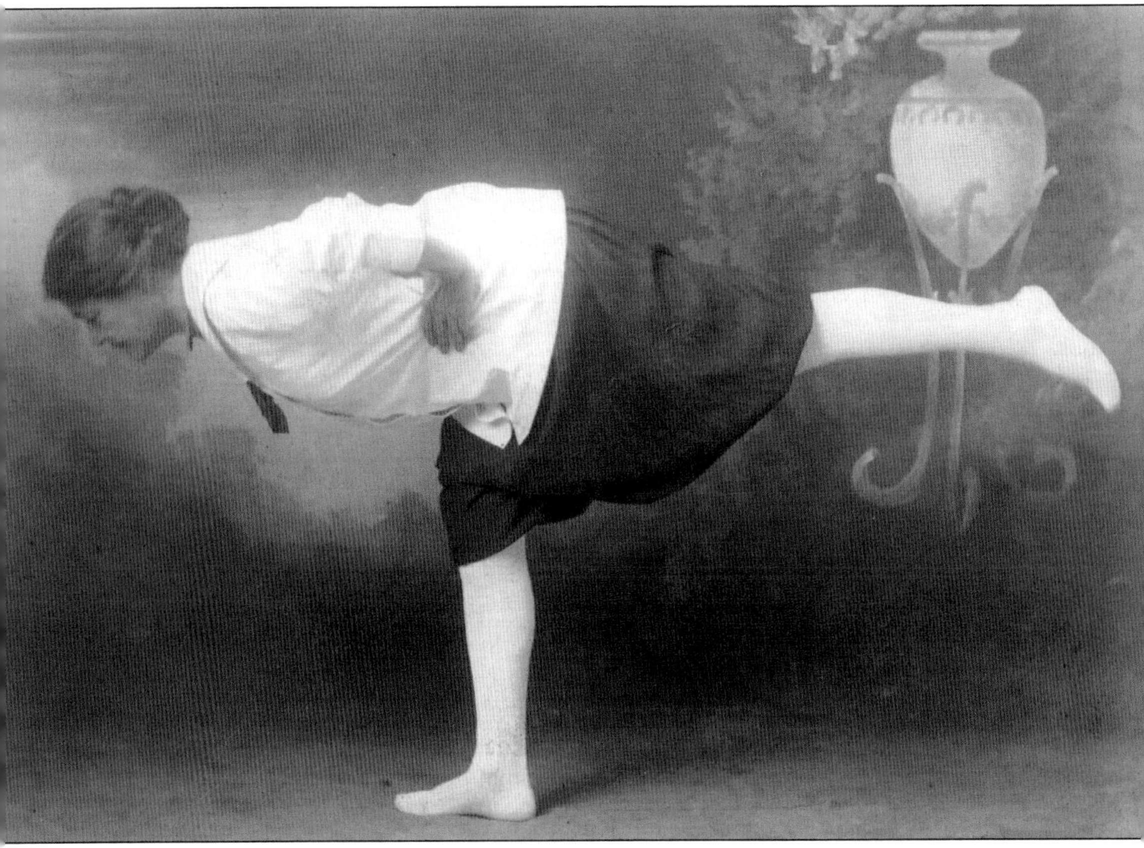

Governor Safford married his third wife, Soledad Bonillas, before coming to Tarpon Springs. A free-spirited individual, she is shown here practicing yoga. Soledad, a devout Catholic who wanted to practice and share her faith, founded the Women's Town Improvement Society in 1892, now the Women's Club. Governor Safford donated the land on Lemon Street west of Pinellas Avenue for the first Roman Catholic chapel, which was built in 1888. It was named St. Ignatius in memory of Soledad's brother Ignacio, who served the governor as an aide and later was the Mexican ambassador to the United States. (Courtesy of Tarpon Springs Area Historical Society.)

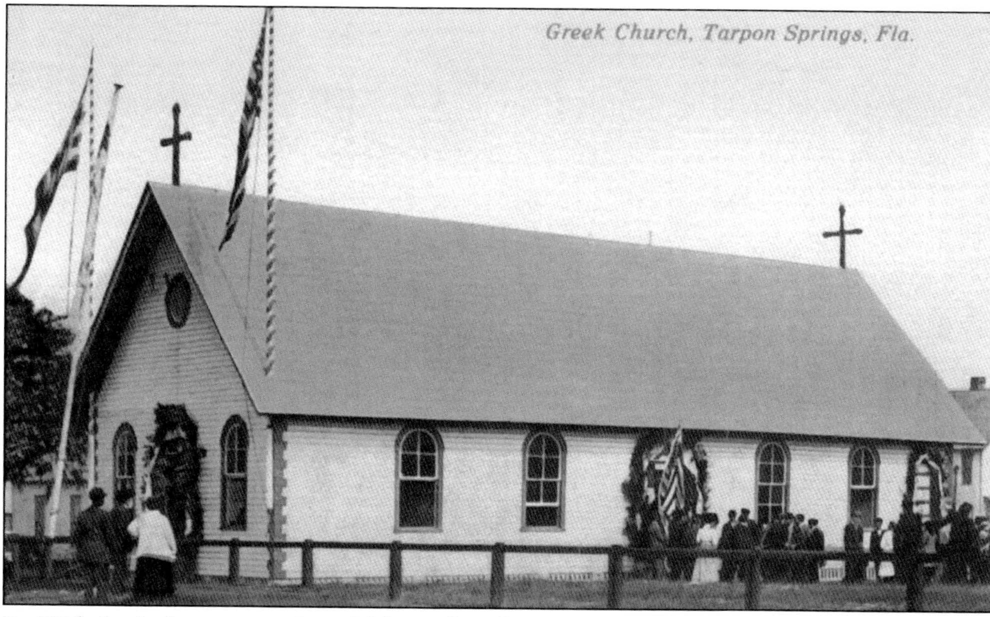

St. Nicholas is the patron saint of ships and seafaring men, whose devout faith remains central to the Greek sponge divers and their families. The first St. Nicholas Greek Orthodox Church, built in 1907, was a wooden structure located at the corner of Orange Street and Hibiscus Street. It would suffer from fire twice before the new church was built to take its place. (Courtesy of Hampton Dunn Collection of Florida Postcards, Special and Digital Collections, Tampa Library, University of South Florida.)

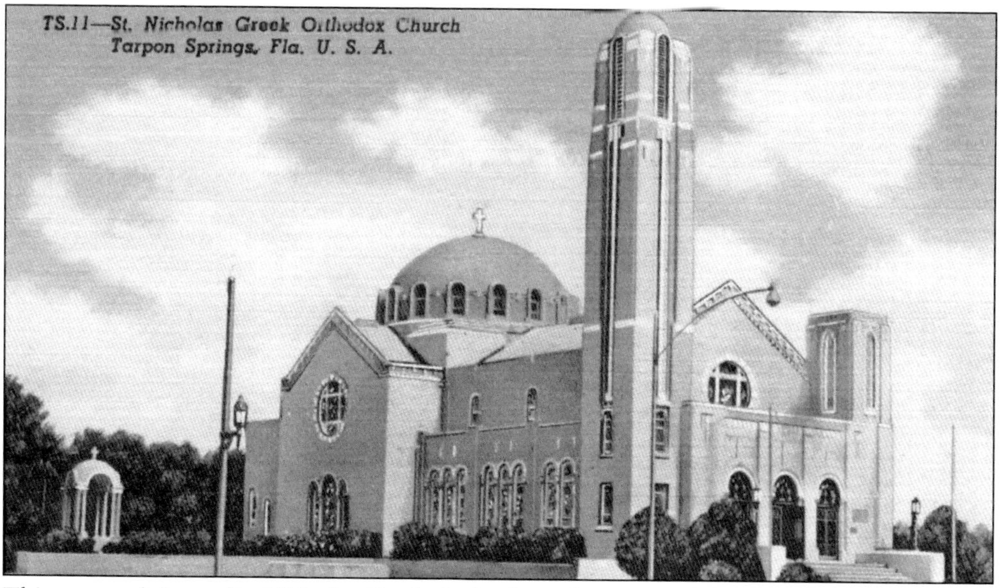

This postcard shows St. Nicholas Greek Orthodox Church as it appears today. Completed in 1943, it was financed in large part by the generosity of the sponge divers who gave a percentage of the sponge gross sales and through donations of the Sponge Exchange. This elegant cathedral by the architectural firm of Eugene Brothers of Chicago has combined Byzantine with Gothic and modern characteristics to make an exquisite style similar, yet different, from all Greek Orthodox Churches.

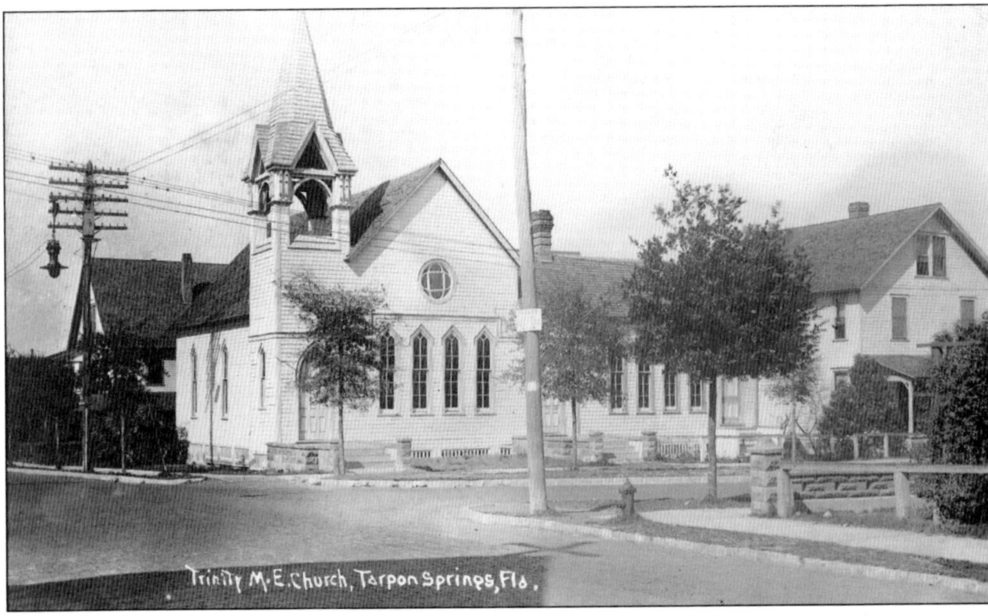

The African Methodist Episcopal Church was established in 1887. Trinity Methodist Episcopal Church, the first white Methodist Church, was founded in 1898 and located at the corner of Orange and Hibiscus Streets. The card, addressed to the writer's sister, says, "We are going to like our new home. We have 12 rooms in the parsonage, have two rooms rented." (Courtesy of Tarpon Springs Area Historical Society.)

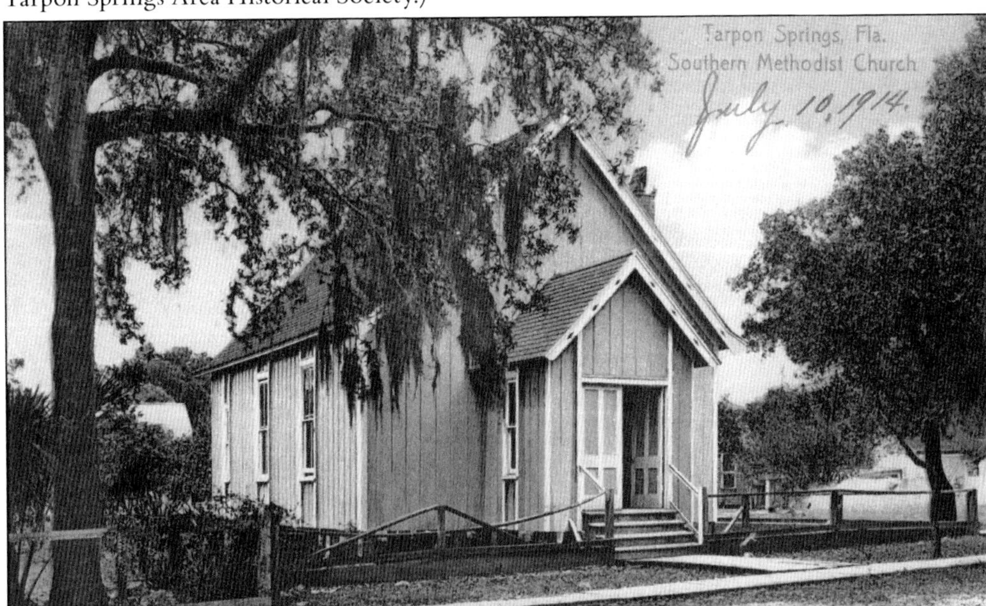

Sometime in the early 1900s, a group of the Northern Methodists left to worship together in the Presbyterian church on Court Street and South Pinellas Avenue. Shortly thereafter, construction was completed for their house of worship on Eagle Street (North Pinellas Avenue) and one lot north of Orange Street. In 1939, the two churches, physically separated by a mere block, joined to become one congregation known as the Methodist Church. (Courtesy of Sam H. Mack.)

Two

The Venice of the South

Of the total area of almost 17 square miles, land in Tarpon Springs comprises barely over nine square miles. Forty-six percent of its area is water, over seven and a half square miles. It is made up of bayous, springs, the Anclote River, salt and freshwater lakes, and ultimately, the Gulf of Mexico. One does not have to look far to find a waterway. Water, the lifeblood of Tarpon Springs, delivered many early pioneers and visitors to town and fed them with abundant fish and seafood. It healed with mineral springs and fresh breezes off of the Gulf of Mexico and employed the masses of immigrants, as well as natives. Its supporting industries developed the wilderness into a cultured, civilized place of residence. Its natural beauty supported a proliferation of the arts. The water offered its playground for fun and folly and blessed all with its wealth.

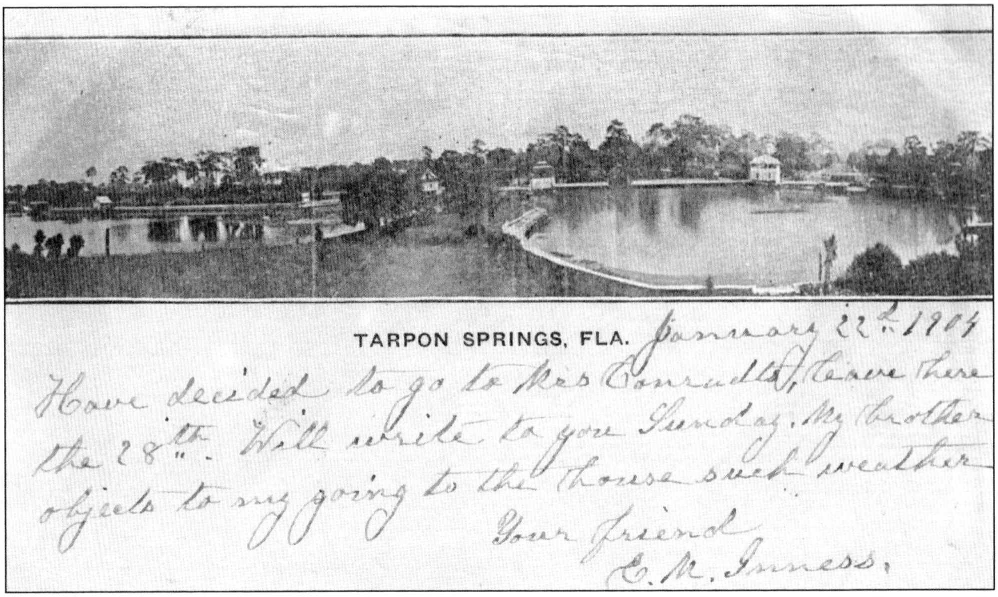

Prior to 1907, US postal regulations required that the address must be on one side of a postcard, leaving the message and view to be on the other. This card, postmarked January 22, 1904, and taken from a different angle on the bayou, shows the point of land directly in the middle and Spring Bayou surrounding it. Signed by E.M. Inness, who probably was married to George Inness Sr., the message on the card refers to objections from her brother. Both George Inness Sr. and Jr. are world-renowned artists. (Courtesy of Sam H. Mack.)

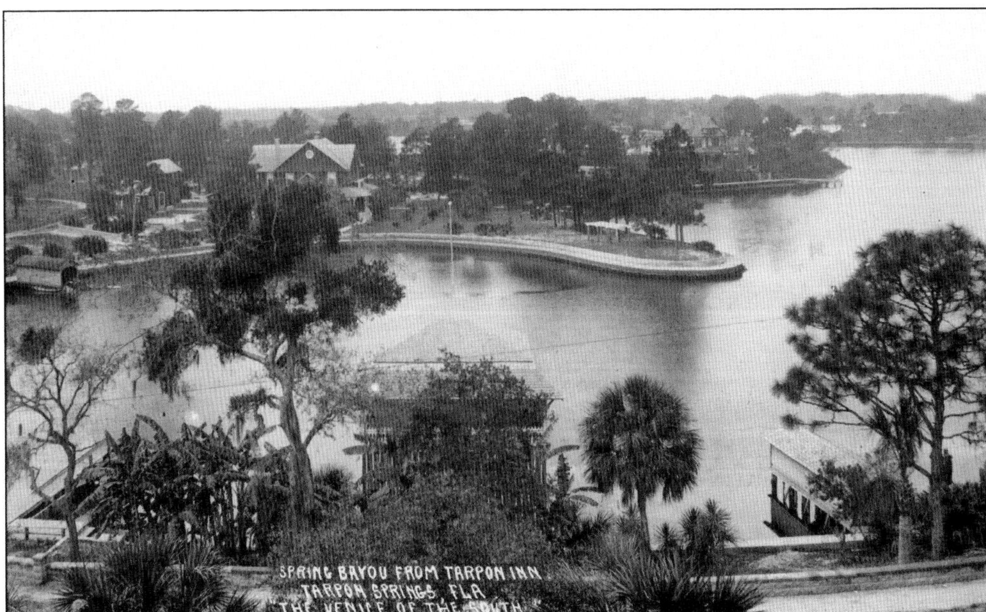

"Tarpon Springs. January 22, 1913. Dear Friend Rob, Am sending you a picture of the Bayou where we go fishing almost every day. I often wish you were here to go along." This view was captured from the top of the Tarpon Inn. (Courtesy of Sam H. Mack.)

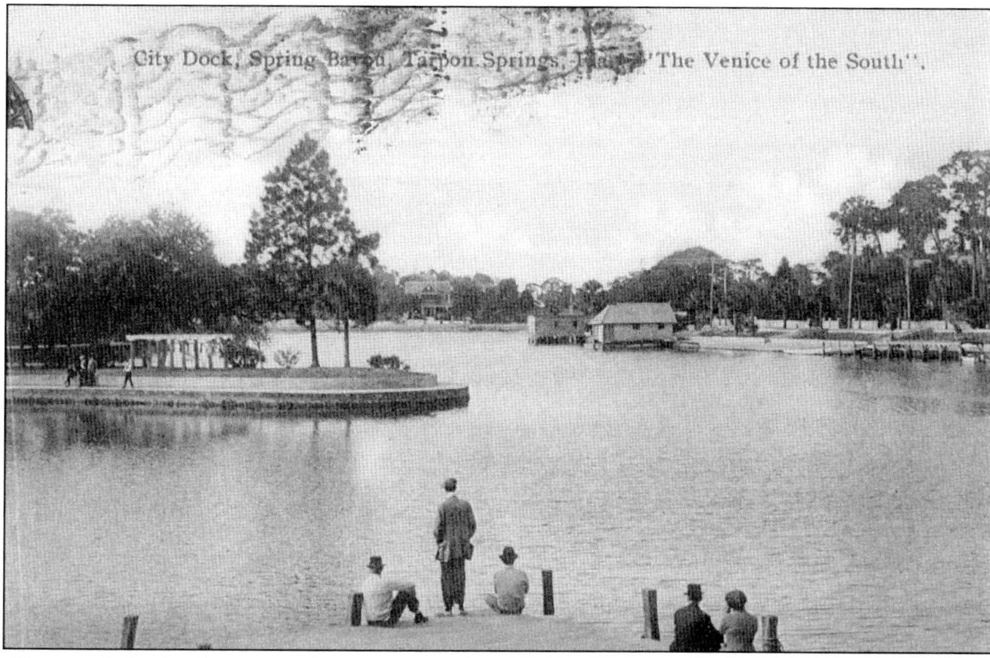

The people in the foreground are at the city's wooden dock, gazing across Spring Bayou to the pergola on the point. Today, there is a war memorial with the names of local missing-in-action and killed-in-action veterans from World War I, World War II, the Korean War, and the Vietnam War inscribed on the 15-foot-tall granite monument. (Courtesy of Tarpon Springs Area Historical Society.)

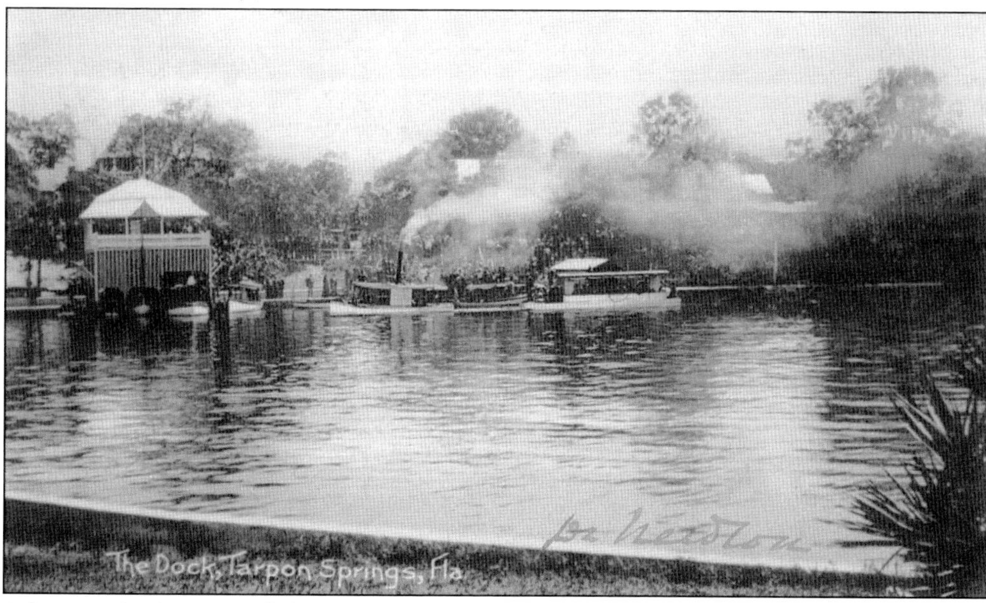

A large gathering around the city dock greets the steamboat's arrival during an unidentified event. The *Governor Safford*, a side-wheel steamer from Cedar Key, disembarked passengers at the pier head in the Gulf near the mouth of the Anclote River. They would transfer to a smaller steamer, the *Mary Disston*, which brought them up the winding Anclote River into the shallow bayou to the city dock. (Courtesy of Tarpon Springs Area Historical Society.)

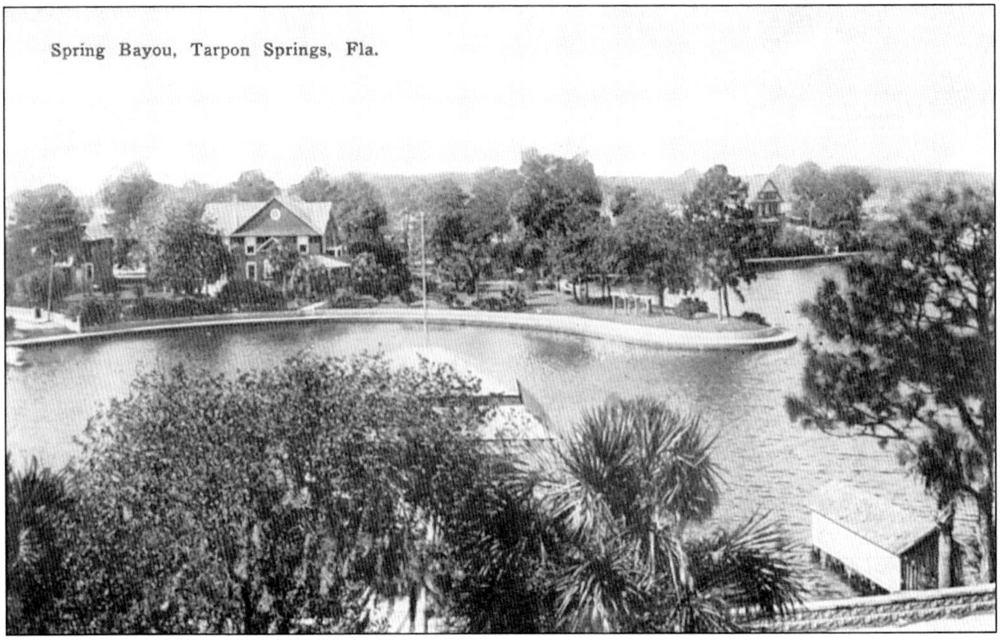

Charles and Viola Keeney built the home named "Glenola," across Spring Bayou and seen on the far right of the image, in 1887. He died in 1891, and she married John Beekman. In 1930, the home and land was given to Tarpon Springs for a park and a library. She organized the Cycadia Cemetery Association to care for the grounds and donated that land in 1887. (Courtesy of Sam H. Mack.)

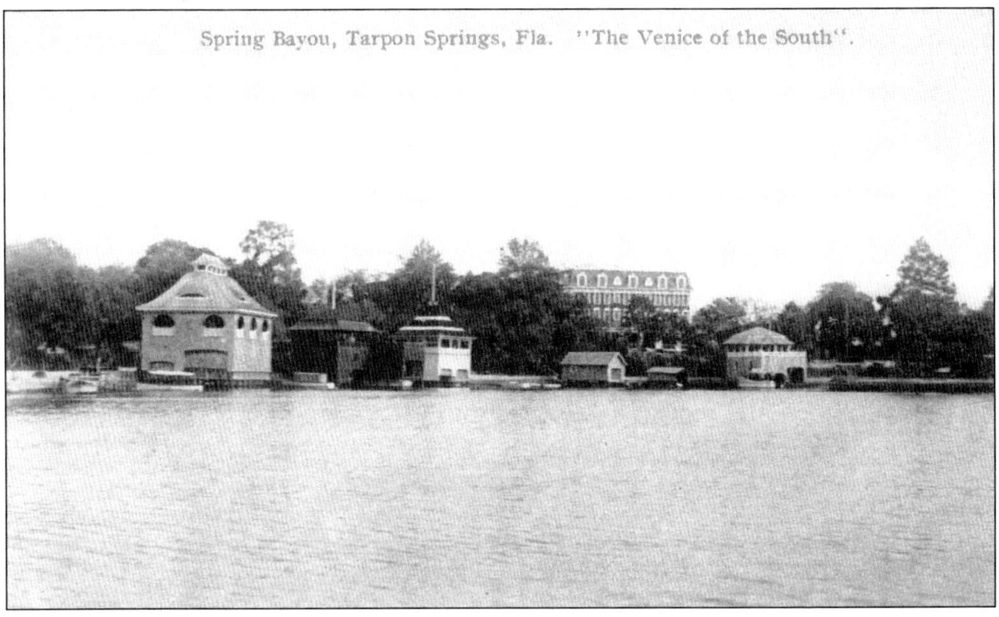

While at the American Medical Society Convention in 1885, Dr. W.C. Van Bibber named "Point Pinelos [*sic*]" as one of the healthiest places in the world. Others attested to the healthy and curative qualities, causing physicians to send their patients to Tarpon Springs for healing. One of the bayou's springs contained sulfur, and its mineral water and vapors were sought as medicinal elixir for all that ails. (Courtesy of Sam H. Mack.)

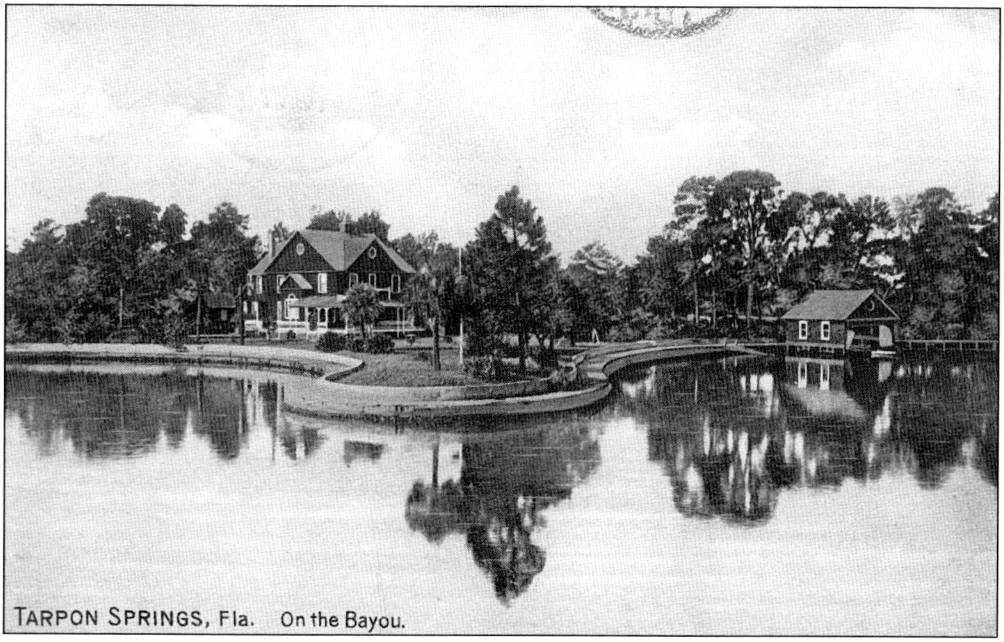

The link between the major spring in Spring Bayou and Lake Tarpon has long been a theory. Saltwater would intrude into the freshwater lake once known as Lake Butler through an underground stream. Robert Edwin Gause and friends wondered about this connection. During low tides in the winter, the spring would appear to boil in the lake. The men poured sawdust into that area and watched it emerge in Spring Bayou. It was a simple and inexpensive way of proving the two were indeed connected. (Courtesy of Sam H. Mack.)

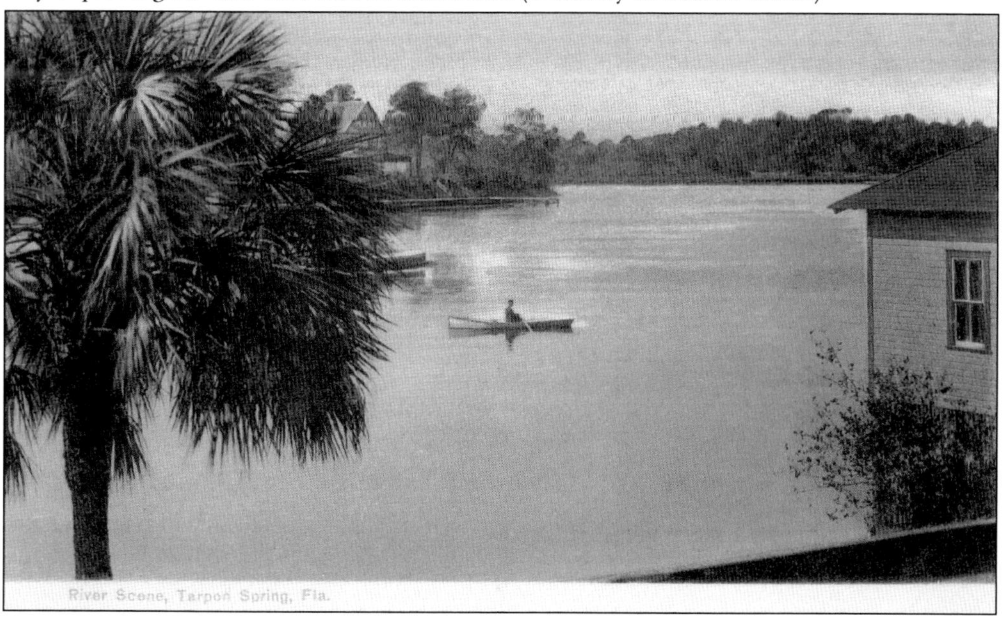

According to R.F. Pent's *History of Tarpon Springs*, George Gause, while diving in the main spring of the bayou, found "ropes, fish lines and anchors from time to time along its rocky ledges—but no bottom." The depth of the spring in Spring Bayou was confirmed in the 1960s by several people at a little over 100 feet to the bottom. (Courtesy of Sam H. Mack.)

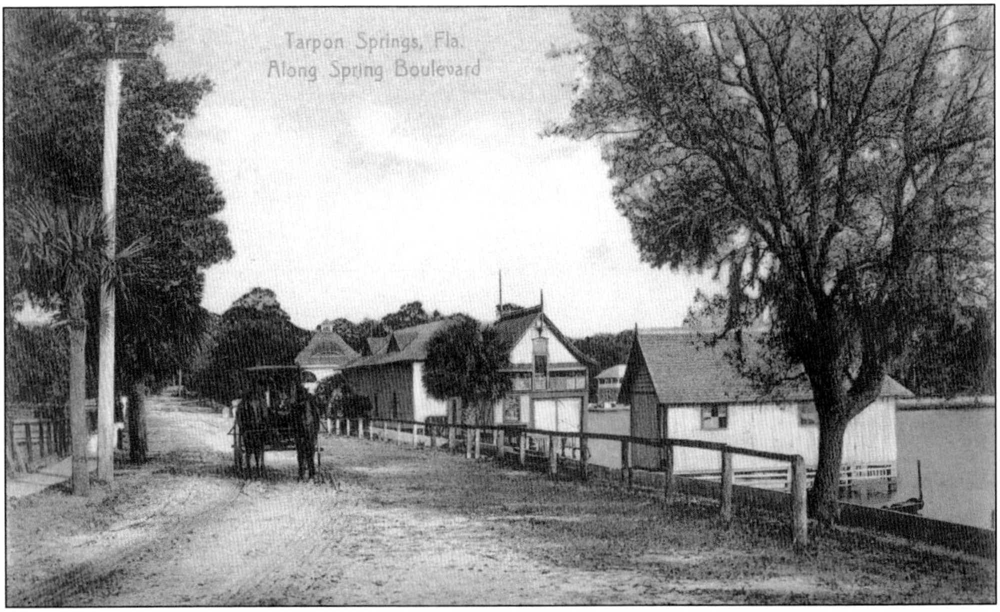

The first settlers' cabins were along the Anclote River and then upriver on the bayous. They consisted of the raw materials at hand. The pioneers timbered their own wood without the assistance of sawmills, which came later. The next wave of residents was primarily wealthy northern business owners who had homes built around the bayous. They would bring lumber from northern mills in by ship, and their homes reflected elegant styles, refined designs, and nonindigenous woods. This view shows the boathouses alongside the road of Spring Boulevard. (Courtesy of Sam H. Mack.)

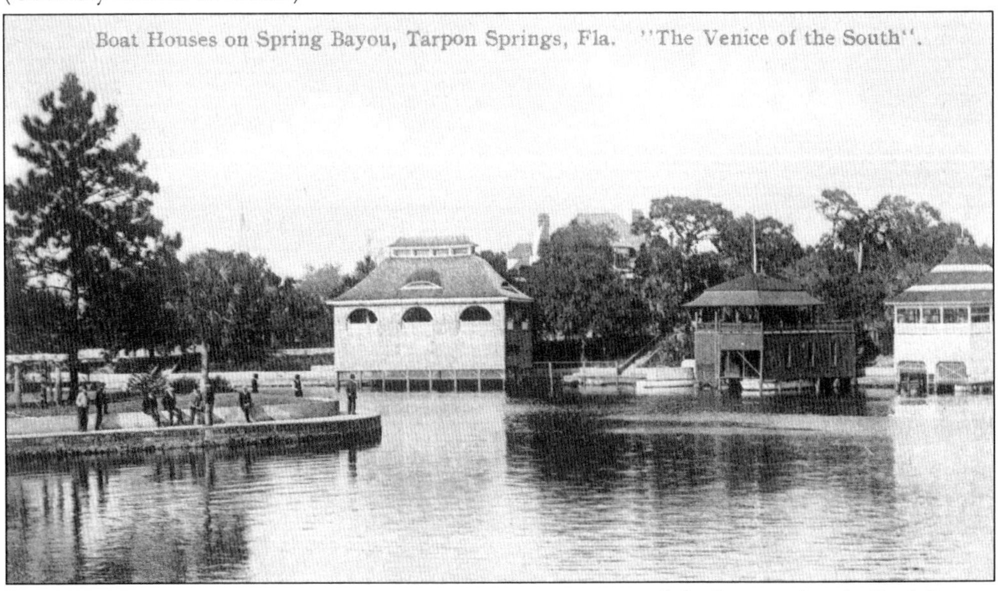

The wealthy northerners who settled in Tarpon Springs around the bayou often built elaborate boathouses. George W. Clemson erected one of the grandest residences on Spring Bayou in the early 1900s that would serve as his winter home. The contract for building his boathouse was awarded for $4,000. While under construction, he took delivery of a new houseboat that would need to be stored during the summer months.

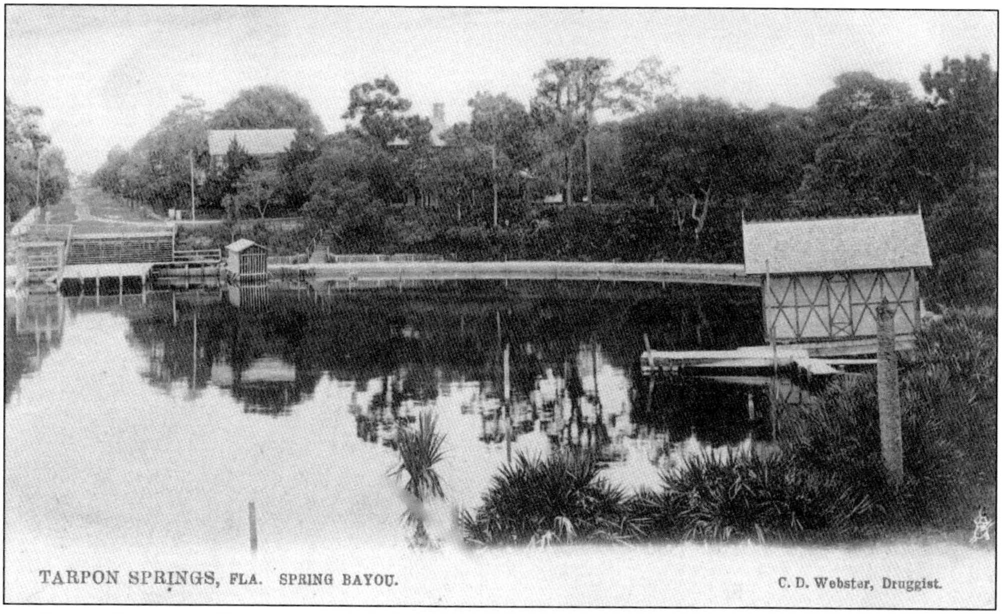

In this early view of Spring Bayou, hardly a ripple can be seen on the surface of the water. The wooden railings are in place, and the dock and stairs leading up to Tarpon Avenue are constructed of wood. Tarpon Avenue can be seen as a single-lane dirt road beyond. Some of the first businesses were the post office (with Edward A. Blum serving as the first postmaster), a general merchandise store, Mrs. George's millinery shop, a grocery store, Decker hardware, Mr. Pent's oyster house, G.E. Noblit's cold drink and confectionery store, and the Tropical Hotel.

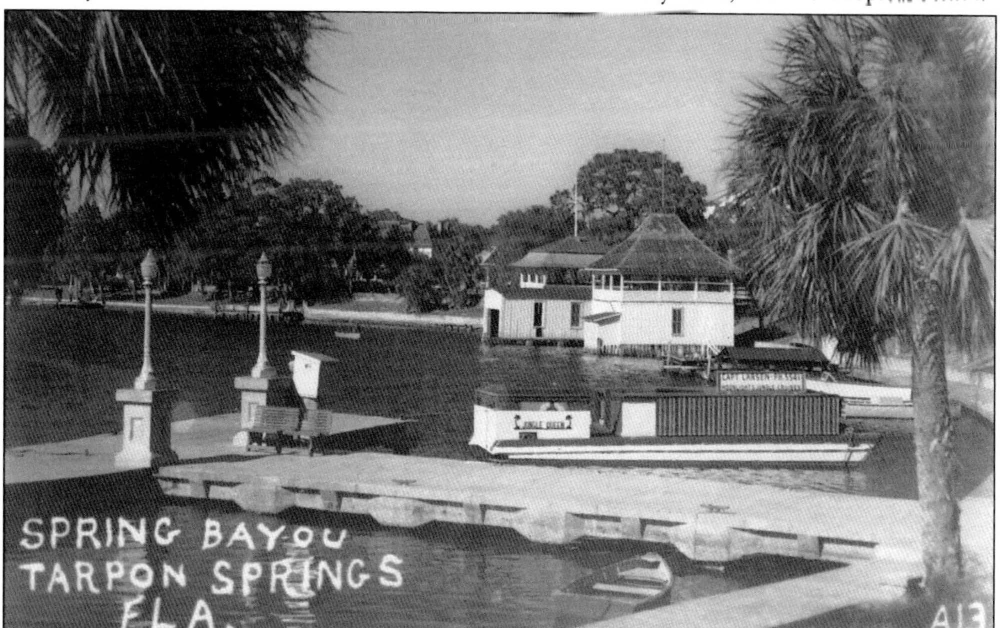

The old wooden city dock, built in the 1880s, was replaced by a concrete dock. The new dock has secured cleats for tying up boats. The design was changed to a T formation, and lights have been added to the tops of pedestal posts. Anchored off to the north of the dock, Captain Larsen's *Jungle Queen* advertises Moonlight Jungle Cruises. (Courtesy of Sam H. Mack.)

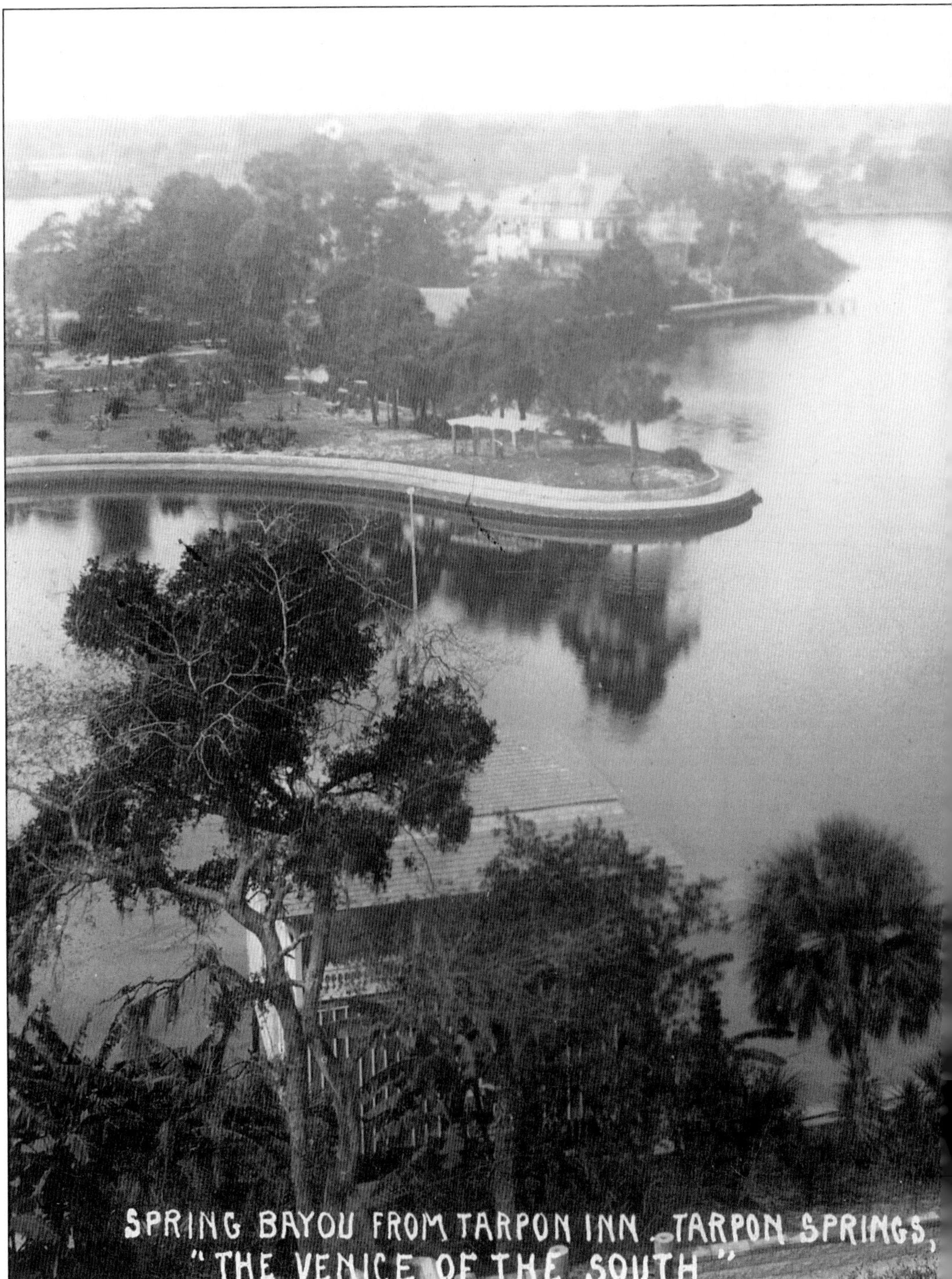

Written with an extra-fine nib in excellent penmanship was the following message to a friend: "Xmas. 1913. What do you think of this for a pretty place. Our boathouse is on the extreme right and our gate just across the road by the big tree. Walk right in. I am as much surprised as you to be here. I caught a nasty cold and cough in Sept. which still hangs on and Dr. Leonard

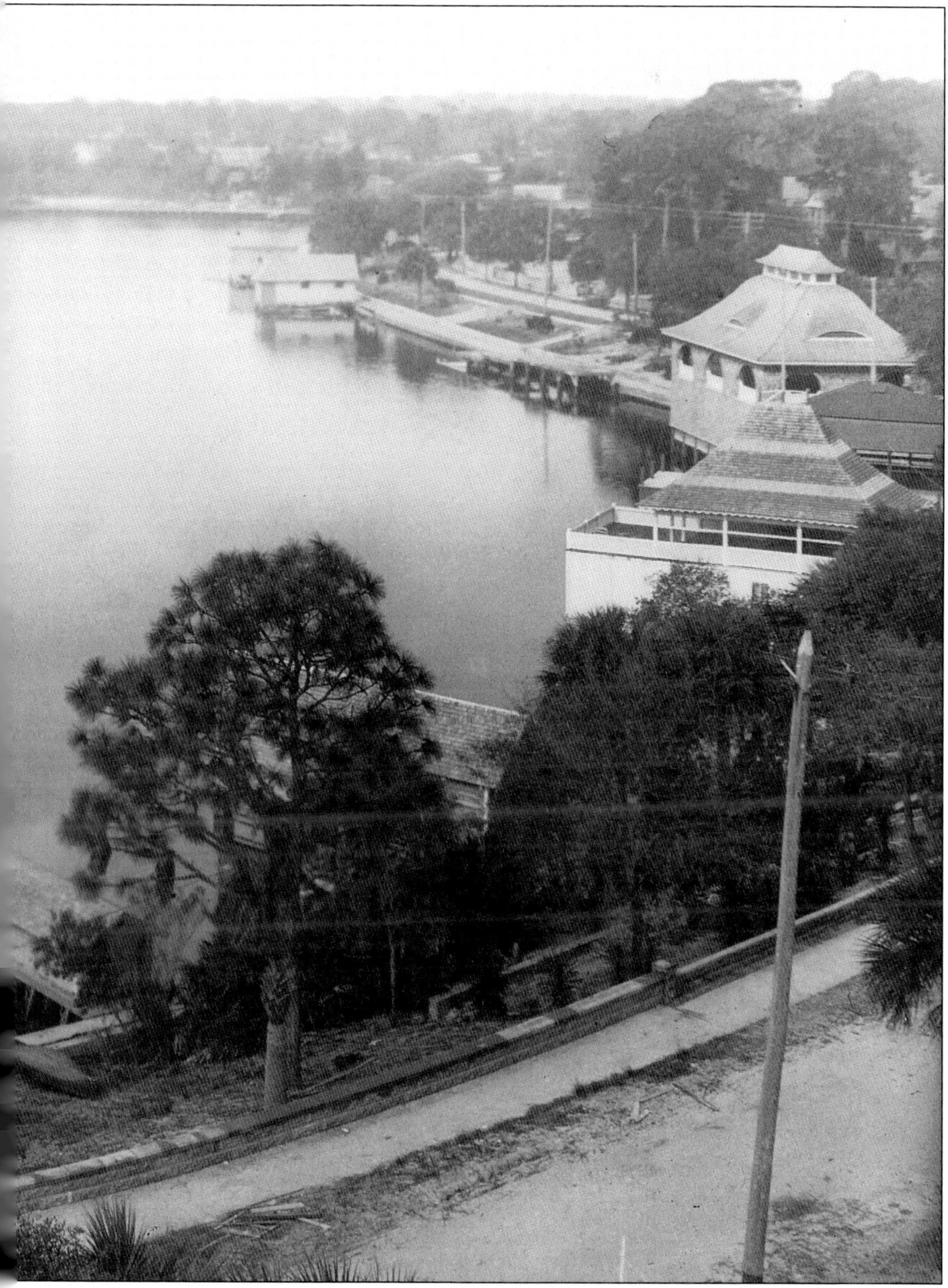

gave me a month's leave of absence to come here and get well. My second dose of 'whooping cough' I fear. I sailed on the Mallory line to Tampa Nov. 29. Five days on the water stopping only at Key West. It was a glorious trip . . . Love and best wishes for a happy Xmas. Barb." (Courtesy of Sam H. Mack.)

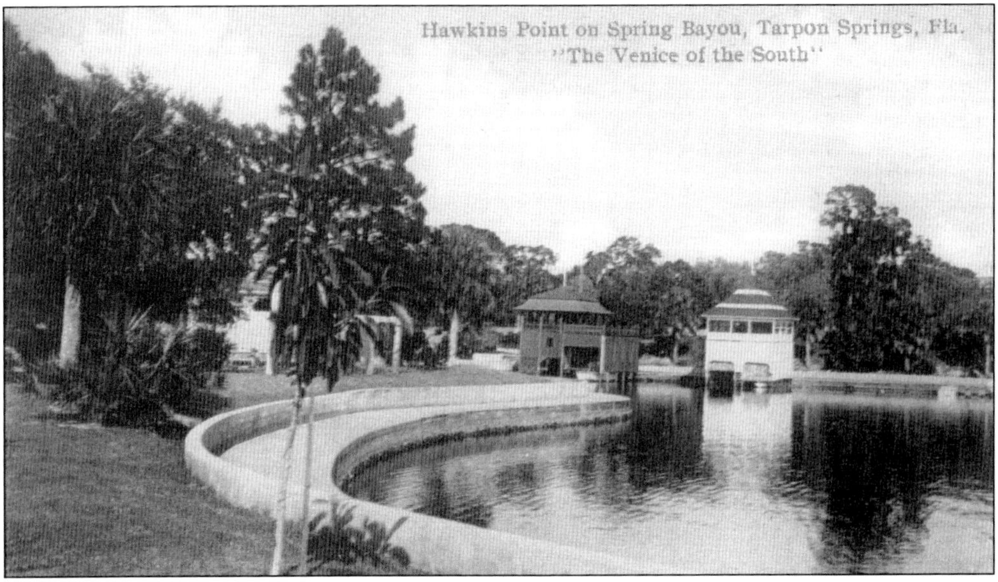

The card above, marked "Hawkins Point on Spring Bayou, Tarpon Springs, Fla. 'The Venice of the South,' " tells it all. Taken from the vantage of Senator Hawkins's home, the view above shows the point with its pergola, hidden behind a newly planted tree. Ebenezer B. Hawkins, a very wealthy iron merchant and Minnesota state senator, hosted many parties and dances here. His niece Mollie Young served as hostess of the gatherings. She married Royal Alworth; his father was the extremely wealthy iron tycoon Marshall Henry Alworth, who loved spending his fortunes on yachts. E.B. Hawkins aided the United States during World War I by loaning his yacht to the government. The postcard below was taken of the same point of land from the opposite side, and in each image two of the same boathouses can be seen across the bayou. (Both images courtesy of Sam H. Mack.)

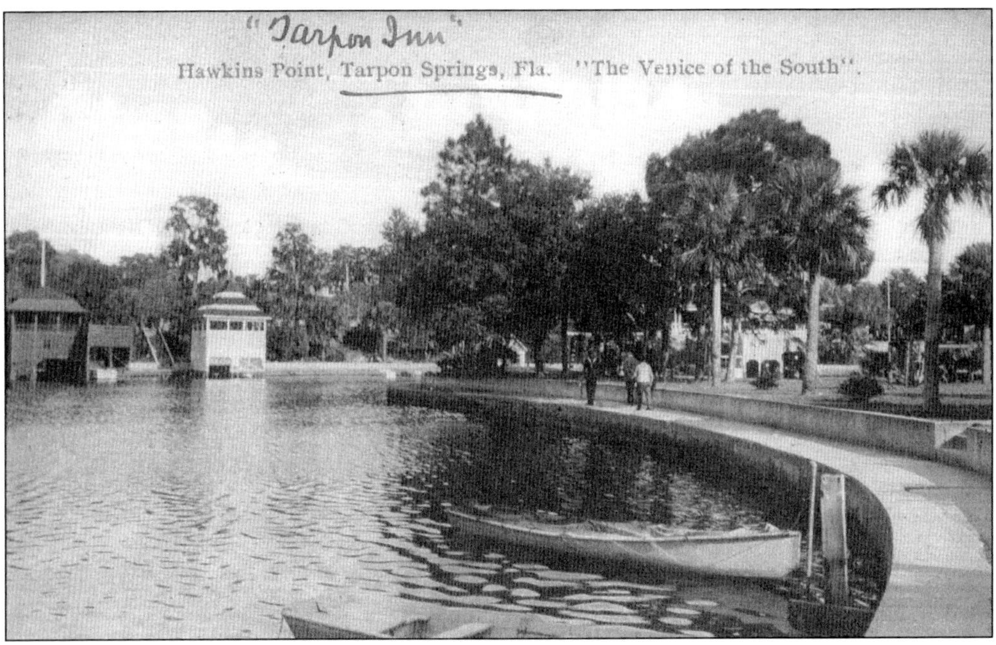

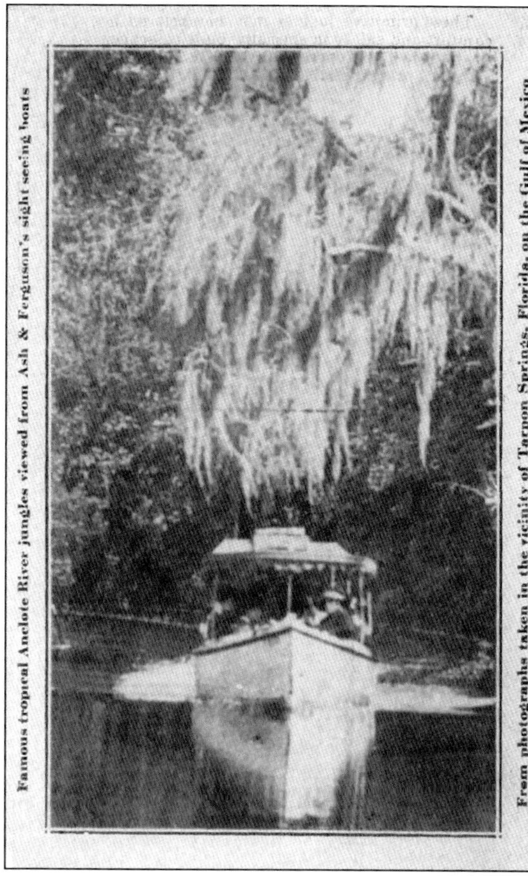

A popular pastime for visitors and residents was embarking on a jungle tour of the upper Anclote River. In relative comfort and safety, passengers could board a motorboat and travel to areas inaccessible by land. Some of these outings would stop along the way for exploring and picnicking. This card advertises "famous tropical Anclote River Jungles viewed from Ash & Ferguson's sight-seeing boats." The upper Anclote was compared to the jungle areas of South America and Africa. (Courtesy of Sam H. Mack.)

The Anclote River flows westward for 29 miles until it empties into the Gulf of Mexico. Its upper tributaries begin in Pasco County, which was a part of Hernando County until a three-part split in June 1887 that also formed Citrus County to the north. Many springs also feed the river. (Courtesy of Sam H. Mack.)

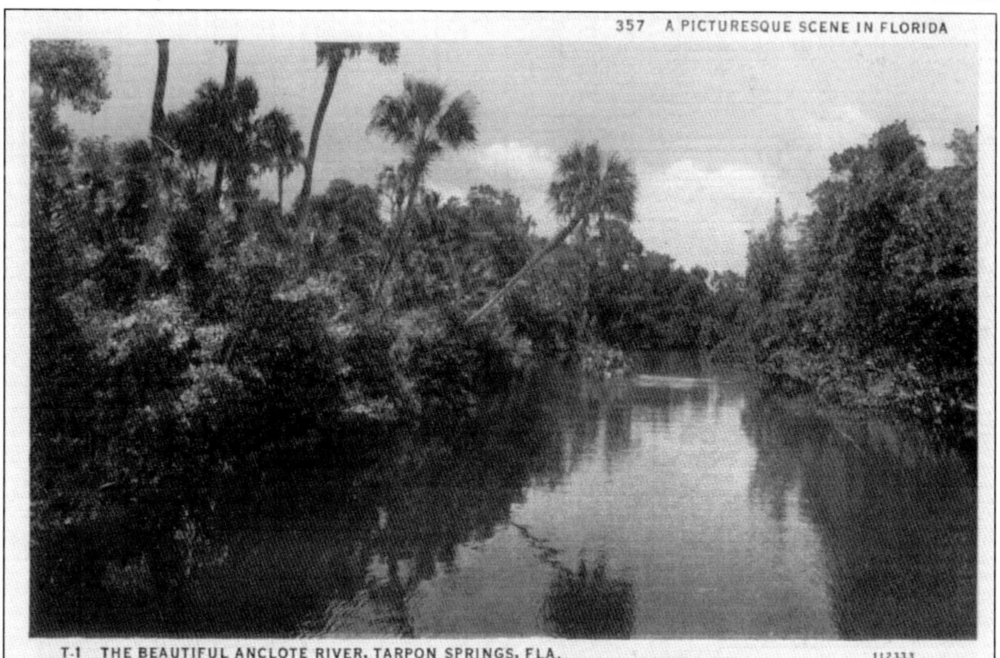

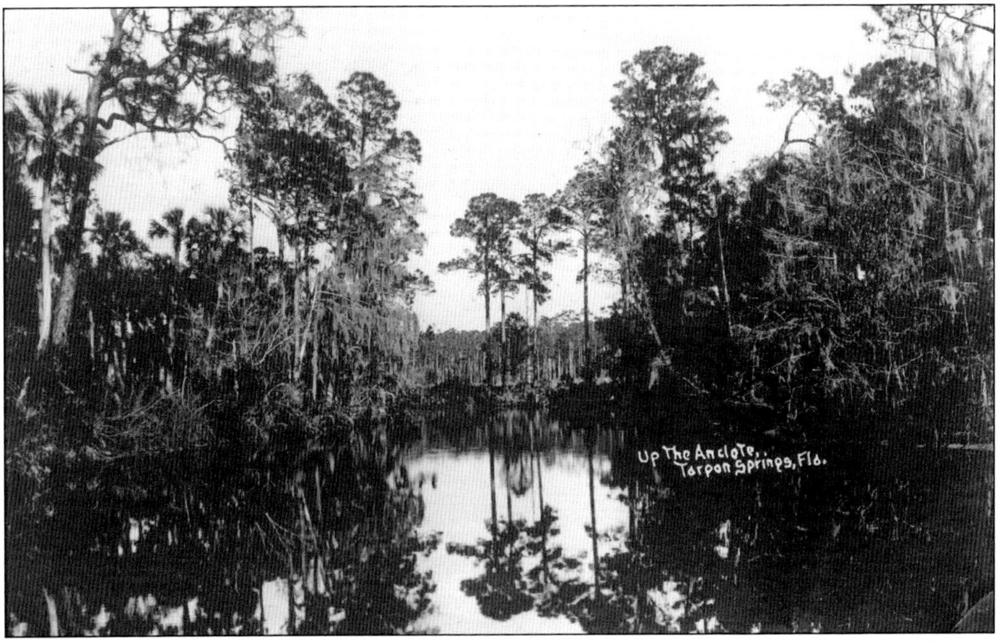

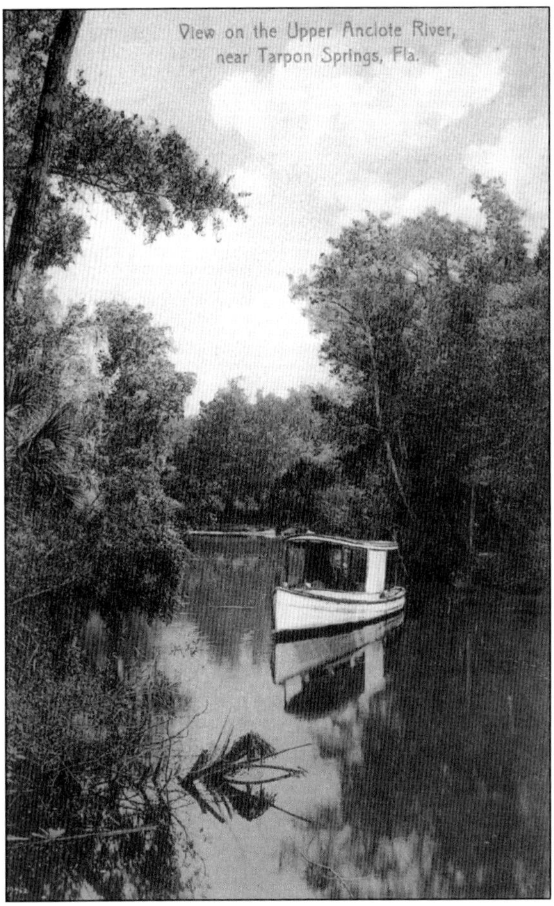

Pinellas County, which separated from Hillsborough County in 1912, took its name from the Spanish origin of *punta pinal*, which means point of pines. In 1528, Panfilo de Narvaez discovered this area, 37 years before St. Augustine was founded. It may be difficult to imagine, but there was a time when Tarpon Springs was a wilderness predominated by the abundance of long leaf pine trees. In this view of the Anclote River, the stately pines that were once prolific can be seen in the glass-like smooth reflection of the water. (Courtesy of Sam H. Mack.)

Anclote is also a Spanish word meaning "kedge," a light anchor used in calm waters to warp a vessel or grapnel, which is an anchor with fluked ends. Near the mouth of the Anclote was a spring-fed well that supplied freshwater to the Indians, Spanish explorers, other fishermen, and, as legend has it, pirates. (Courtesy of Sam H. Mack.)

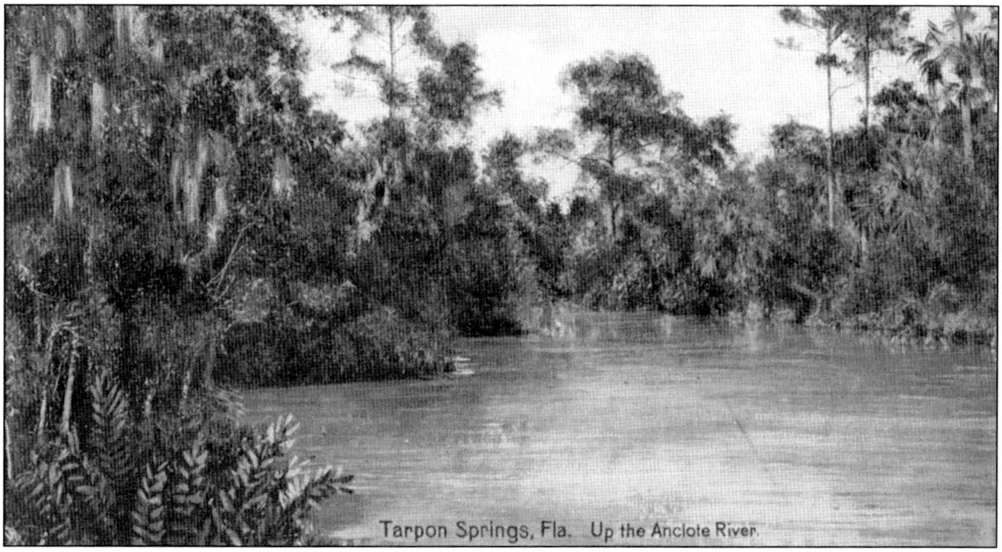

Anclote was also a settlement formed a short while after the Civil War ended. Brothers Frederic and Benjamin Franklin Meyer came within a few months of each other and settled about three miles north of Tarpon Springs on the Anclote River. Benjamin, while at his sawmill in Cedar Key, contracted yellow fever. He returned home and died. His brother Frederic died shortly after, also of yellow fever. Their wives, both named Sarah, and the children stayed and grew up along with the settlement. With the popularity of travel by train, which delivered passengers directly to the downtown area of Tarpon Springs, Anclote remained less populated. (Courtesy of Hammond Salley.)

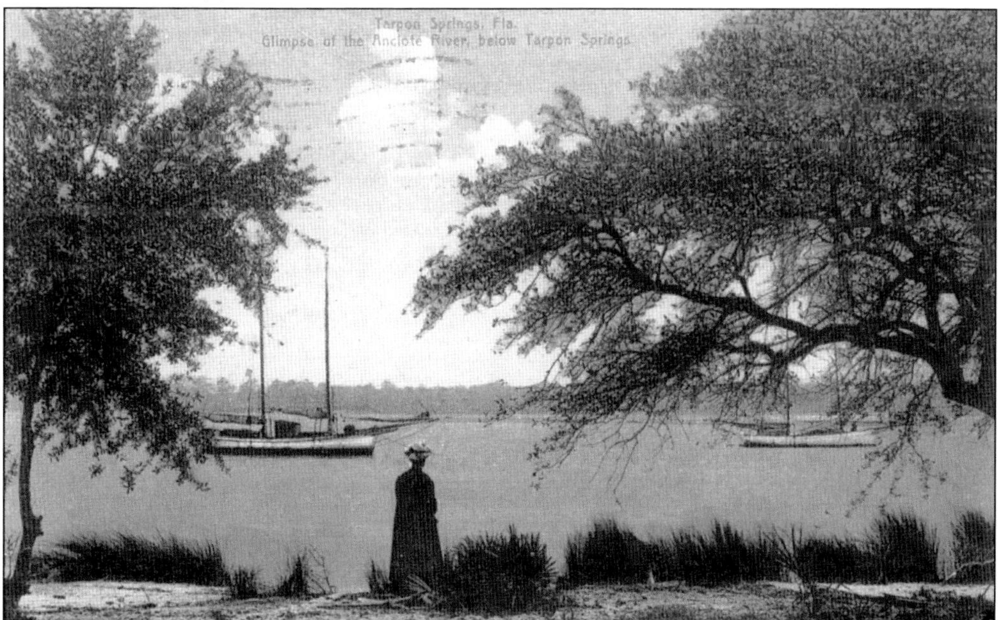

Salt Lake is an area feeding into the Anclote River. In *History of Tarpon Springs* by R.F. Pent, it was recalled that Edward A. Blum built a 14-ton schooner that he named after his granddaughter, Gracie Blum. Built on Salt Lake, it had to go under the bridge northeast of town. This was just barely accomplished during a low tide. (Courtesy of Hammond Salley.)

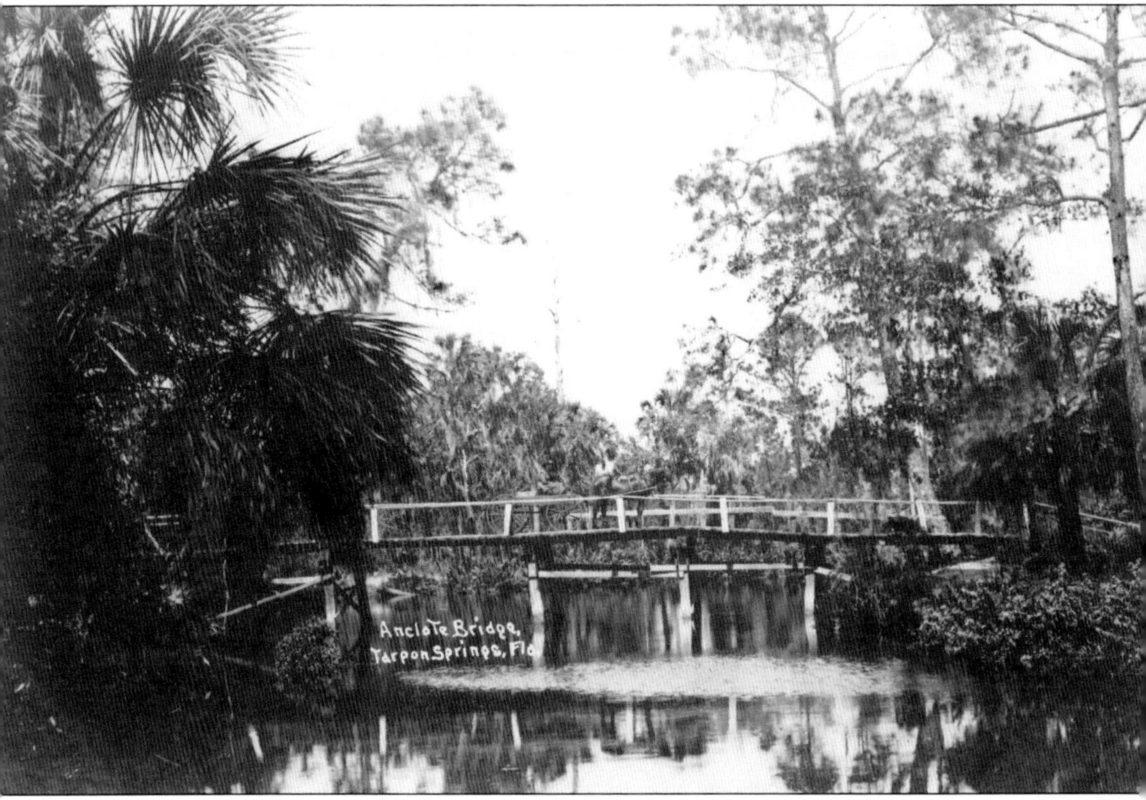

When Anclote was settled, there were no bridges crossing the river, but it could be forded at Mr. Ferguson's Ferry Point in Seven Springs. The first bridge was reported to be at the end of Huey Avenue, and the bridge at the foot of Athens Street was the way to Bailey's Bluff. In 1916, the county commission approved construction of a drawbridge over the Anclote River. It was originally a wooden bridge with a concrete pier and a drawbridge span made of steel. Constructed in 1924, it was reconstructed in concrete in 1956. However, the original 1924 wooden pilings and single leaf movable bascule draw span is still in use today. Currently, there is not a permanent on-site bridge tender, and two hours notice must be given to the county prior to opening. At one time, the bridge tender and his family lived in a very small home on the side of the bridge. From its build date of 1924 to the 1960s, and from 1994 to present, this bridge is the only single leaf moveable span of its kind in Pinellas County. Another Tarpon Springs bridge has an ill-famed history. Tragedy occurred when the bridge crossing the Anclote River on Highway 19 collapsed on December 17, 1968, resulting in one death and five injuries. (Courtesy of Tarpon Springs Area Historical Society.)

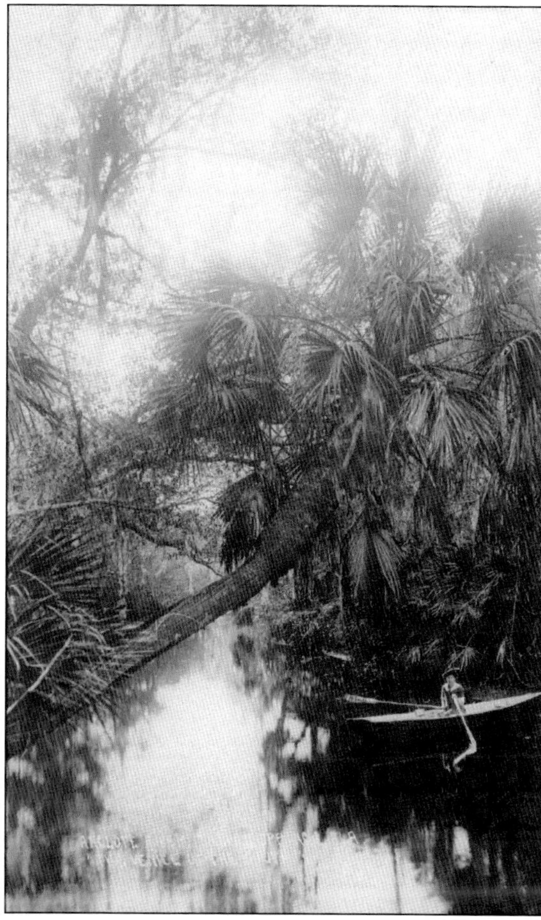

Boating was a popular sport, whether sailing or by a motor. It was equally popular to take a small boat out and go rowing, as seen in this postcard. One can only guess if the name on the oar, "E.M. Smith," was that of the rower and owner of the boat or was the name of a rental boat owner. (Courtesy of Sam H. Mack.)

In 1824, the first surveyor general of Florida was Col. Robert Butler. Lake Butler had its name changed in 1949 to Lake Tarpon by a state legislative official act; it seems there was another Lake Butler, which is the seat of Union County in northeast Florida. It was thought that changing the lake's name to Lake Tarpon would be appropriate because the lake is found in the Tarpon Springs area. The Lake Butler Villa Company, with A.P.K. Safford as president, sold land that was deeded over by Hamilton Disston in 1885. The last acreage was sold in 1969. Safford got the lands for $1. (Courtesy of Tarpon Springs Area Historical Society.)

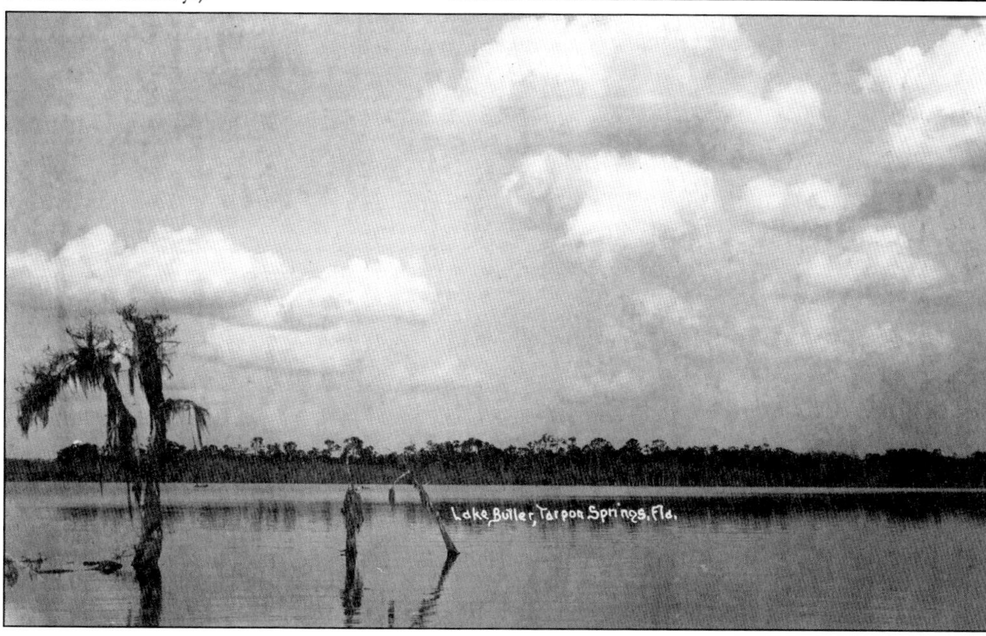

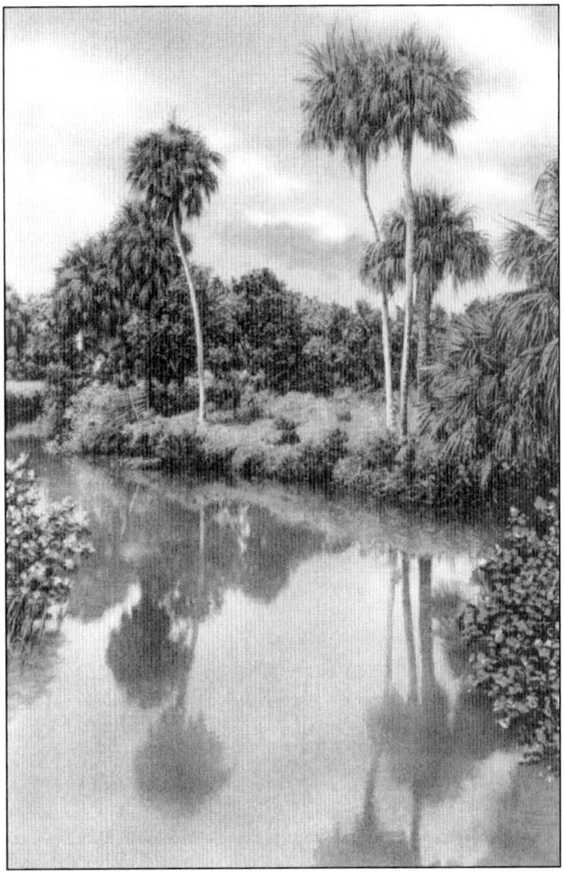

An advertisement for realtor H.W. Davis reads, "Lake Butler, crystal clear, The rippling murmurs you can hear, Come to Tarpon Springs. Boost, Brother Boost, Prosperity's come to roost, Florida beckons, so heed her call, Tax free homes await one and all. Life giving sunshine for grown up and tot, Come, live in your country's garden spot." Lots were selling from $50, and "Easy house-keeping bungalows" sold for $1,250.

Another Davis advertising card features the Crooked Oak at the Health Springs, now known as Wall Springs. On the back, a man named Henry wrote, "Indians said to have bent this tree reasons unknown. We drove into this place right near road on our way home. A spring for drinking and bottling—supposed to be healthful for both interior and external use to the body. Florida is full of health giving springs mostly sulphur." (Courtesy of Sam H. Mack.)

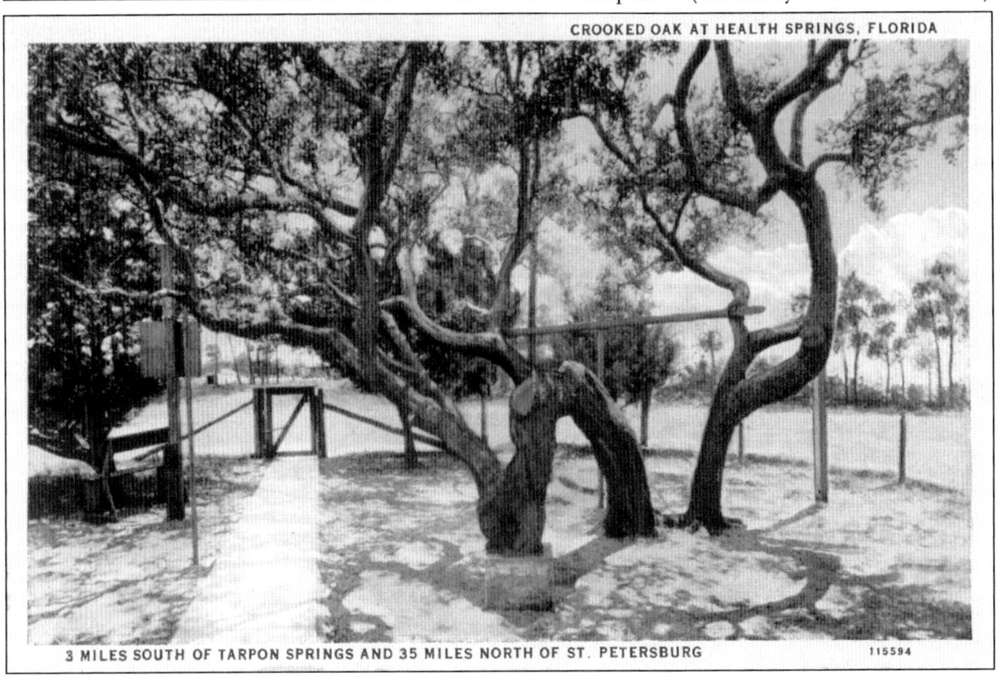

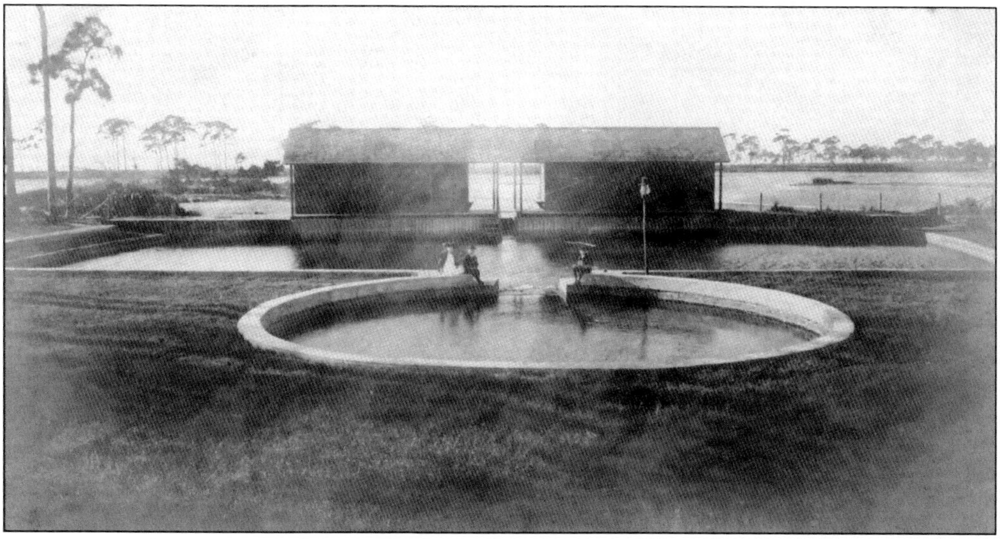

In 1860, Joseph W. Gause from North Carolina found a spring and suggested to his son William Reuben Gause that the area would make a good home. Shortly afterward, William homesteaded the spring and its surrounding area. The family stayed there until the early 1880s when they moved to Gauseville, which was a settlement east of Tarpon Springs. In order to raise capital for the move, William sold the property to Charles F. Wall for $50, a wagon, and a pair of mules. The family moved back to the region when William died. His son Robert Edwin Gause was born at Wall Springs in 1873, and upon returning to his birthplace, he operated the pool area, a general store, and post office and fished commercially. (Courtesy of Sam H. Mack.)

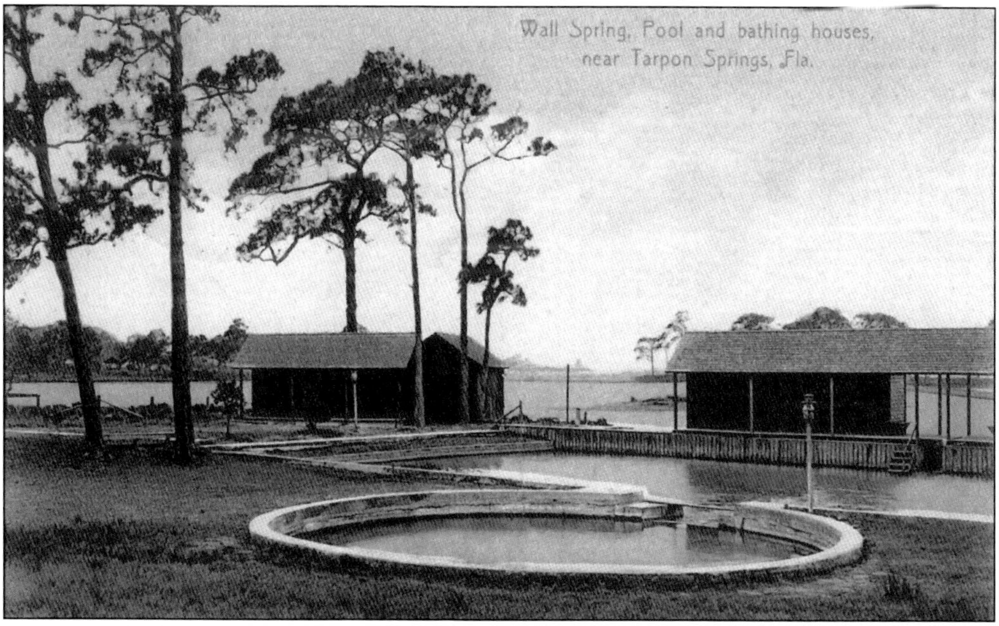

In 1884, Charles F. Wall purchased the property. He and his family maintained ownership until 1927, giving the springs the current name of Wall Springs. Wall would compete at the trap-shooting facility located northeast of the pool area. People from Tarpon Springs, Palm Harbor, Dunedin, Clearwater, and as far away as Tampa would all participate. (Courtesy of Sam H. Mack.)

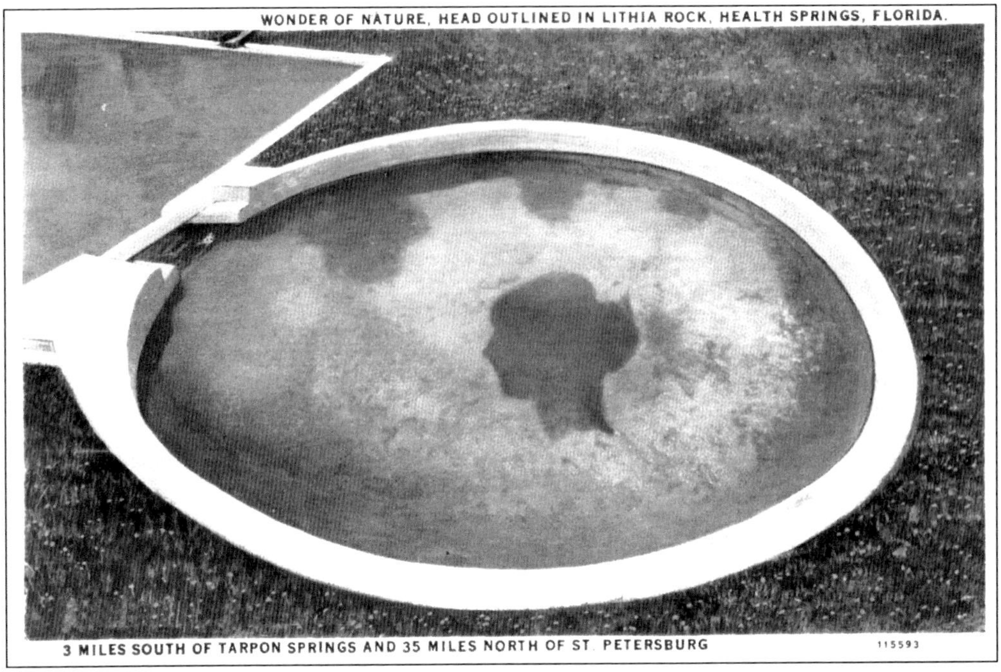

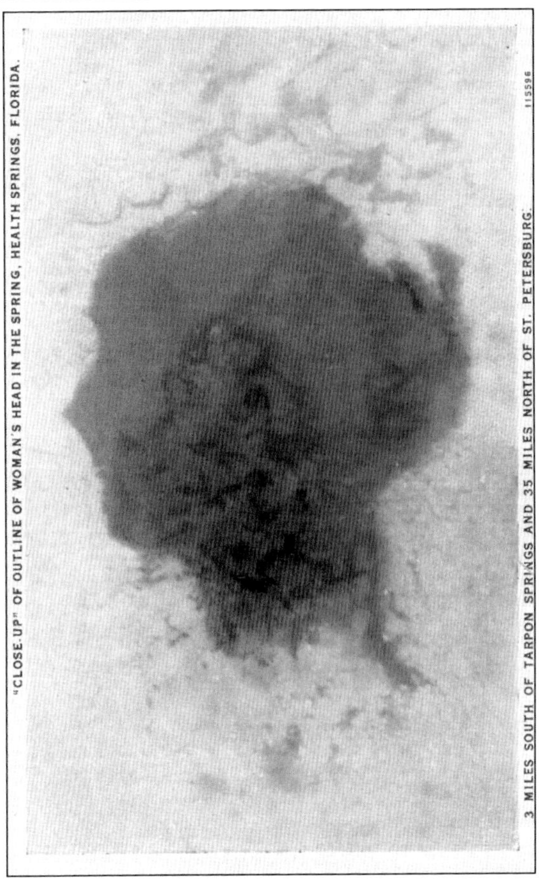

The next owner of Wall Springs was realtor Harry Wentworth Davis. During this time, the spring was said to produce 200,000 gallons an hour. Information from the back of this postcard claims that the spring is "the healthiest swimming pool in Florida" and that it makes free drinking water available to all. The water flow now varies from none at all during droughts to 444,300 gallons per hour with an average water flow around 175,000 gallons an hour. During the time of the Davis family's ownership, the name became Health Springs, reflecting its use as a health spa. (Courtesy of Jackie Payne.)

This postcard shows a close-up view of the outline of the women's head that reportedly belonged to Ponce de León's wife. The depth is nine feet below the water's surface at her nose. The spring is more than 60 feet deep at the center of her head. It was said that a swim in the pool is an "invigorating tonic," perhaps due to the mineral content of the water or because the water temperature constantly remains around 74 degrees.

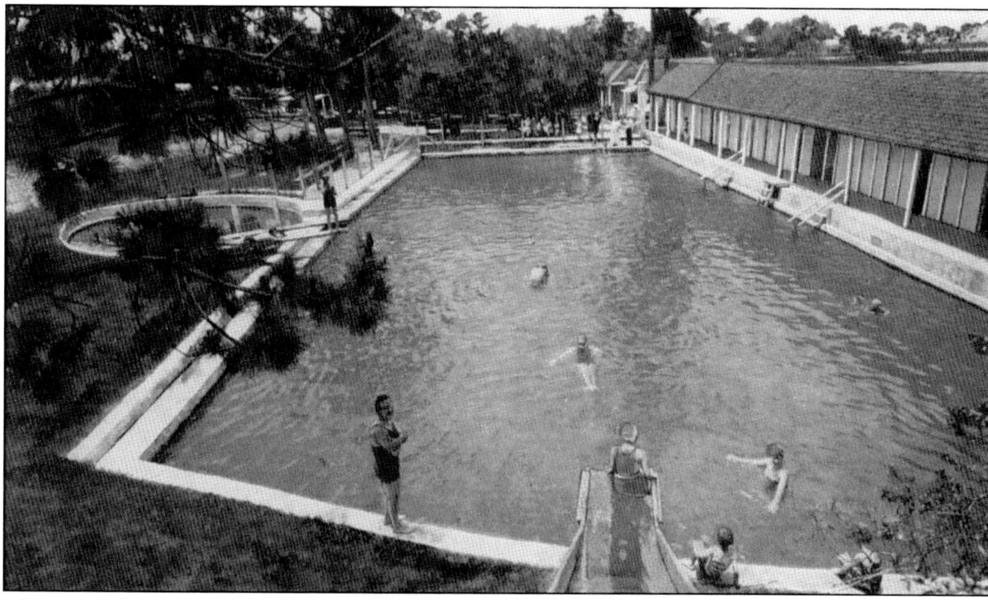

This view shows a diving board just north of the smaller pool and a slide. H.W. Davis sold the springs to the Cullen family in 1948. In 1988, Pinellas County started to purchase the property for use as a park. The swimming areas are now closed to protect the ecosystem. (Courtesy of Tampa Bay History Center.)

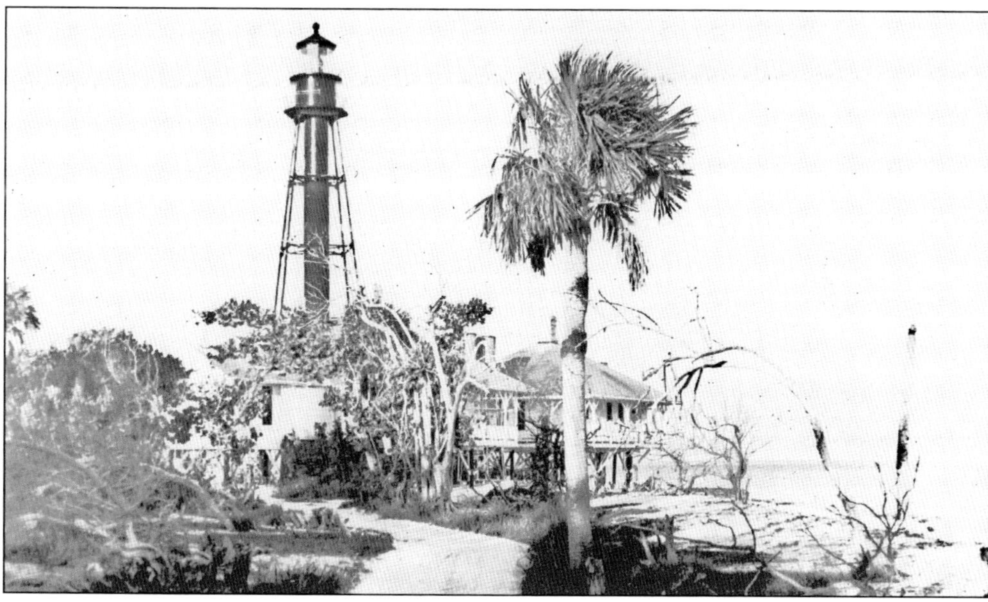

Anclote Key is an island three miles offshore from Tarpon Springs, close to the mouth of the Anclote River. In 1887, Tarpon Springs was incorporated as a city and the railroad chugged into town. One of the brightest and highest points of the year was the Anclote Key lighthouse becoming operational on September 15. The lighthouse used a third-order Fresnel lens to concentrate the light emitting from the oil lamp. The lens was rotated by a clockwork-type assembly driven by a weight that was wound by a lighthouse keeper. This lighthouse was constructed of cast iron in a narrow, cylindrical core with an outer skeletal bracing. (Courtesy of Tarpon Springs Area Historical Society.)

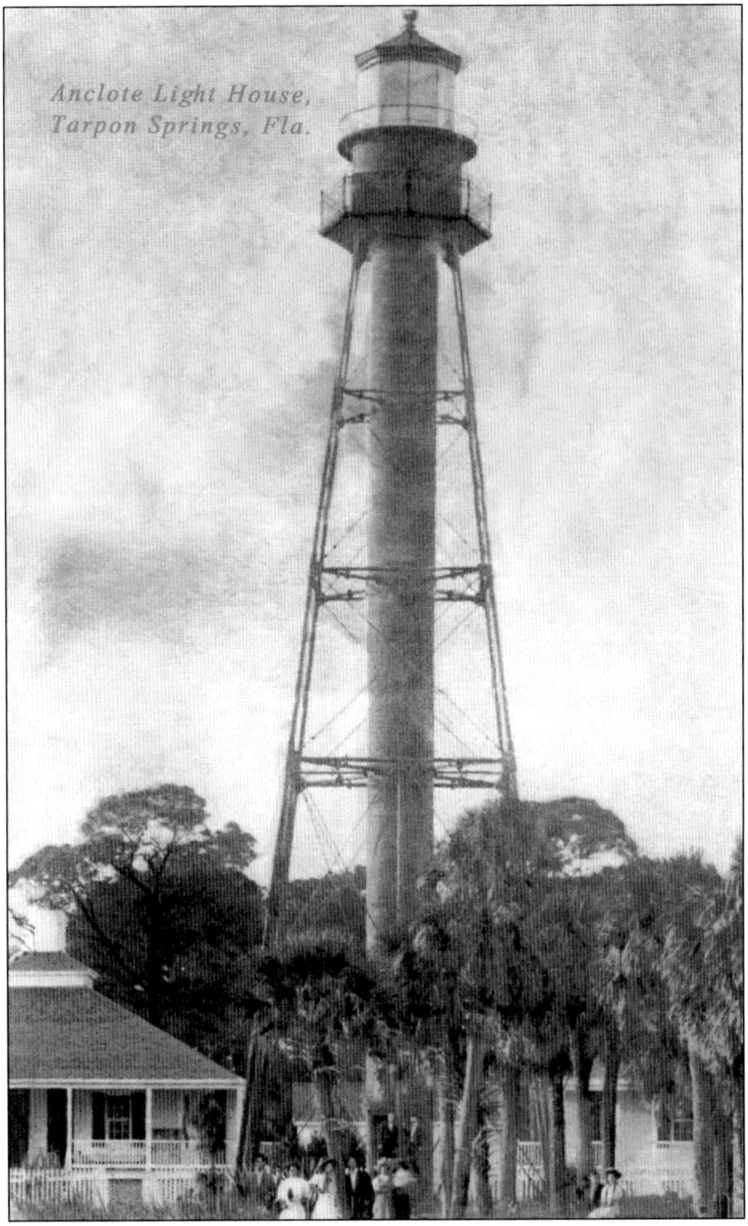

The lighthouse keeper had the job of keeping wicks trimmed, stocking the fuel from the oil house to the tower, and winding the clockworks, along with other maintenance tasks. There were two houses on the island: one for the keeper and another for his assistant and their families who would live there with them. A dock went out into the gulf, and there was an onshore boathouse with rails that were used to hoist the boat in and out of the water. A series of brick walkways connected the buildings. Robert E. Meyer performed his duties for 35 years as the second keeper. It was a popular destination for outings from the mainland. The Coast Guard took over control of lighthouses in 1939, automated Anclote's light in 1952, and decommissioned it in 1984. In September 2003, a celebration to "Relight the Light" took place, signaling the restoration of the Anclote Key lighthouse, a beacon to welcome all home. (Courtesy of Pauline Pavlis Phillips.)

Three

Our Accommodations Are Beautiful

Florida has long been a destination for travel. As early as the 1870s, Florida became a place where the rich and famous would come for a vacation or an extended stay. The northerners were known to visit during the winter months, and they still do so today. Often times, health physicians would recommend to their patients a period of time for recuperation in the sunny south, with its warm weather and fresh ocean breezes. The sunshine and natural beauty, like that of the white sand beaches, was an anecdote for whatever ailed people. Fishing and hunting were available for the sportsmen. Visitors came to Tarpon Springs for many different reasons, but one thing was for sure: once people visited Tarpon, they were smitten.

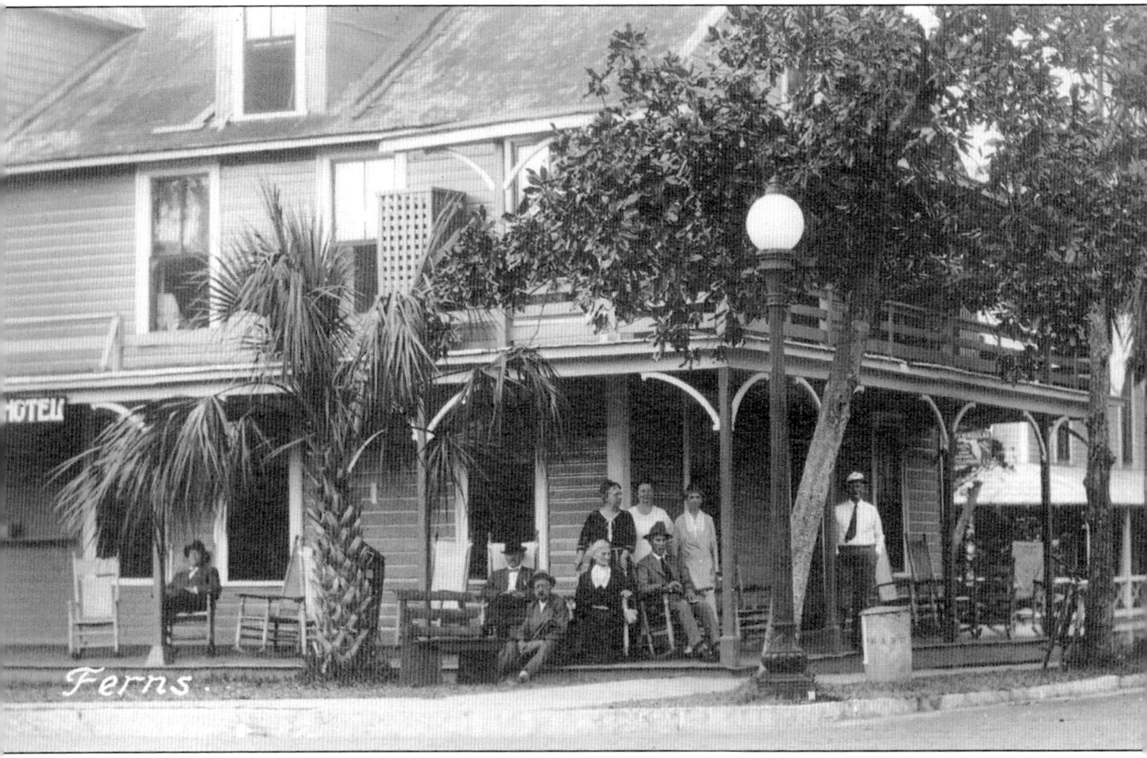

From its hospitable early beginnings in 1882 at the Boyer family cabin, Tarpon Springs grew quickly within the first few years, creating a need for accommodations. There are many reasons why people travel from their homes to another locale. At times it is dictated by opportunities not present in one's home town, such as the role of a traveling salesperson or a person conducting business in another locality. At other times, people travel for enjoyment, visiting friends and relatives, or exploring new territories. What was once an uninhabited wilderness became a thriving community offering a selection of lodging. The definition of hospitality is to welcome guests, being both generous and warm, and well disposed to strangers. In this c. 1908 photograph, the Ferns Hotel, with the kindly "Mother Meres" as its manager, hosts a large group of guests. (Courtesy of Tarpon Springs Area Historical Society.)

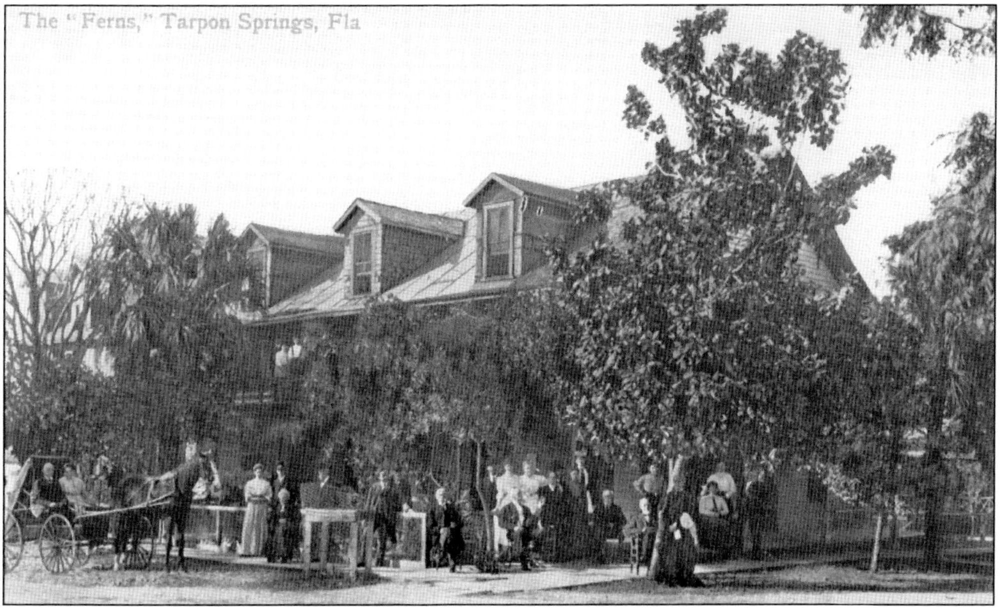

Perhaps the first hospitality offered in Tarpon Springs was in the cabin of Mary and Joshua Boyer, who wrote about the developing community's early residents arriving with no place to stay. The Tropical was the first hotel, located on the southwest corner of Tarpon and Pinellas Avenues. It was later named the Ferns, as shown in this c. 1900s postcard. The Tarpon Springs Hotel, the second hotel in the area, burned in the late 19th century. (Courtesy of Hammond Salley.)

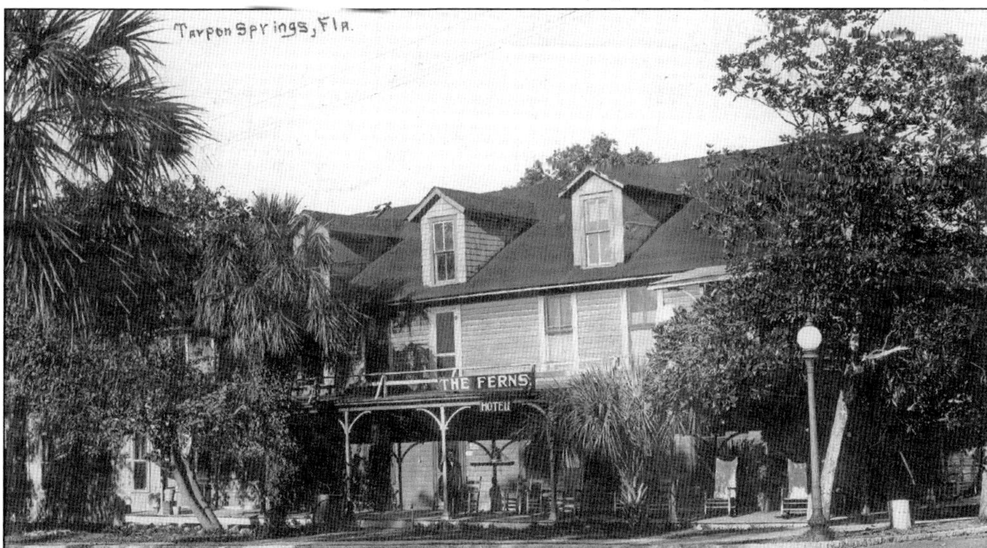

Walter and Amelia (Petzold) Meres owned the Tropical Hotel, which was located on the southwest corner of Tarpon and Pinellas Avenues. Amelia, also known as Mother Meres, ministered to sick or lonesome travelers who stayed at the Tropical and treated friends and acquaintances with equal care. The hotel's name was changed to the Ferns because of the surrounding lush vegetation that Mother Meres planted. At that time, Pinellas Avenue was not a through street and was known as Citron Street south of Tarpon Avenue. (Courtesy of Jackie Payne.)

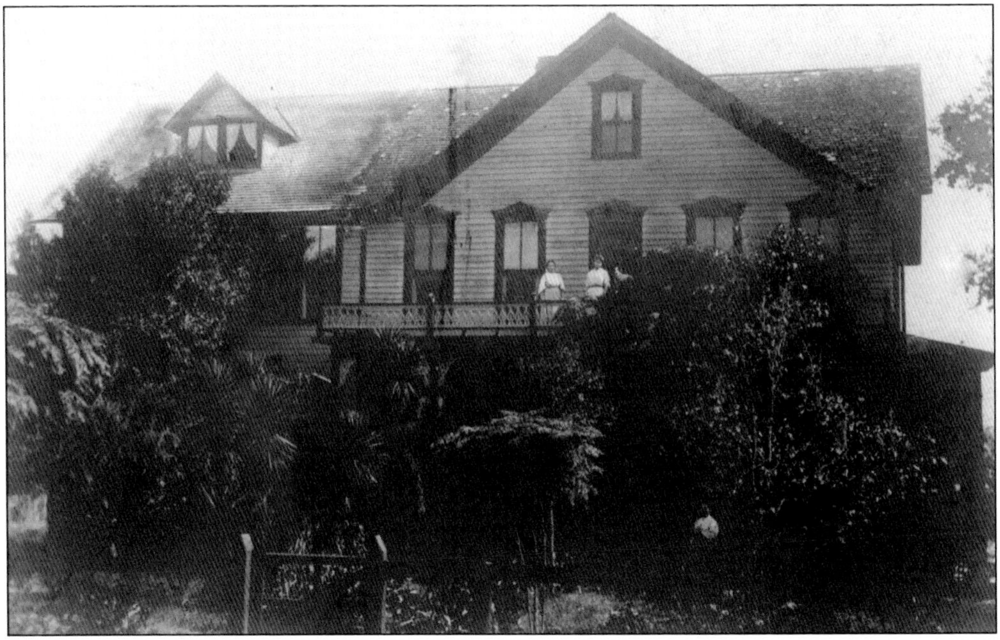

Amelia Meres was the oldest child in a large family, and her youngest sibling was Theodore J. Petzold. The above postcard shows Theodore's daughters, Clair and Alice Petzold, on the porch while Amelia is in the yard. At the time this real-photo postcard was taken, the building was being used as a residence and had been purchased for $1,000. Reportedly created out of a need to house the workmen building the George Clemson mansion, the residence was turned into the Homeworth Inn. It was located on Court Street between Safford and Pinellas Avenues. After repairs and some enlargements, it became a small hotel, as shown in the c. 1912 postcard below, catering to tourists, transients, and town people. It could accommodate 15 guests. (Courtesy of Tarpon Springs Area Historical Society.)

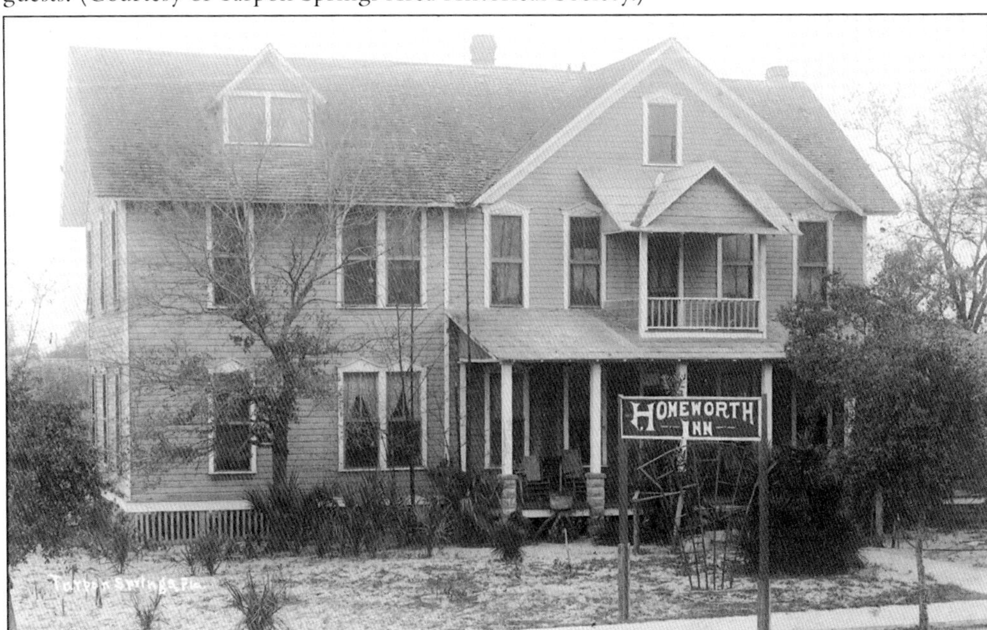

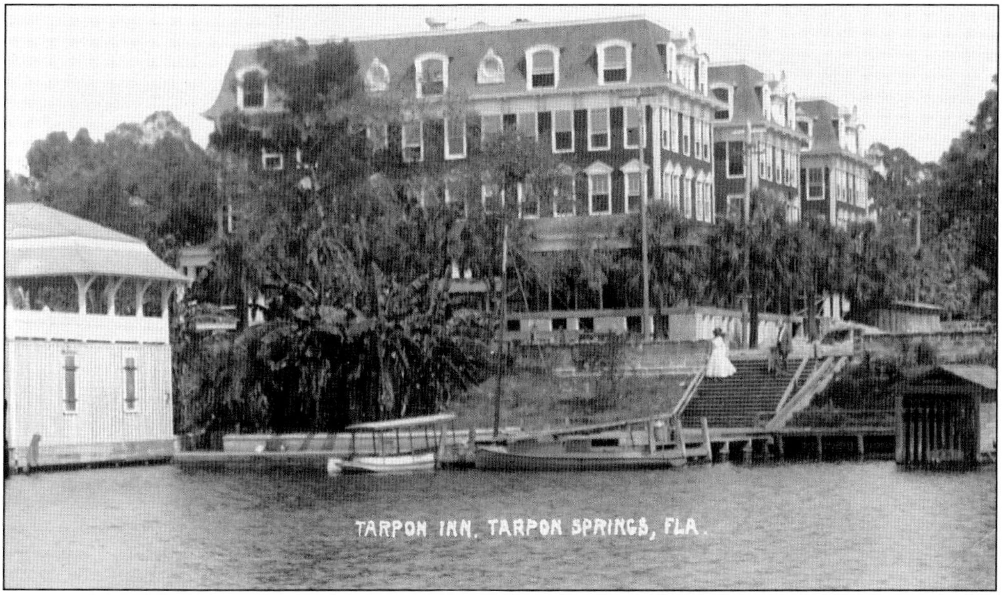

The inscription on this November 7, 1913, postcard reads, "This hotel is just being completed. They hope to open the 15th of Jan." A close look at this image reveals that the ground floor work has not been completed; stucco has not been applied, and the columns have not been completed. (Courtesy of Sam H. Mack.)

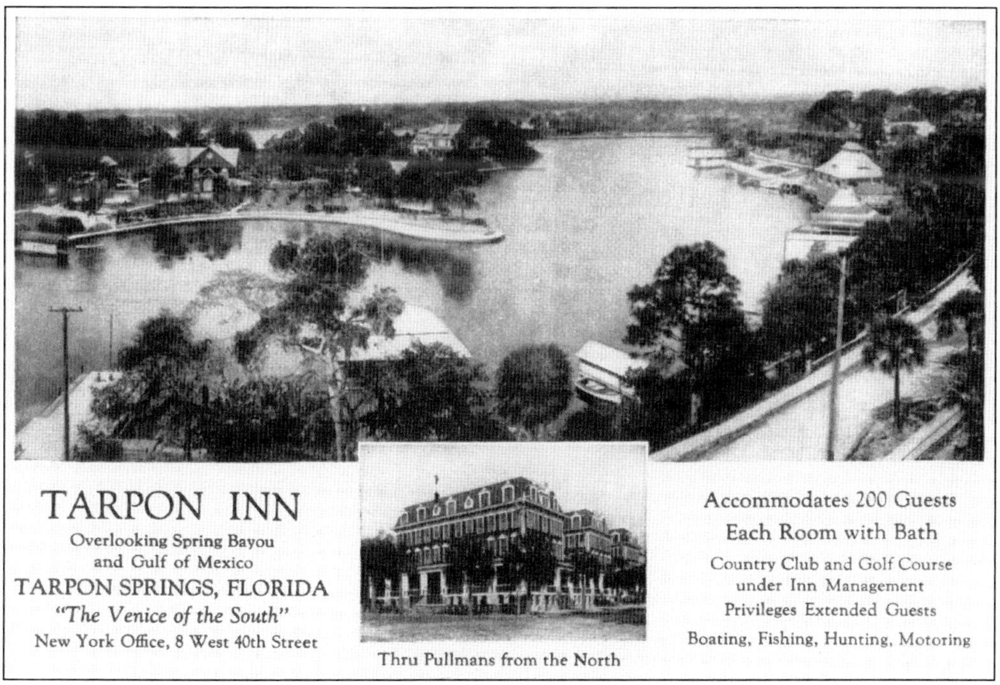

The Tarpon Inn, located at the corner of Tarpon Avenue and Spring Boulevard, overlooked the bayou, and at night the fountain would illuminate a 70-foot-high spray of water. It had all the luxury indulgences one could want at that time. In this later version of a promotional postcard, the words "Country Club" are added and the golf course is "under Inn Management." (Courtesy of Sam H. Mack.)

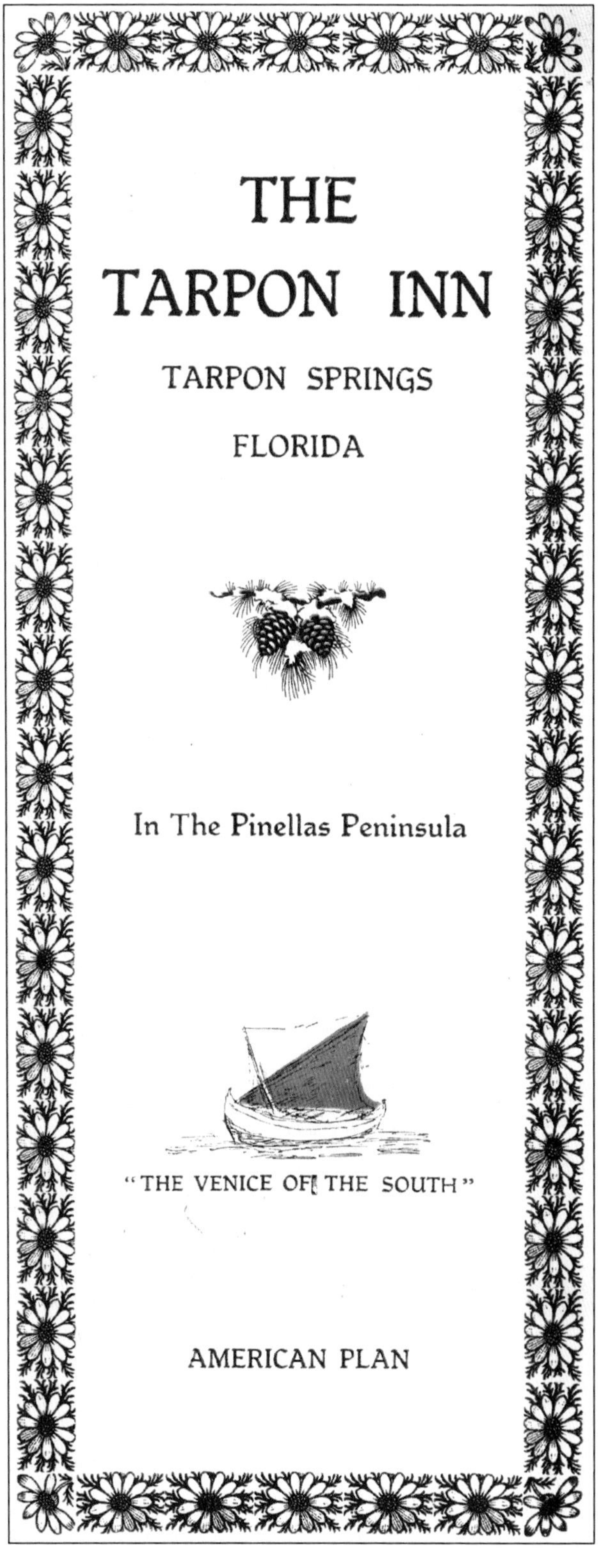

In order to entice upper-class northern residents to travel to this new hotel, manager Howard V. Dalton was available in a New York office to furnish rates and information about the Tarpon Inn, as well as travel by railroad. These are three panels of an attractive eight-panel brochure sent out upon request to potential customers. The first panel at left, the front cover, features a border of flowers surrounding two pine cones and pine needles covered in snow above a sailboat with the words "The Venice of the South." It suggested to the northerners that they would be smart to winter in the sunny south. (Courtesy of Sam H. Mack.)

The Tarpon Inn

Tarpon Springs Florida

"THE VENICE OF THE SOUTH"

the west coast. The present management aims for itself a high reputation. The meats are always fresh and of ample variety, and the breadstuffs unsurpassable. The drinking water is from the famous Tarpon Springs of fresh water, which are located on the Inn property.

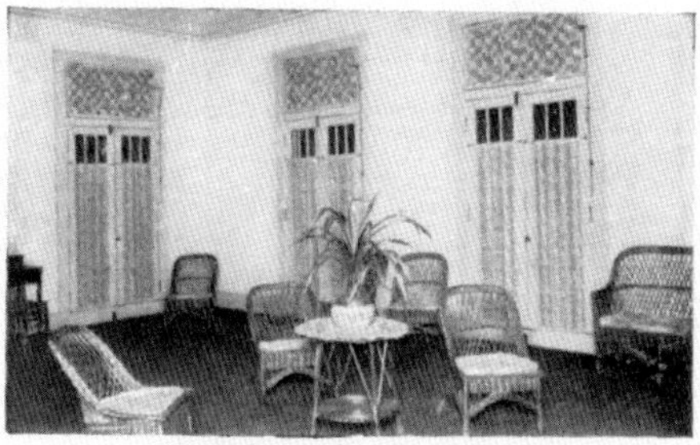

CORNER OF LADIES' RECEPTION ROOM

Tarpon Springs is the center of a great fishing industry, and the Inn serves all the varieties of fish for which the Gulf shore is famous, fresh from the water and prepared after most appetizing recipes.

Early Florida vegetables and fruits make delightful additions to the menu.

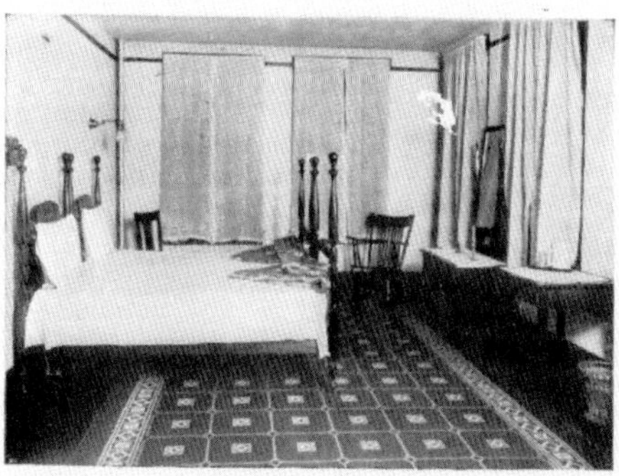

A BEDROOM INTERIOR

The Tarpon Inn

Tarpon Springs Florida

"THE VENICE OF THE SOUTH"

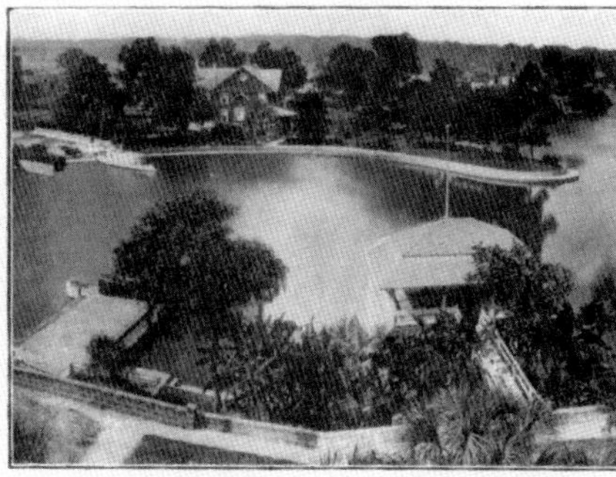

VIEW OF THE SPRING BAYOU—FROM INN PORCHES

Along the Boulevard is a large cottage colony, including winter residents from nearly all the cities in the Eastern and Central States. The Inn is thus the center of a delightful social life, with all that this implies.

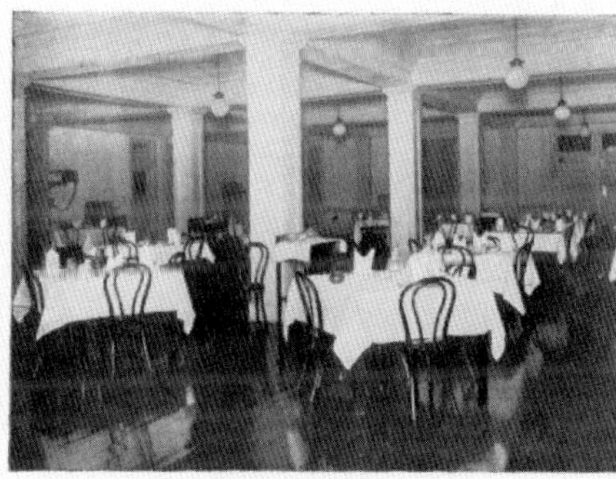

THE MAIN DINING ROOM

Nothing contributes more to the comfort and health of hotel guests than well selected and well cooked food. The Inn is in this respect easily the leader along

The advertising booklet begins by promoting the climate, stating that there are "more sunny days and a more equable daily temperature than any other county in the state." The reason given is that Pinellas County is surrounded by water. The inn is promoted in these panels; further, it endorses the Tarpon Springs Country Club and golf course. Information on transportation by railroad, steamship, and "brick motor road" is included. A photograph of the Epiphany, also known as Greek Cross Day, is included in the brochure. The back page provides tourist activities suggestions such as visits to the Anclote River, Wall Springs, Lake Butler, Sponge fisheries, Anclote Keys, and lighthouse, as well as the New York office and address. (Courtesy of Sam H. Mack.)

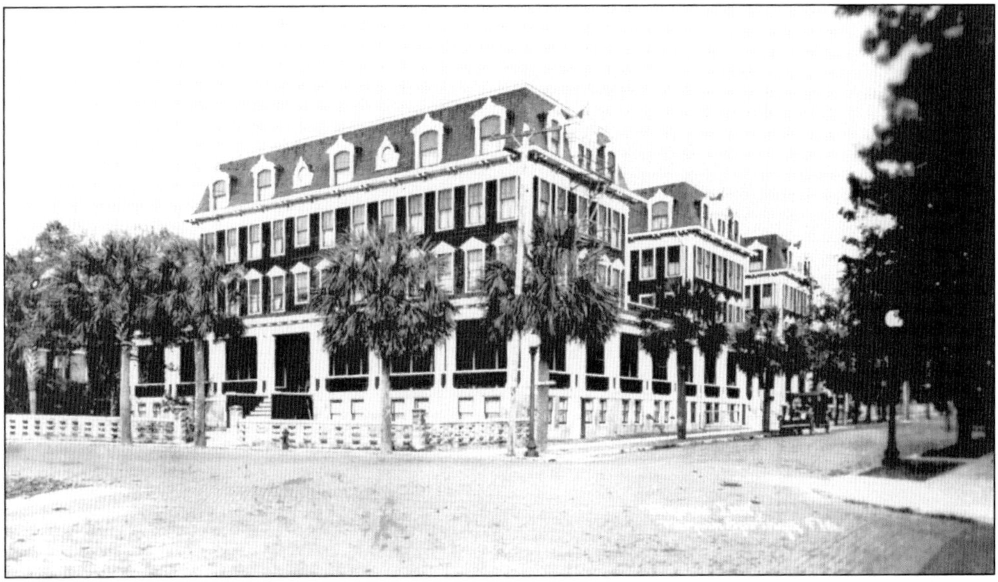

Built at a cost of $150,000, the Tarpon Inn offers the latest of modern conveniences. The inn was "a modern, semi-fire-proof building. It has all the conveniences of an up-to-date city hotel." Rooms featured an attached bath, steam heat, hot and cold running water, a telephone, and six windows in the larger rooms. The inn also boasted an electric elevator. In spite of its purported ability to withhold a fire, the Tarpon Inn burned down in 1927. (Courtesy of Pauline Pavlis Phillips.)

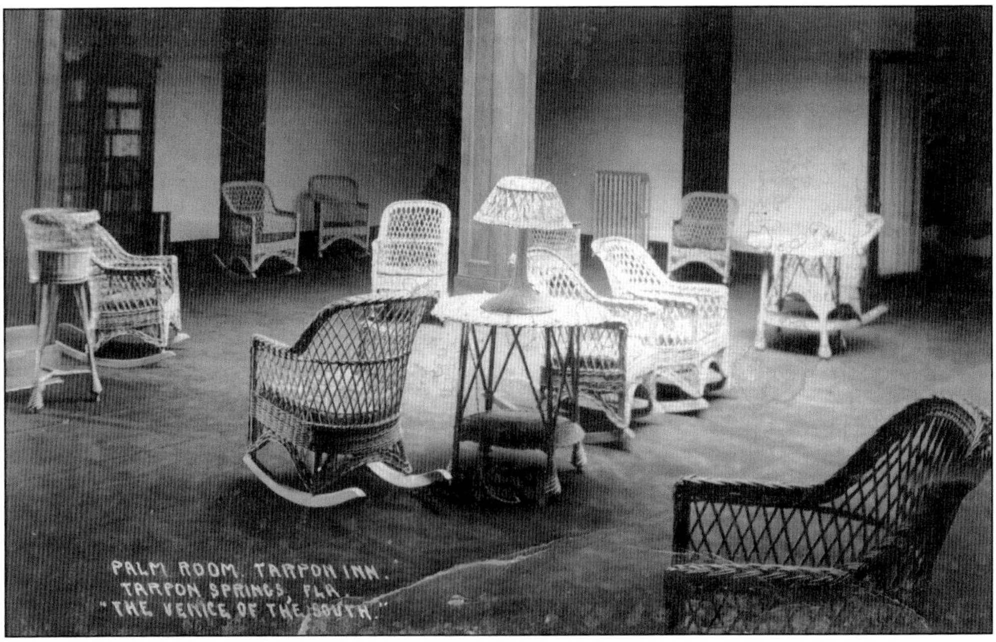

Shown here is the Palm Room at the Tarpon Inn. Its furnishings were promoted as, "modern twin beds, and the finest most comfortable mattresses to be found in any hotel in Florida. Each room is equipped with all the conveniences which add so greatly to the comfort of the winter resident, writing tables, long mirrors, ample closet space." Almost the entire first floor was comprised of spacious and well-ventilated public rooms.

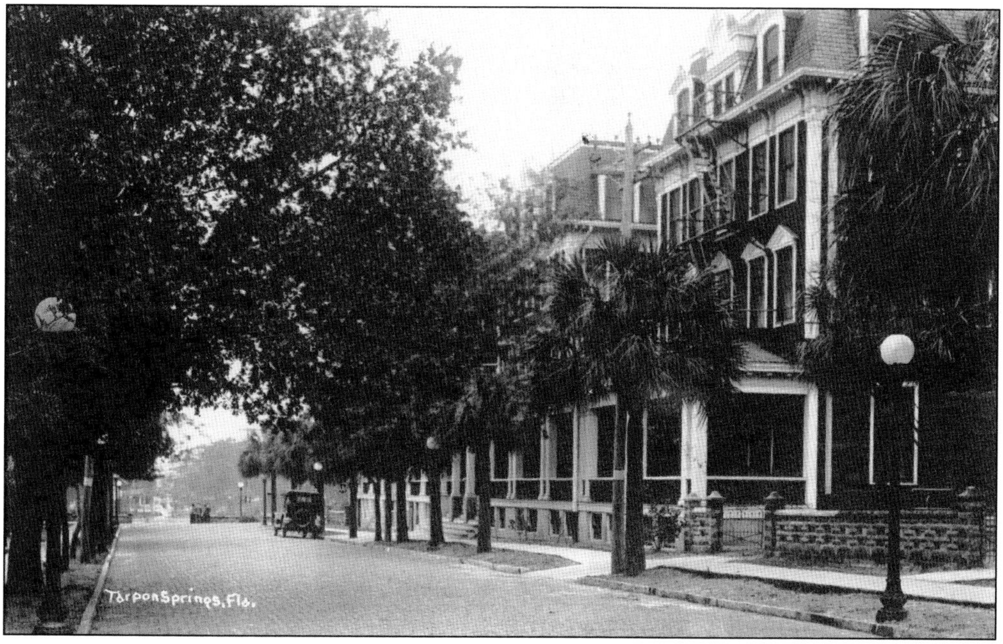

A hurricane with maximum winds recorded at 100 miles per hour hit Tarpon Springs on October 25, 1921. It was later estimated to be a category 3 hurricane. Thankfully, there was no loss of life or injuries in Tarpon Springs and most of the harm was done to roofs, windows, and trees. The telephone and electrical lines were also damaged; however, all employees worked to return normal service as quickly as possible. The Tarpon Inn and the Hotel Stratford both suffered water damage. The former (above) had many broken windows. Part of the Hotel Stratford's roof had been blown away. (Both images courtesy of Sam H. Mack.)

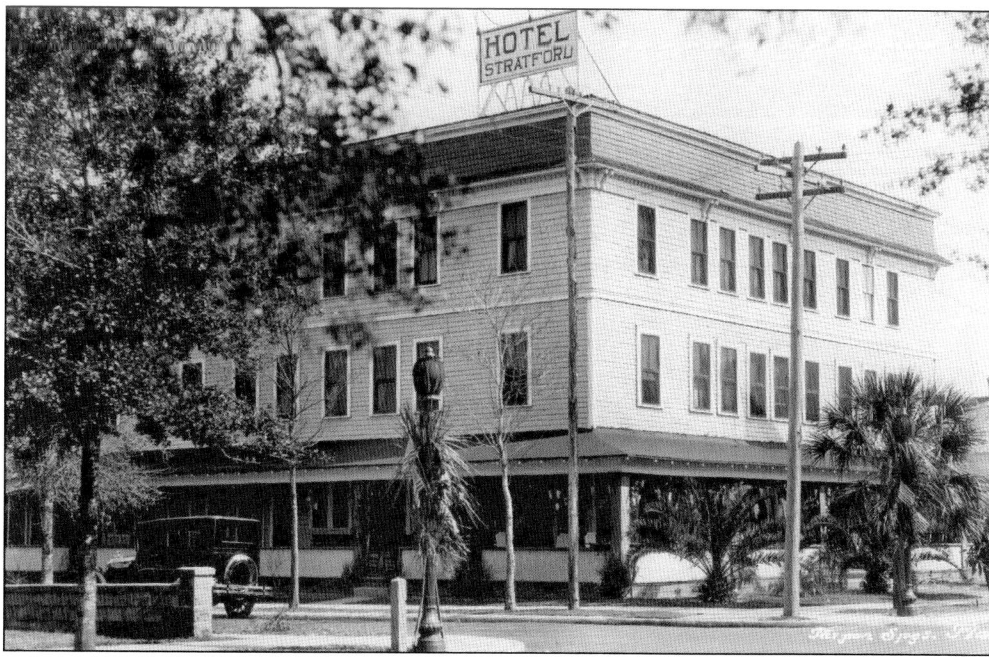

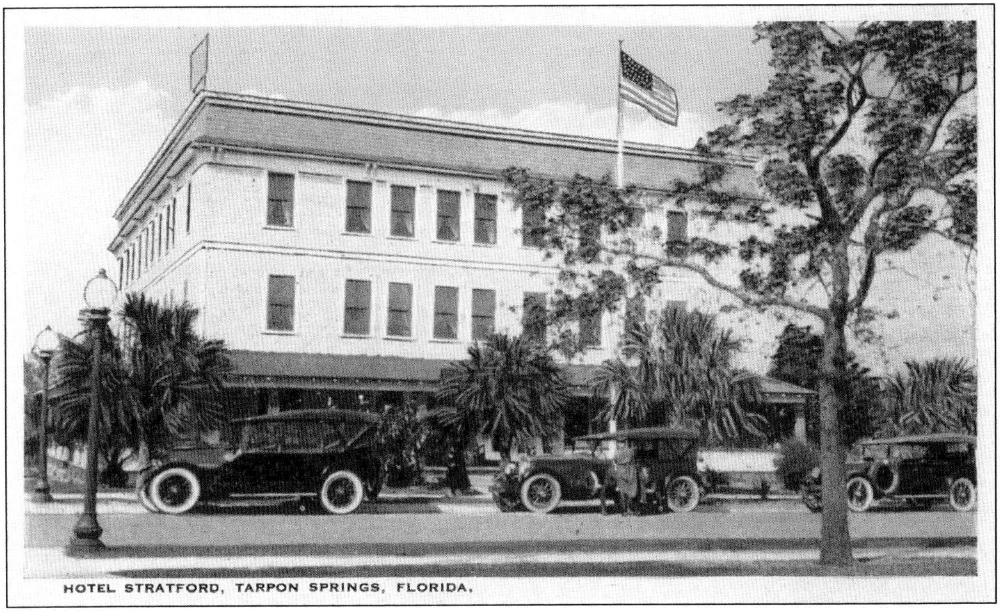

The Hotel Stratford faced Tarpon Avenue at the corner of Gross Avenue. It was a three-story hotel built from lumber left over from the Fivay lumber mill. Tarpon Springs High School's class of 1922 had their banquet here on June 8. On the menu were olives, dill pickles, fruit cocktail, filet of fish, chicken au printemps with dressing, French fried potatoes, string beans, fresh carrots, rice, salad, ice cream, roll cake, hot rolls, muffins, coffee, and iced tea. (Courtesy of Tarpon Springs Area Historical Society.)

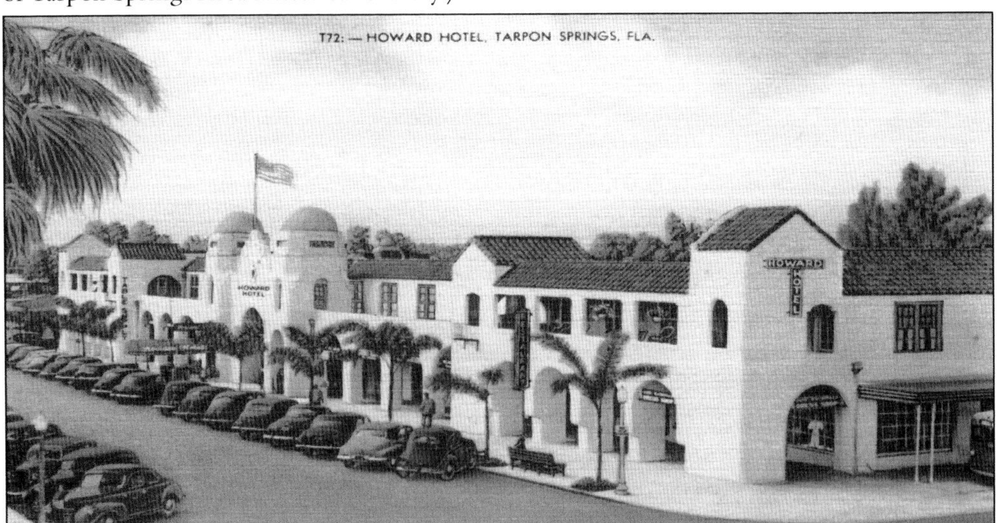

The Shaw Arcade, designed as a prime example of Mediterranean Revival architecture, was built on South Pinellas Avenue in the mid-1920s. The lower story had 10 small shops, and the Howard Hotel, comprised of 40 hotel rooms, was on the upper floor. The archway between the twin copper-domed towers was once a drive-through area. The post office used to be located downstairs, and the bus station was on the north side. A 1976 fire destroyed much of the second floor; however, it was renovated and added to the National Register of Historic Places on January 12, 1984.

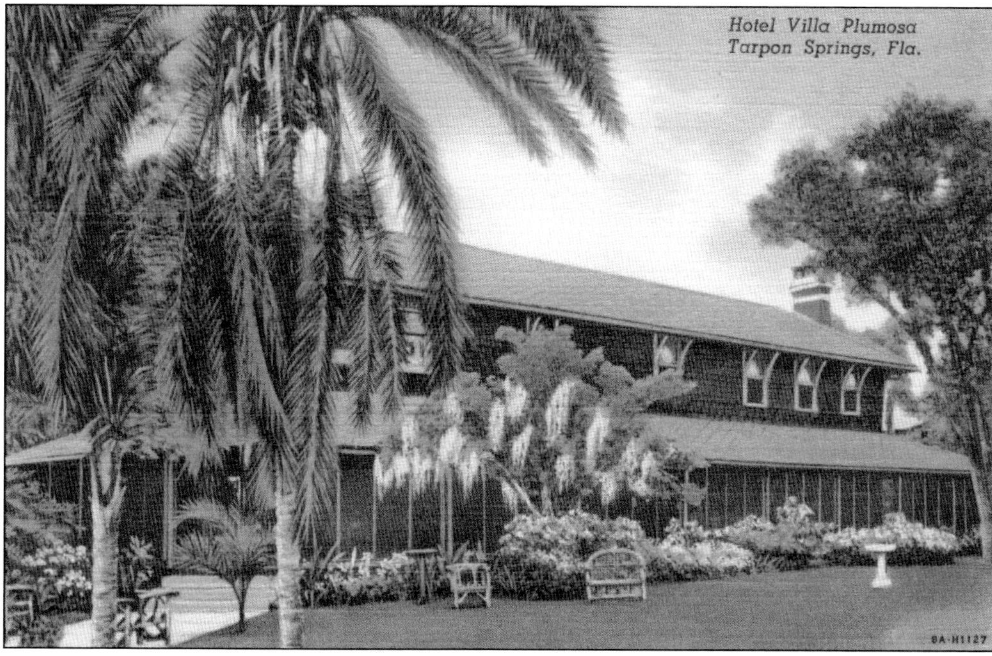

The Hotel Villa Plumosa, originally a private residence with a boathouse, stood at the corner of Orange Street and Grand Boulevard. Bonnie Staley, the owners' daughter who worked as a mermaid at Weeki Wachee, used to dive from the roof of the boathouse to swim in Spring Bayou. When the movie ***Beneath the 12 Mile Reef*** was filmed in Tarpon Springs, most of the actors, including Robert Wagner, Terry Moore, Gilbert Roland, J. Carrol Naish, Richard Boone, and Peter Graves, stayed there. The location is once again residential, known as the Villa Plumosa Condominiums.

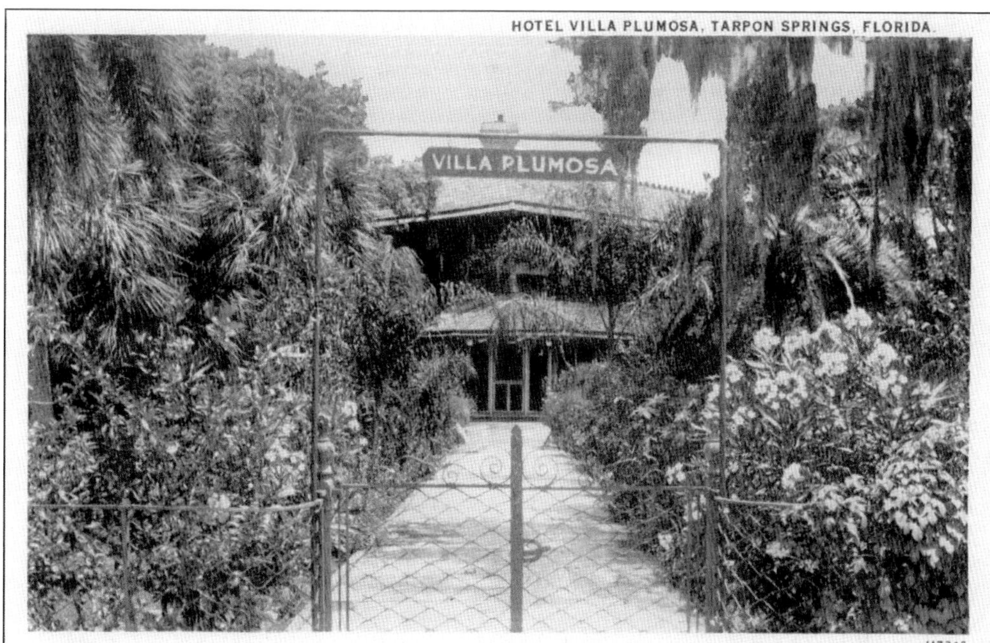

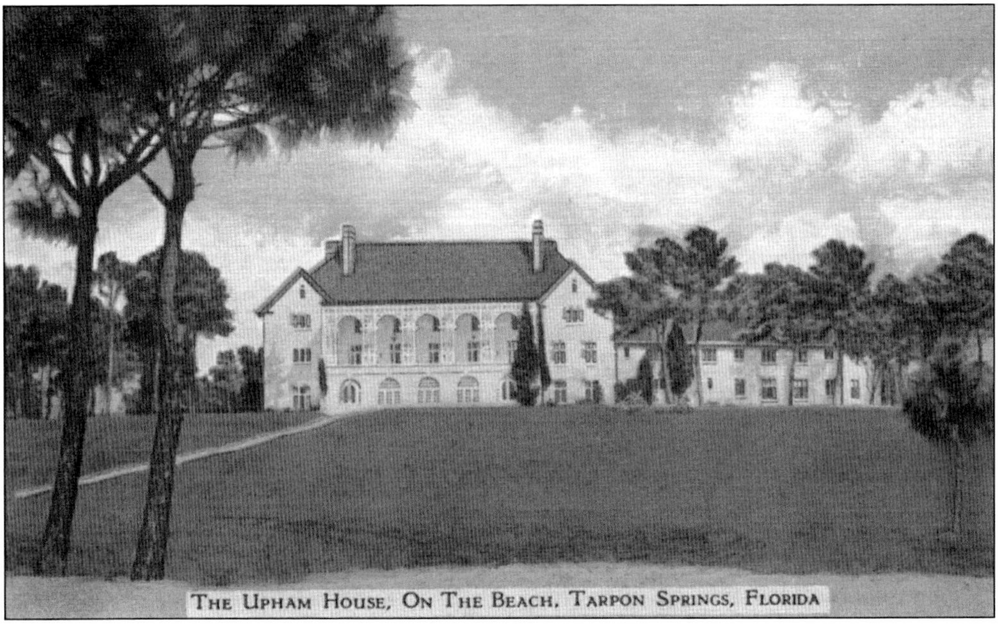

First developed as the Sunset Hills Country Club, this beautiful property was located between the Anclote River and the Gulf of Mexico and featured its own golf course; however, it was open for only three years before being repurposed as a hotel. Al Capone was rumored to have stayed at the elegant resort hotel called the Upham House when he vacationed in Florida. It then became Anclote Psychiatric Center, later called the Manors, and was eventually torn down to make a housing subdivision. (Courtesy of Sam H. Mack.)

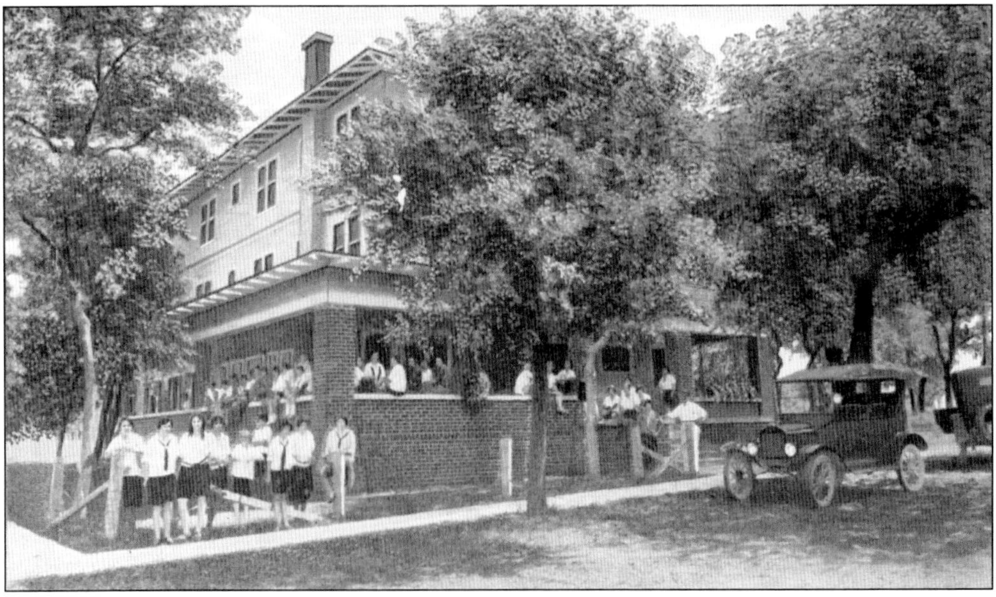

Crystal Beach was the location of the Blue Heron Hotel. When the hotel fell on bad times during the Depression, it was sold to Reverend Fred and Cora Markert, Canary Island missionaries who had returned home due to language barriers. They established Faith Mission in 1923, and in 1928 they began using the hotel as a home for orphans and unwanted children. (Courtesy of Tarpon Springs Area Historical Society.)

Four

The Sponge Capital of the World

Before Tarpon Springs earned a reputation as the Sponge Capital of the World, the sponge industry was centered in the Mediterranean. In the United States, sponge harvesting took place from Apalachicola to Key West, where the market for selling and buying sponge was located as early as the 1840s. The early spongers harvested by a hook method. Two men would use a smaller boat that one would row while the other passenger would look through a glass-bottomed bucket. When a sponge was found, a 15-to-40-foot-long pole with a pronged hook was used to reach down and pull the sponge loose to the surface. The man who would change this common practice was John K. Cheyney. He formed the Anclote and Rock Island Sponge Company in 1891 with Hamilton Disston's financial backing, bringing the industry into the Bailey's Bluff area. Cheyney had hired Greek sponge buyer John Cocoris, who convinced Cheyney that the relatively new hard-helmet diving method would yield vast amounts more. The two became a team and brought over the first hard-helmet sponge divers from Greece.

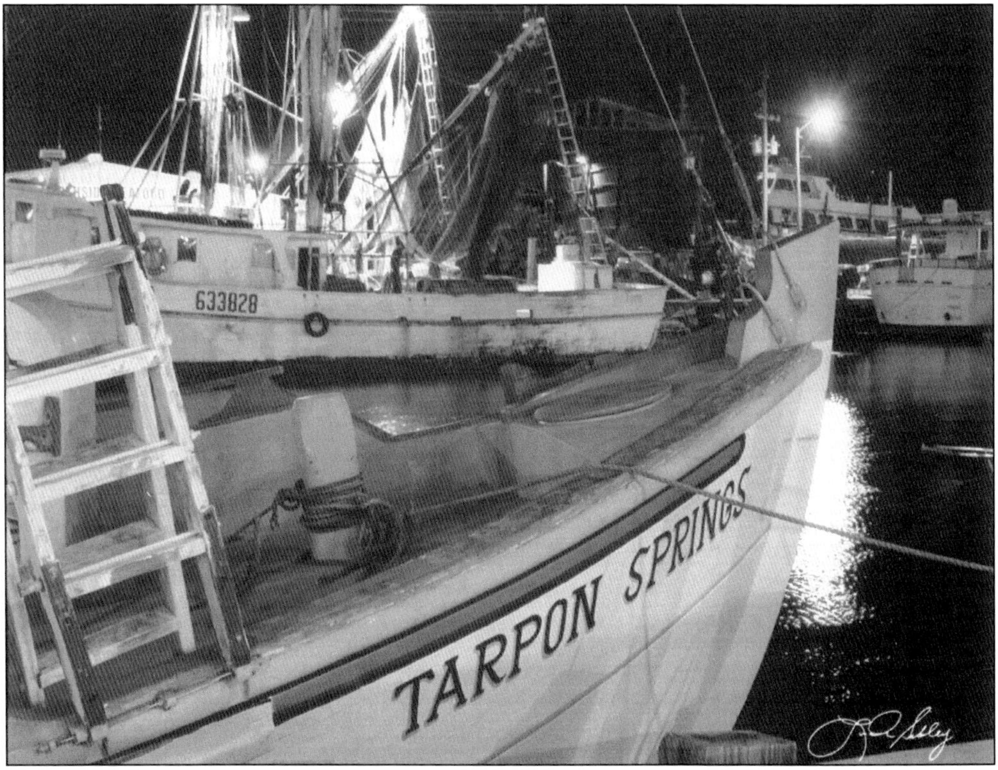

All is quiet in the nightfall. This distinctive Greek-style sponging boat, the *Tarpon Springs*, has its ladder prepared for a diver. Moored across the river is a working shrimp boat. Its crews will soon leave to earn their wages and bring in a much desired catch for dinner. (Courtesy of Lisa Sibley, photographer.)

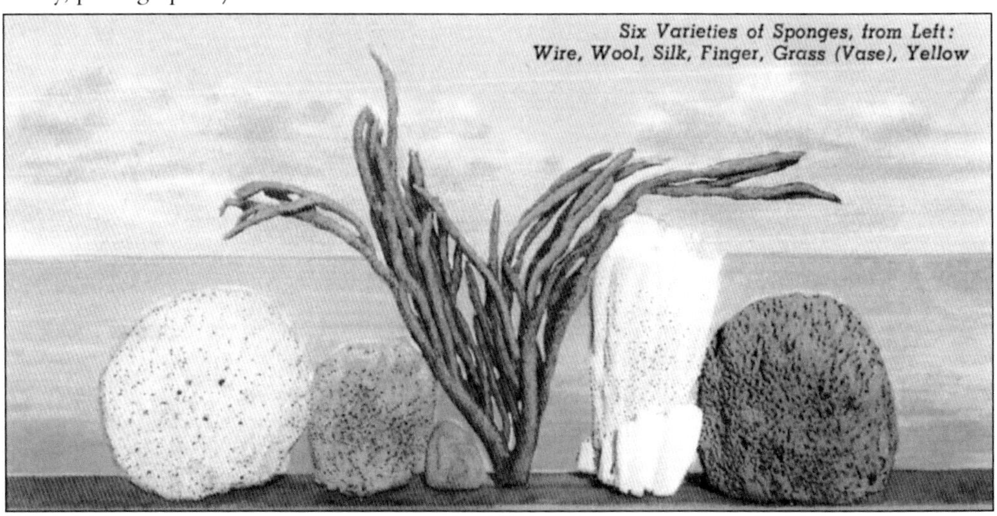

Sponges are a renewable resource harvested from the bottom of the ocean. Here are six of the main varieties of sponges that are brought in from the Gulf of Mexico off Tarpon Springs. The most sought after sponge is the wool sponge, second from the left, due to its absorbency and its pliability. It can be used for cleaning, painting, or bathing, which the Roman empresses did. (Courtesy of Tampa Bay History Center.)

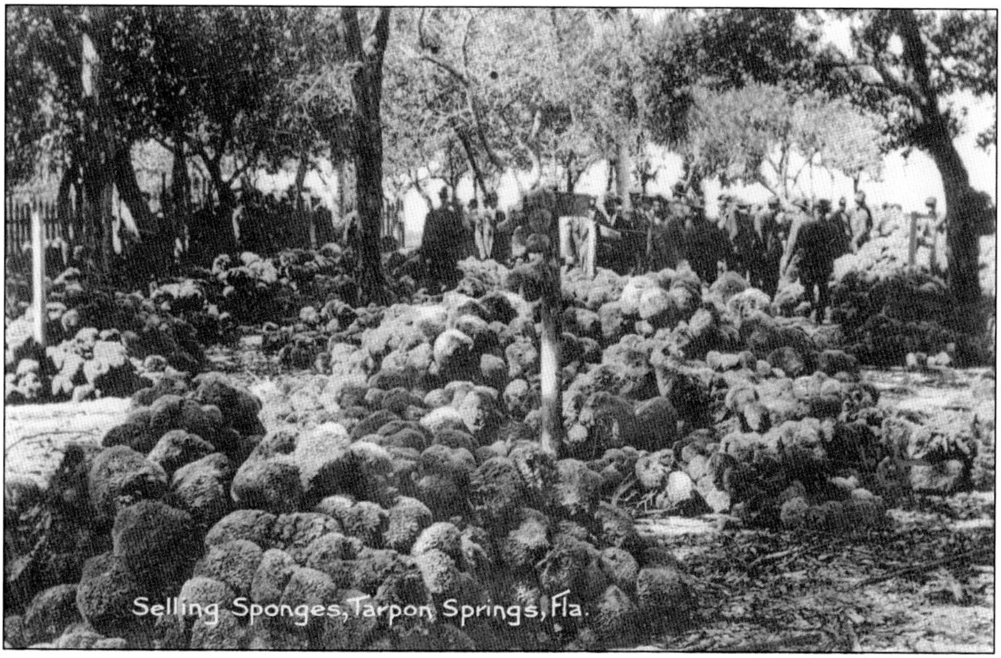

Searching back in ancient Greek history, Aristotle spoke of sponges, claiming that they are somewhere between plants and animals, yet primitive, and lacking in nervous systems, stomachs, and brains. Found in every ocean and at every depth, there are thousands of species. The skeleton of the sponge is the final product sought after. These sponges are possibly being sold at Bailey's Bluff. (Courtesy of Tarpon Springs Area Historical Society.)

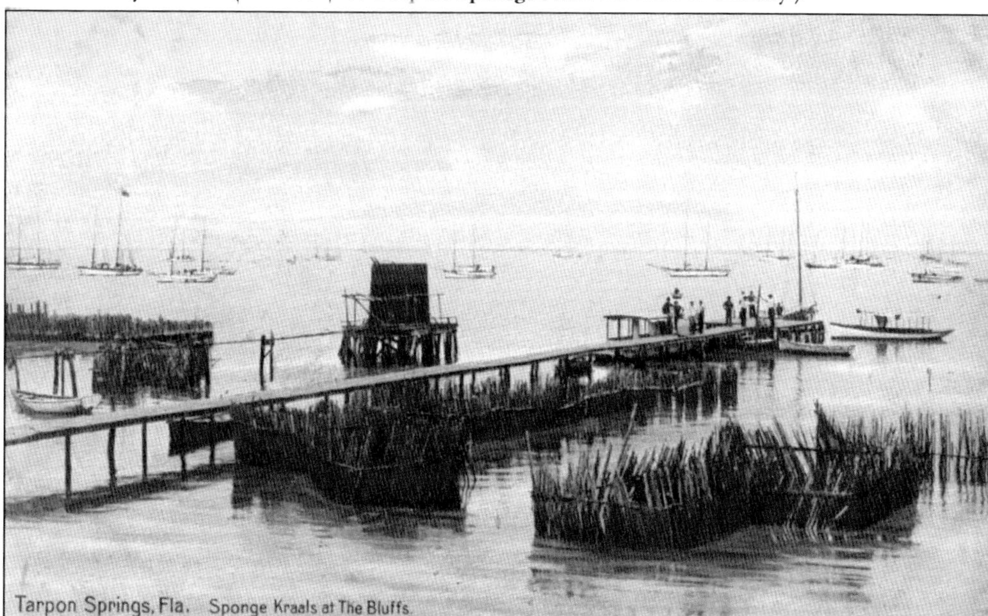

The early spongers brought their catches to the kraals at Bailey's Bluff, close to the Anclote River. The kraals, or crawls, would contain the sponges, while the ebb and flow that naturally occurs with the tide helped to wash and clean them. Visible in the background are the boats with one unloading its catch on the dock. (Courtesy of Heritage Village Archives and Library.)

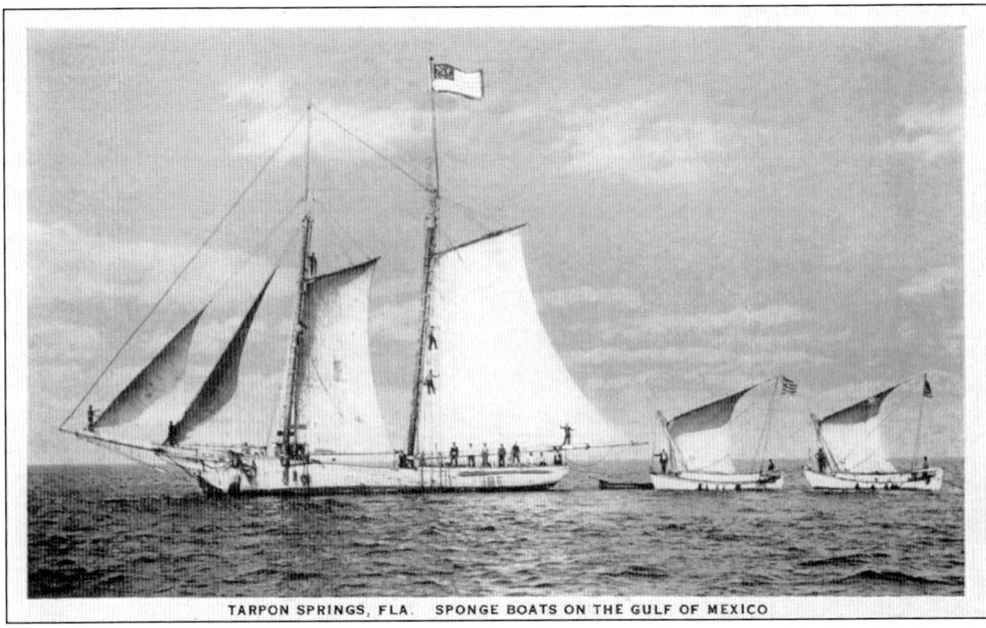

In the book *Strangers at Ithaca,* the name of the schooner in this postcard is identified as the *Telegram* with two diving boats the *Pelagia* and *Androniki.* An account of the sinking of the *Telegram* in March 1921 is told by its captain, J.M. Thompson, who had gone to explore alternate sponge beds in waters off of Mexico with a crew of three. (Courtesy of Tampa Bay History Center.)

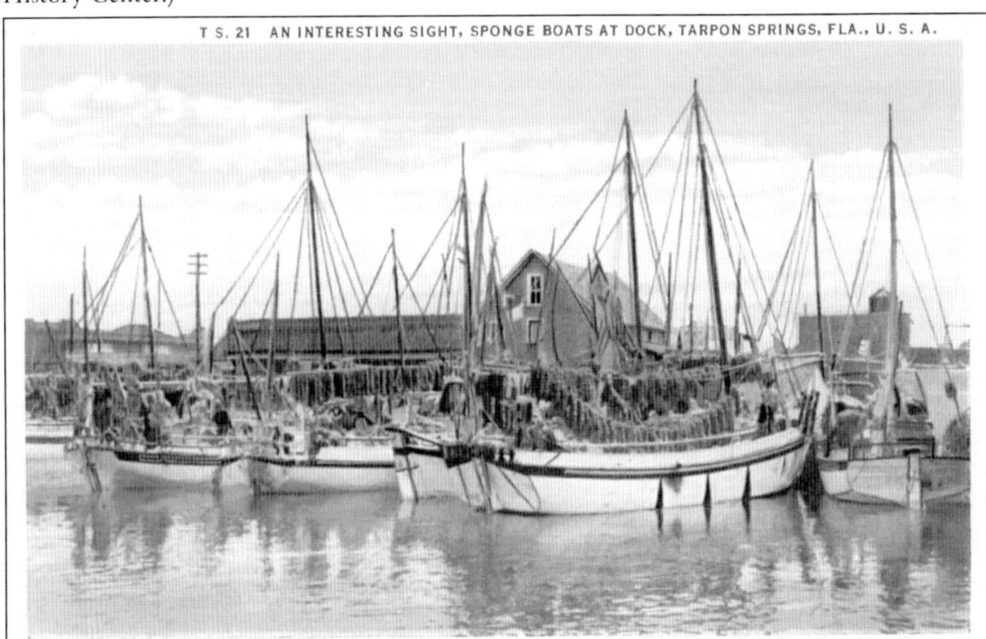

Animosity ran high at times between the Conchs and the Greeks when one group would venture into the other's territory. *Beneath the 12 Mile Reef,* a movie made in 1953, illustrated the plight of the Greek people and the Conchs. Many local "Tarponites" were in the movie. (Courtesy of Tarpon Springs Area Historical Society.)

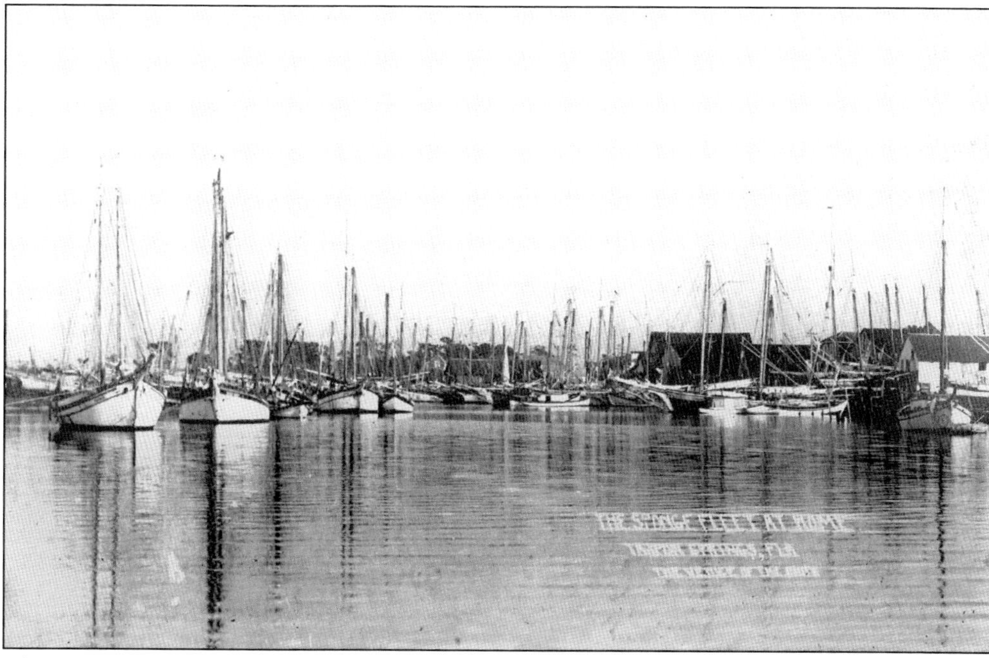

This card is titled "Sponge Fleet at Home." Some of the first spongers were from the Keys or Bahamas, and many of them were of African American descent, working side by side with the locals and Greeks. Most men working in the sponge industry spoke Greek, so communication was not a problem. (Courtesy of Tarpon Springs Area Historical Society.)

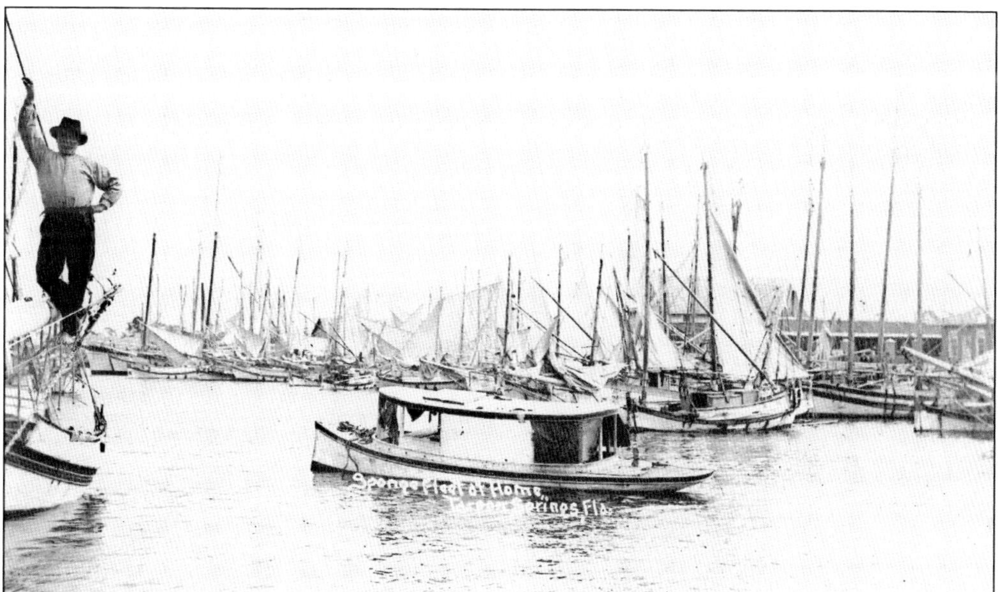

Another card with the same title above offers a close-up view. The sails are up on many of the boats (probably to dry them), as a deckhand stands on the bow. When the industry developed from hook boats to diving boats, there was a shortage of dive boats. A variety of vessels were used, although their original intent was not that of a dive boat. (Courtesy of Sam H. Mack.)

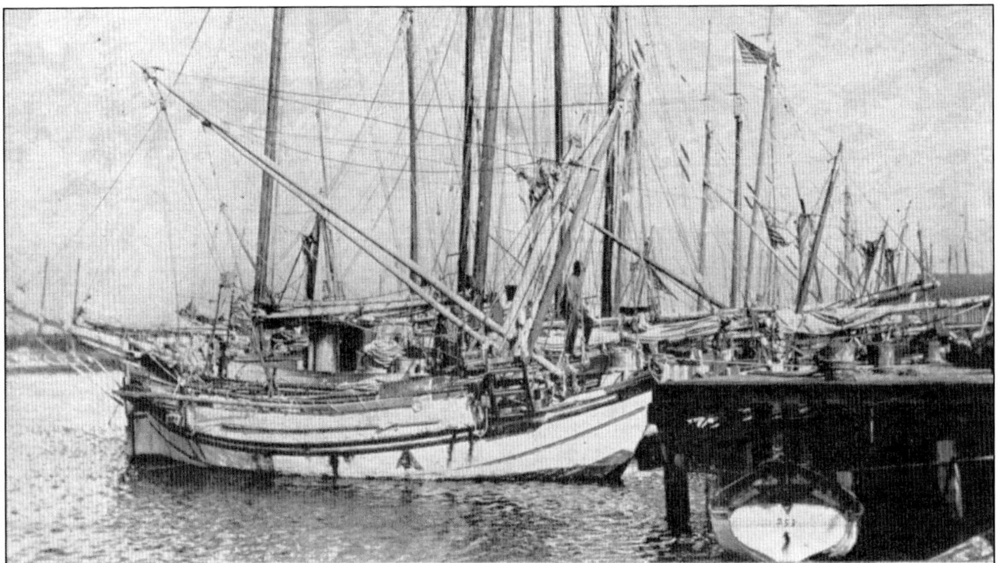

Sponge Fleet in Harbor, Tarpon Springs, Fla.

This postcard illustrates the differences between a hook sponge boat and a dive sponge boat. On the bottom right is a Greek dinghy. At times, these boats were used for hook sponging in shallower water, their lower sides being helpful in both rowing and hooking. Using a diving suit meant that the sponger could remain under water longer and, therefore, go to a deeper bottom for harvesting. This typically meant the use of a somewhat larger vessel. Additionally, the hook boats would have a two-man crew and the dive boats would have a captain, divers, and several other crewmembers. (Courtesy of Sam H. Mack.)

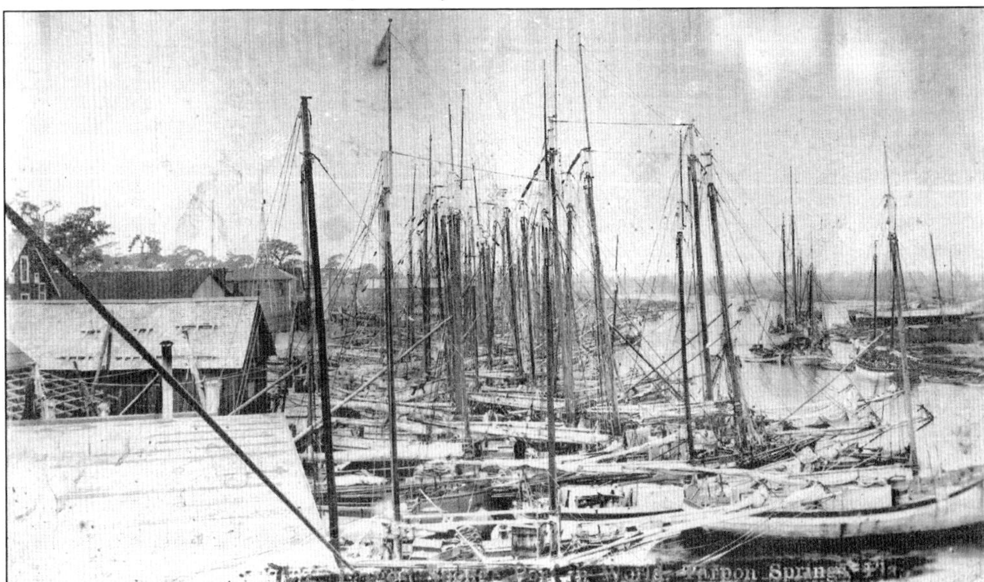

This faded card is titled "The Largest Sponge Port in World, Tarpon Springs, Fla." In 1916, it was reported that Tarpon Springs was the largest sponge market in the western hemisphere. Certainly, with over 100 schooners, Tarpon Springs had the fleet as well as the people, with an estimated 2,000 Greeks, most of them employed in the sponging business. (Courtesy of Tarpon Springs Area Historical Society.)

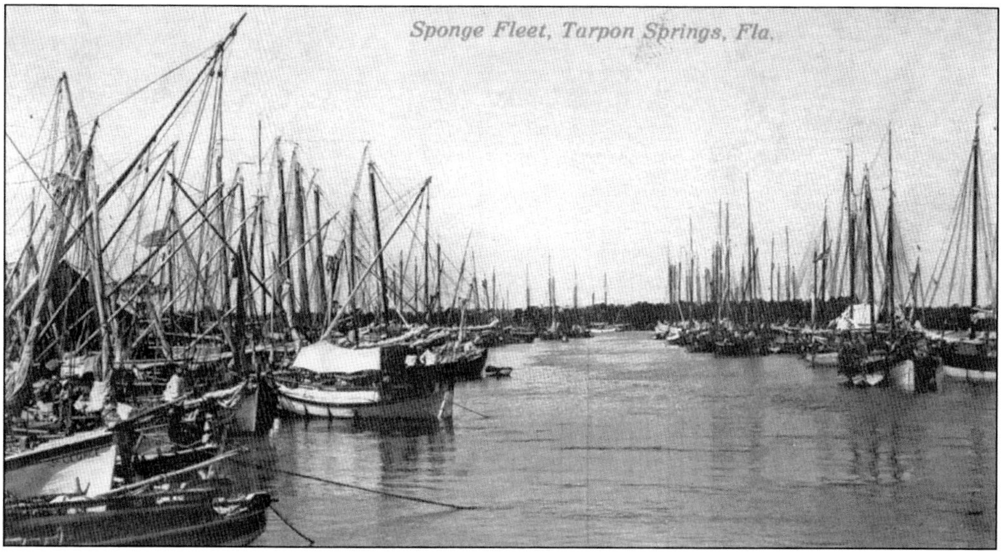

As far as the eye can see, the sponge boats are moored and anchored in the Anclote River. When the auctions were held at Bailey's Bluff, there was a place for the boats to remain closer to the mouth of the river. Sponge Harbor had the facilities to handle the vessels and crews with a wharf and a general store. When the processing, sales, and distributing warehouses relocated up river, so too did the men and their boats. (Courtesy of Sam H. Mack.)

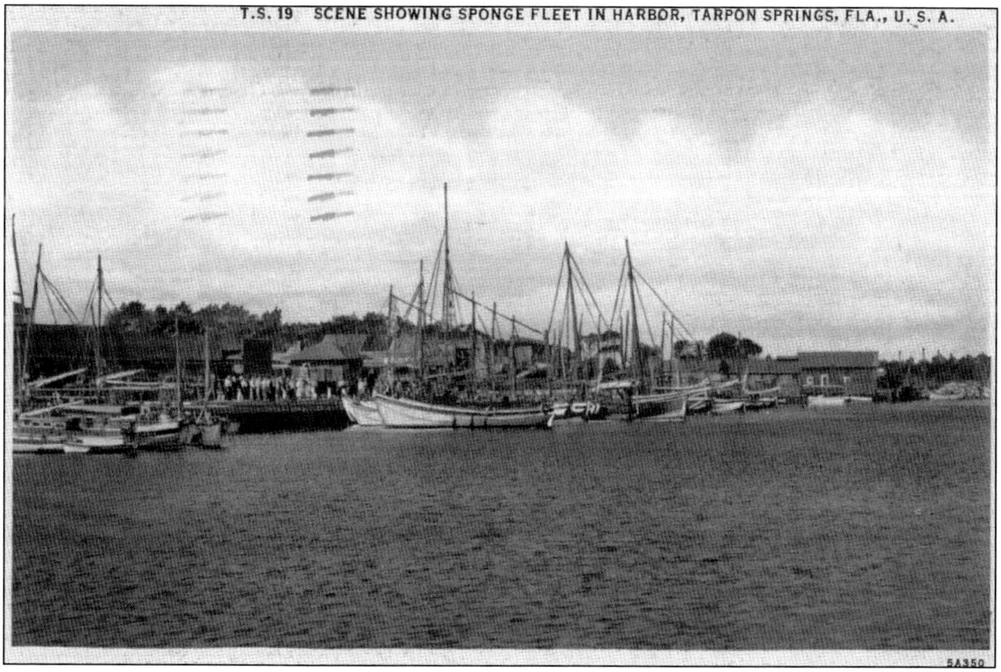

In this image, the sky's winter sunset reflects in the water on a beautiful calm day; however, weather could be unpredictable at times. During the hurricane of October 1921, reports stated that two smacks (fishing vessels) were wrecked and the hulls were found adrift five miles west of the Anclote Key. It was believed that the 15 crewmen were lost at sea, and additional reports were made of several schooners and crew who had gone missing. Later, all men were accounted for. (Courtesy of Sam H. Mack.)

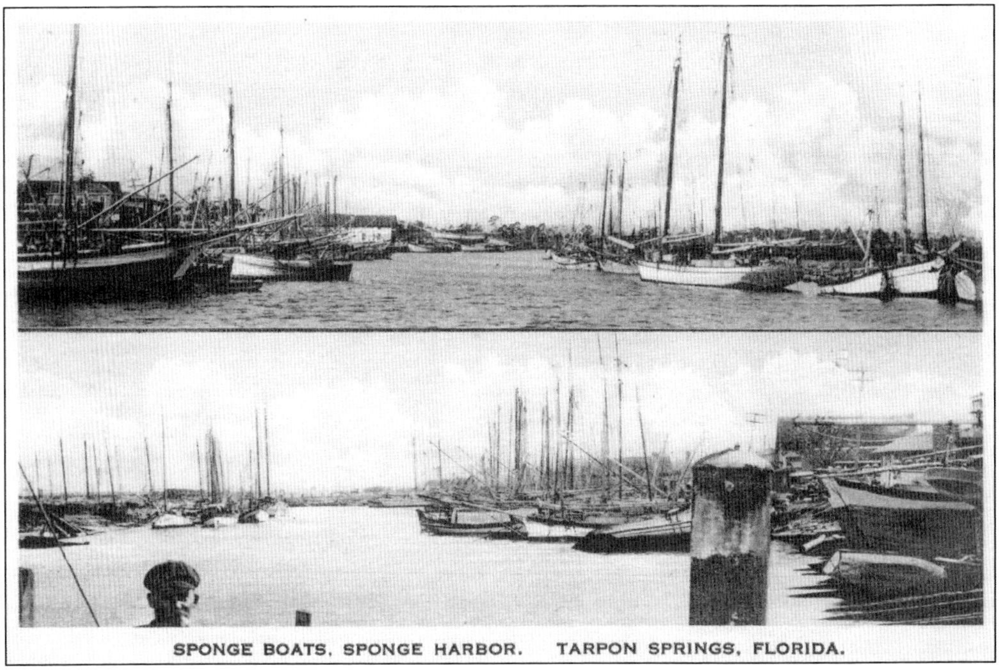

This interesting postcard offers two views on the front. It identifies the location as Sponge Harbor, a settlement that supported the Bailey's Bluff sponging boats. There, supplies could be purchased from the general store and repairs could be made at the marina. There was also some housing for the primarily African American spongers. Once located at Point Alexis, there are no remains of it today. From this postcard, it is difficult to tell if this actually is a view of Sponge Harbor or if it is up river on the Anclote. (Courtesy of Sam H. Mack.)

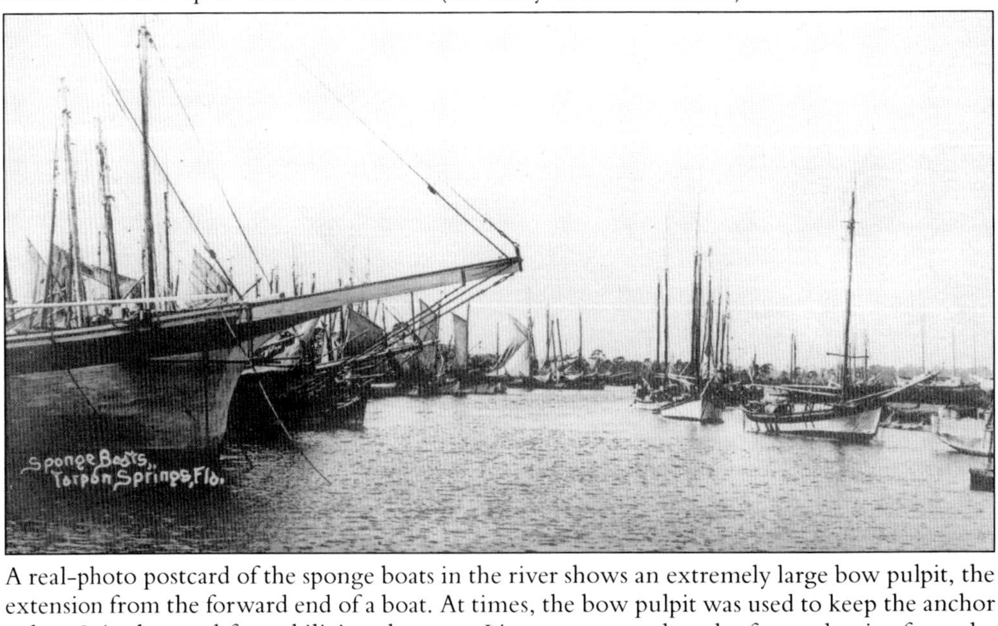

A real-photo postcard of the sponge boats in the river shows an extremely large bow pulpit, the extension from the forward end of a boat. At times, the bow pulpit was used to keep the anchor at bay. It is also used for stabilizing the mast. Lines are secured to the forward point from the top of the mast to give it strength. Larger boats would occasionally supply the smaller working boats. (Courtesy of Sam H. Mack.)

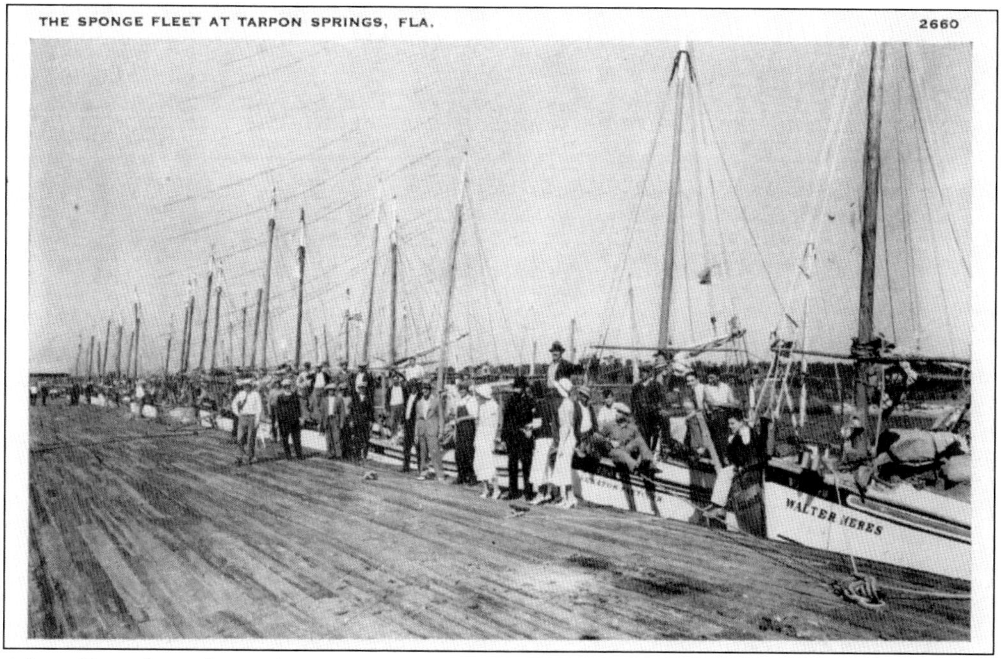

A long line of vessels can be seen at the docks on the Anclote River. At one time, the Sponge Docks were wooden. Ernest Meres would play an important role in the formation of the Sponge Exchange. The *Walter Meres* can clearly be seen as the first schooner, although it is unknown if the name Walter refers to Ernest's father or son. Tourists pose along with boat crew men for a photograph. (Courtesy of Sam H. Mack.)

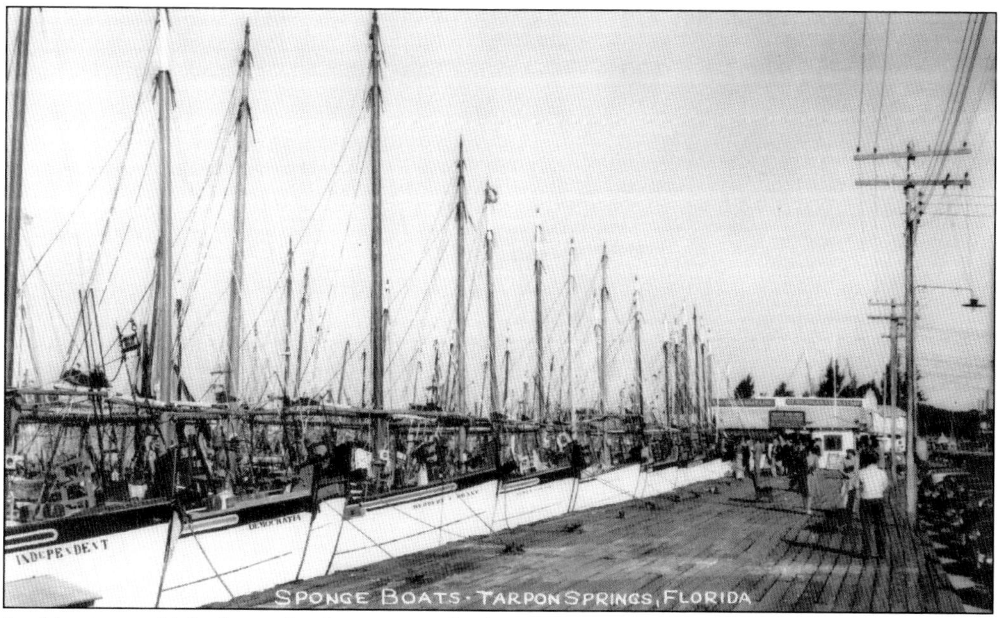

In this view, which shows the Sponge Docks from the other direction, some of the boat names can be seen. The first boat in line, the ***Independent***, was owned by Peter Leondakos from Sparta and his son-in-law George A. Hourdas from Halki. Both were owners, captains, and sponge divers. Descendants of this family still reside in Tarpon Springs. (Courtesy of Sam H. Mack.)

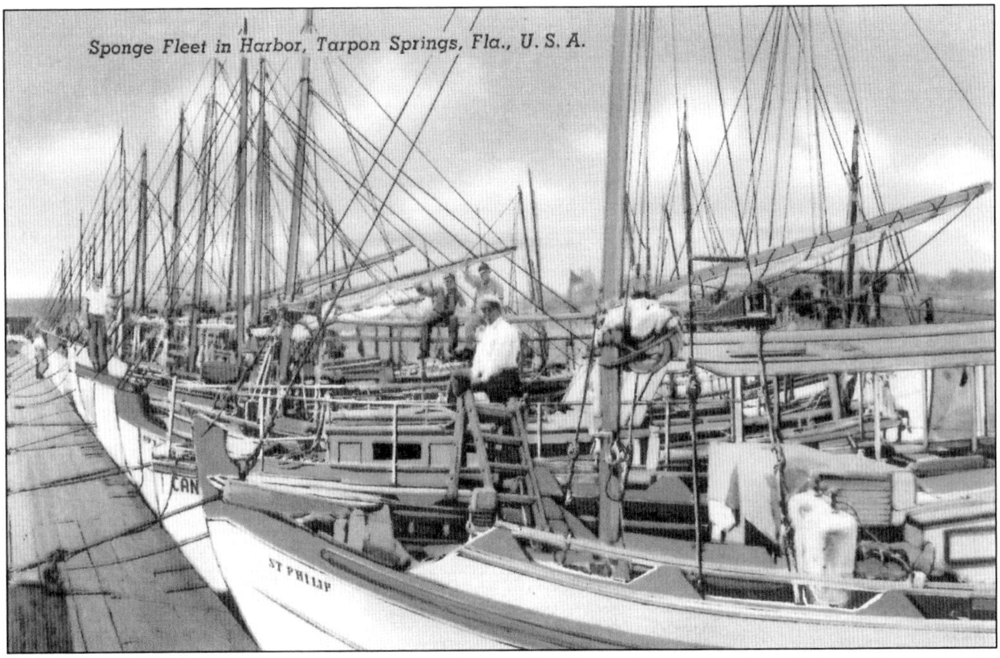

The sponge boats, featuring white hulls and many bright colors, are painted along the gunnels, the topmost plank of a wooden vessel. A source of pride in their occupation kept their schooners cleaned and cared for. (Courtesy of Tampa Bay History Center.)

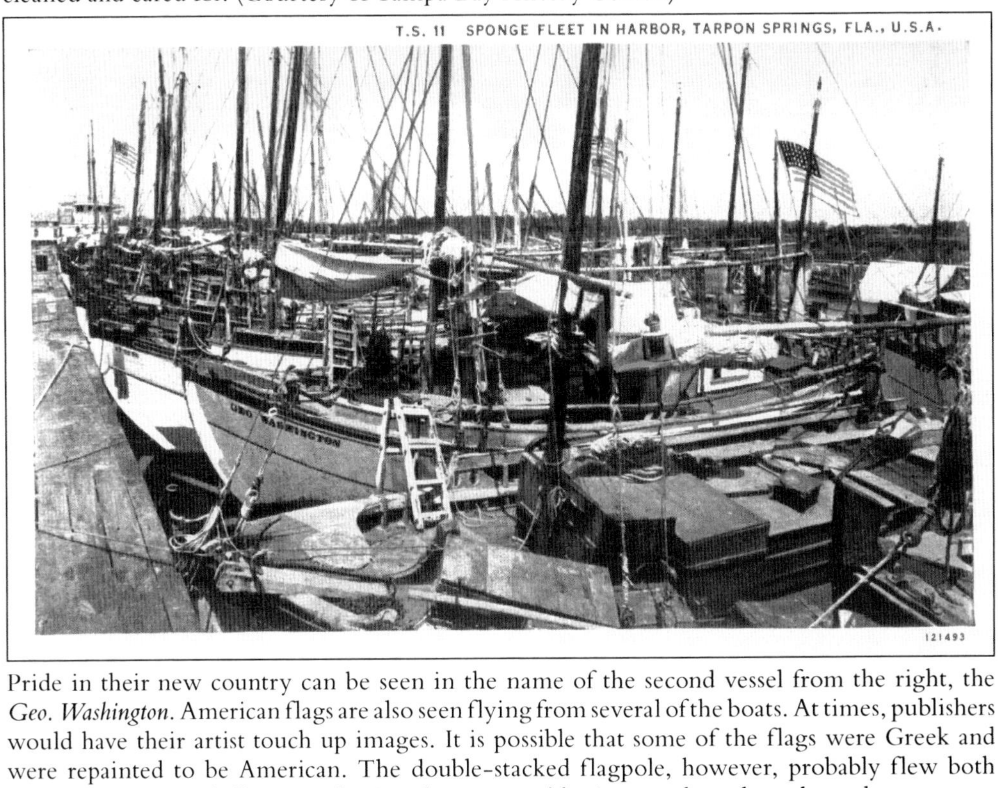

Pride in their new country can be seen in the name of the second vessel from the right, the *Geo. Washington*. American flags are also seen flying from several of the boats. At times, publishers would have their artist touch up images. It is possible that some of the flags were Greek and were repainted to be American. The double-stacked flagpole, however, probably flew both American and Greek flags, reinforcing the spongers' heritage and newly embraced country.

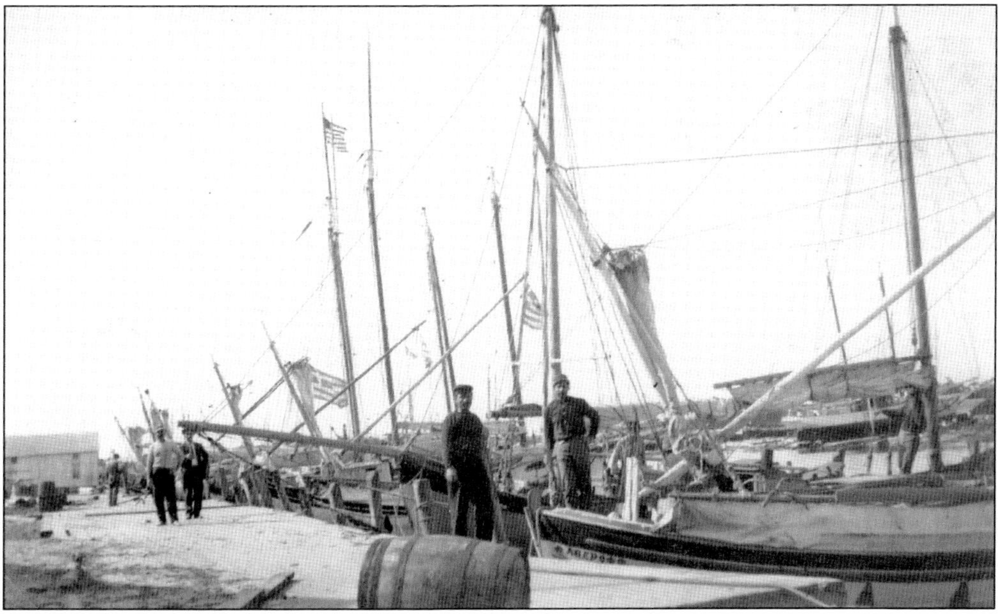

In this real-photo postcard, both Greek and American flags are flying. The docks are now concrete, and a supply barrel is seen in the foreground. Spongers could go out for weeks at a time, necessitating food and water aboard. Kavourma, a Greek specialty, is meat cooked in lard. The lard cools, becoming the meat's preservative. It is still made today and enjoyed by the Greeks. (Courtesy of Sam H. Mack.)

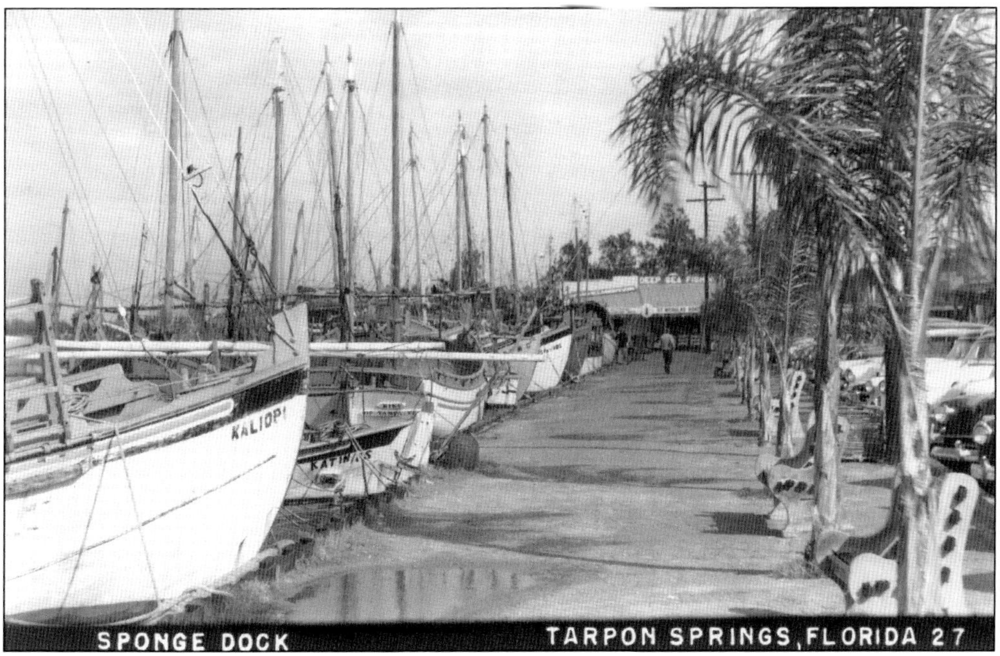

When the sponge industry was at its peak, there were more boats than there was slip space at the docks. After the first two boats, the next in line is tied parallel to the docks, enabling several other vessels to be moored alongside so that more could be accommodated. (Courtesy of Sam H. Mack.)

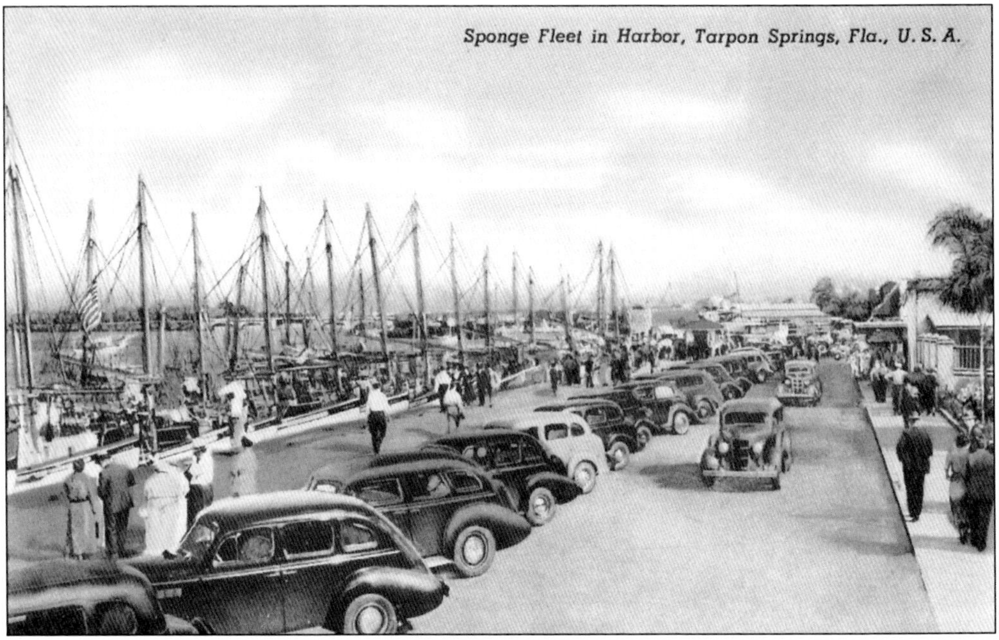

In this c. 1950s card are the concrete docks, street, and sidewalk where the edge of the Sponge Exchange is visible on the far right. In the distance, the Alternate Highway 19 (North Pinellas Avenue) concrete bridge crosses the Anclote River. (Courtesy of Tampa Bay History Center.)

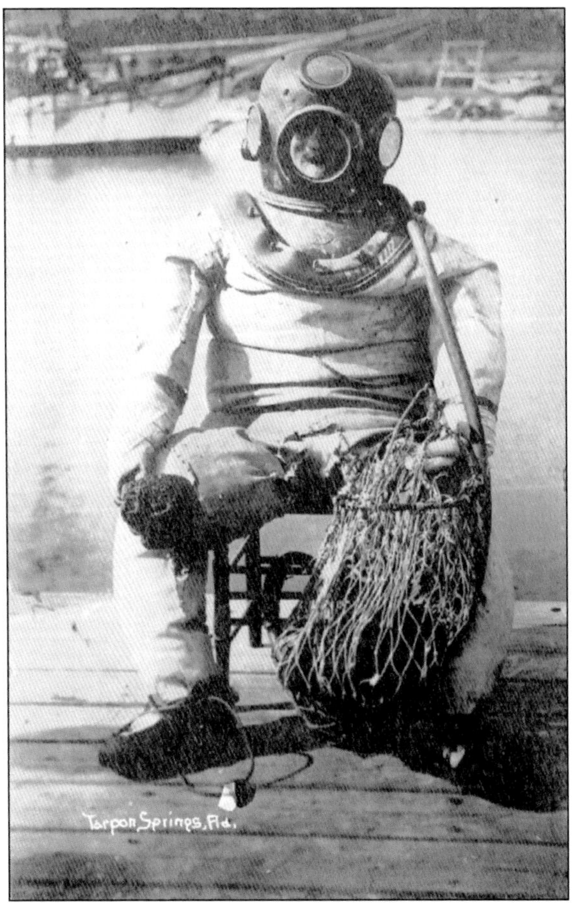

A sponge diver wearing a suit of double-waterproof canvas and holding a net basket of sponges poses for this photograph. The suit boasts an inside layer of rubber and rubber cuffs, and the breastplate's collar uses clamps, forming a watertight seal. The shoes have brass or lead soles and tips, and the air hose is seen laid over his shoulder. The helmet for these kinds of suits was usually made of bronze. (Courtesy of Tarpon Springs Area Historical Society.)

This diver has his suit inflated and helmet on; however, his helmet would be placed on and clamped down after he was on the ladder to descend into the water. There is a tremendous amount of weight involved with a dive suit, as a fully dressed diver's suit can weigh about 200 pounds. A dive suit is called a *skafandro* in Greek. (Courtesy of Sam H. Mack.)

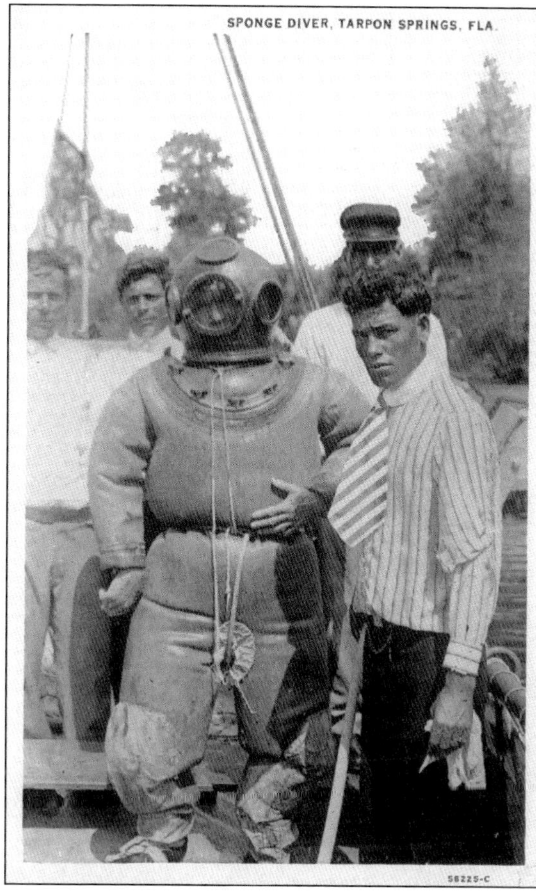

In 1886, John Cheyney came to Tarpon Springs to buy and sell in the sponge industry. He formed the Anclote and Rock Island Sponge Company, initiating a change that would take the sponging business from the Mediterranean Sea into the Gulf of Mexico. This postcard was made from a publicity photograph of the 1934 film *Sixteen Fathoms Deep.* (Courtesy of Jackie Payne.)

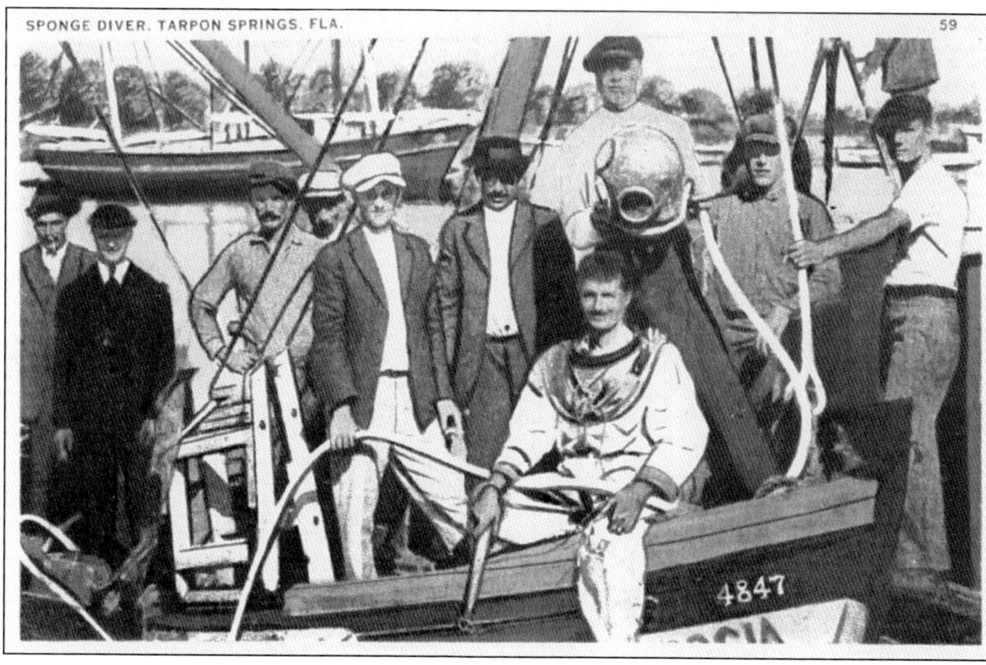

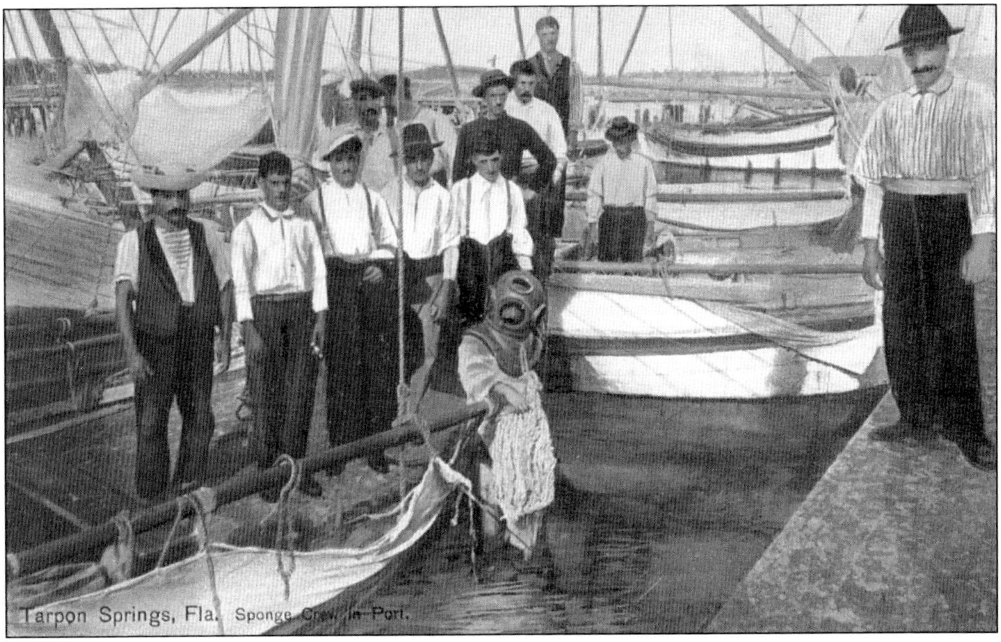

Hook sponging usually employed two men in a dinghy or rowboat—one would row while the other would use a glass-bottom bucket to view the bottom of the seafloor. When he saw sponges, he would use a lightweight pole of 15 to 40 feet with a three to five-pronged end to pluck the sponge from the bottom. These spongers were arranged to pose for this tourist postcard.

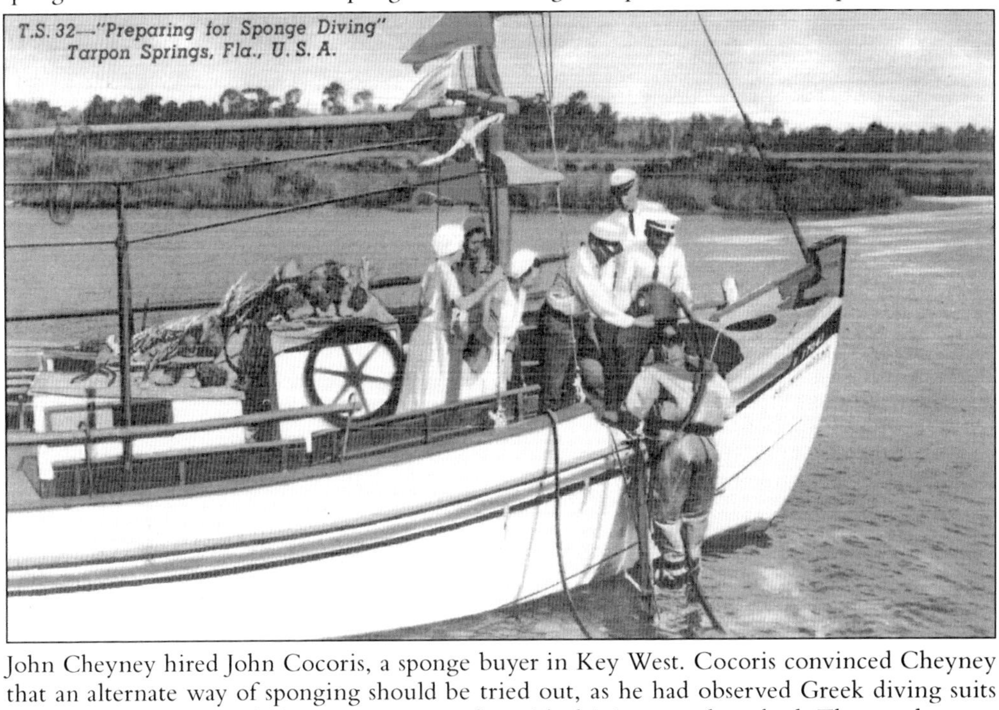

John Cheyney hired John Cocoris, a sponge buyer in Key West. Cocoris convinced Cheyney that an alternate way of sponging should be tried out, as he had observed Greek diving suits and knew that they could bring in more profits with this improved method. The two became partners. In 1905, Cocoris arranged for dive equipment and a crew to leave Greece and come to Tarpon Springs. (Courtesy of Tampa Bay History Center.)

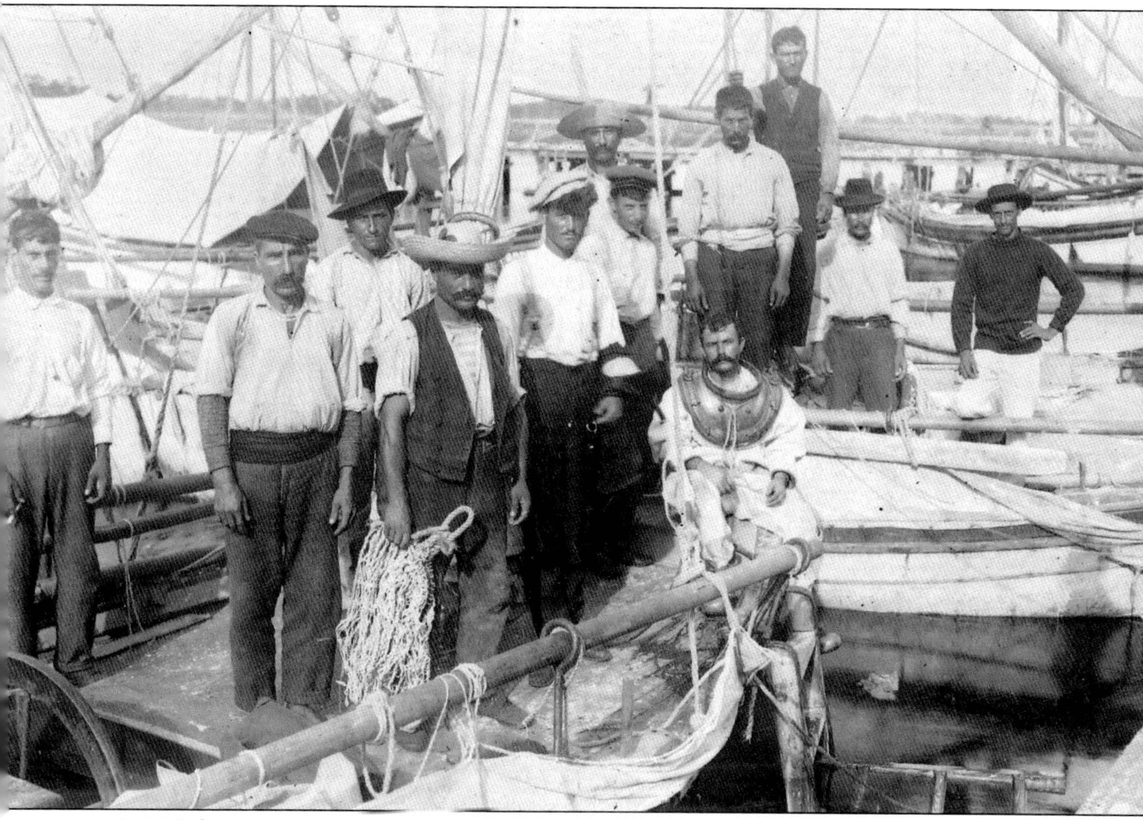

In mid-1905, hard-helmet diving proved profitable by the crew John Cocoris brought in. Two divers would take turns going down, changing in and out of the one helmet. One can imagine the surrealistic quiet and beauty seen by the divers. This would be the first time that a diver's footsteps would walk on the floor of the Gulf of Mexico. It was said that the diver could fill up his net and send it topside every 10 minutes. Any doubts of this new method that may have been thought or spoken previously were now put to rest, as the boat, which had been renamed *Hope* in Greek, was filled by the day's end. (Courtesy of Irene Giannaras Garner.)

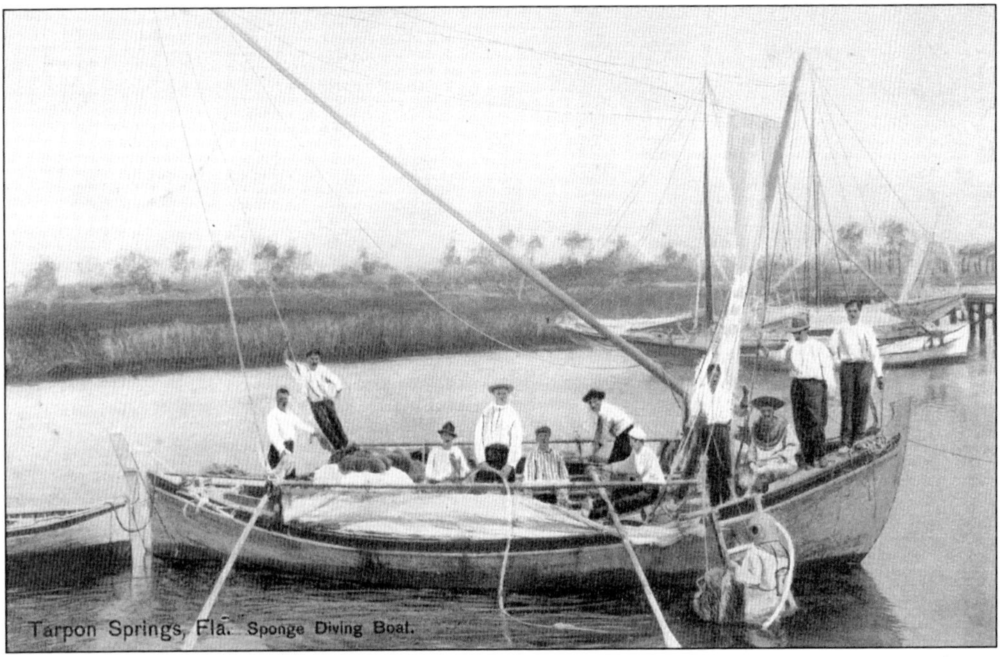

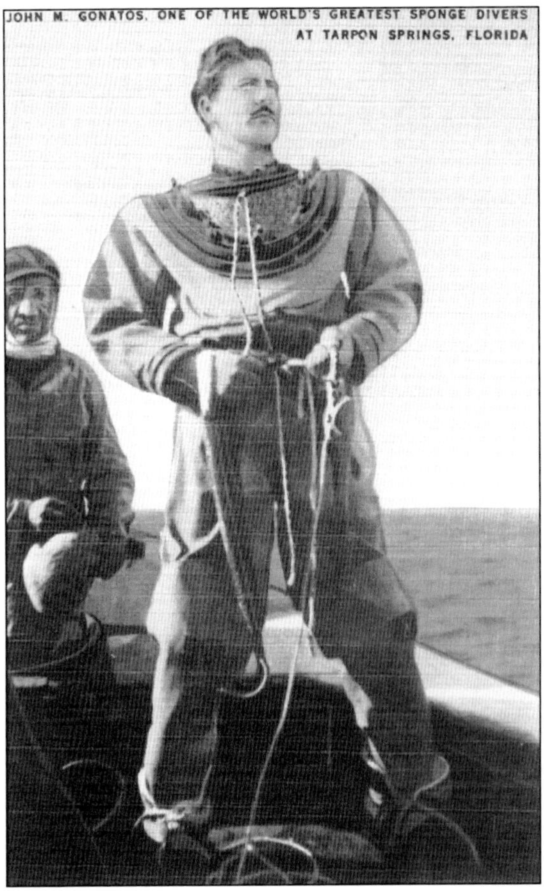

A conventional sponging crew on their boat with two divers can be seen in the photograph. The divers share the helmet, so one can rest while the other sponges, maximizing the amount of time harvesting. A lifeline tender holds the airline, and behind him to the right is a man operating the hand-cranked air pump, which supplies air to the diver. (Courtesy of Hammond Salley.)

Born in Tarpon Springs, one of the greatest sponge divers in the world was John Michael Gonatos. He attended the University of Florida and became a nationally known heavyweight boxer. He learned to use the diving suit and, in 1939, made a 16-millimeter motion picture shown at the Sponge Docks, the 22-minute documentary *The Story of the Sponge*. He also starred in the 1948 feature film *16 Fathoms Deep*. His photograph appeared in the January 1947 issue of *National Geographic*. (Courtesy of Sam H. Mack.)

Here, a diver ascends with a full net basket of sponge. The three-pronged hook used to detach the sponge from the hard surface on which it has grown is also visible. Sponges that have had their gurry, a gelatinous substance, cleaned out are drying from stringers hanging from the boat's boom. Spongers pounded and squeezed the day's catch while rinsing it. It was then covered on deck where gas created from the heat of the sun helped clean the waste off.

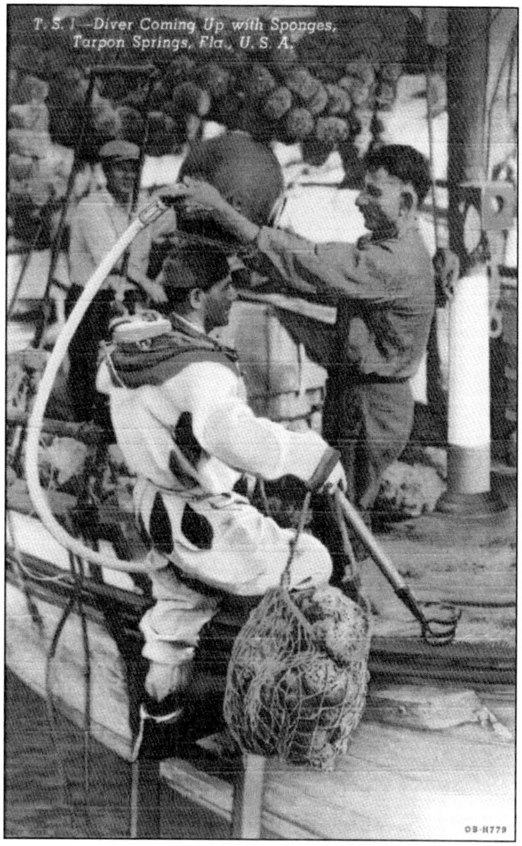

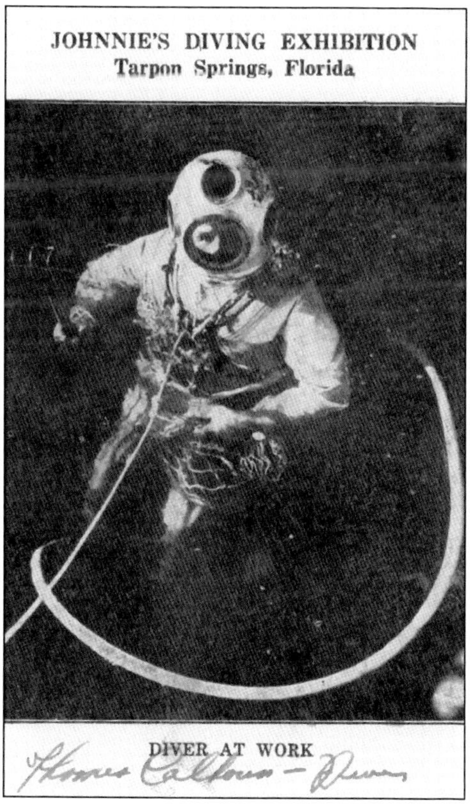

Cards such as this one were used during diving exhibitions to promote their work. A photograph of the diver, along with the pertinent information, is given to each attending guest as a souvenir. Sometimes, the divers would personally sign their cards. (Courtesy of Sam H. Mack.)

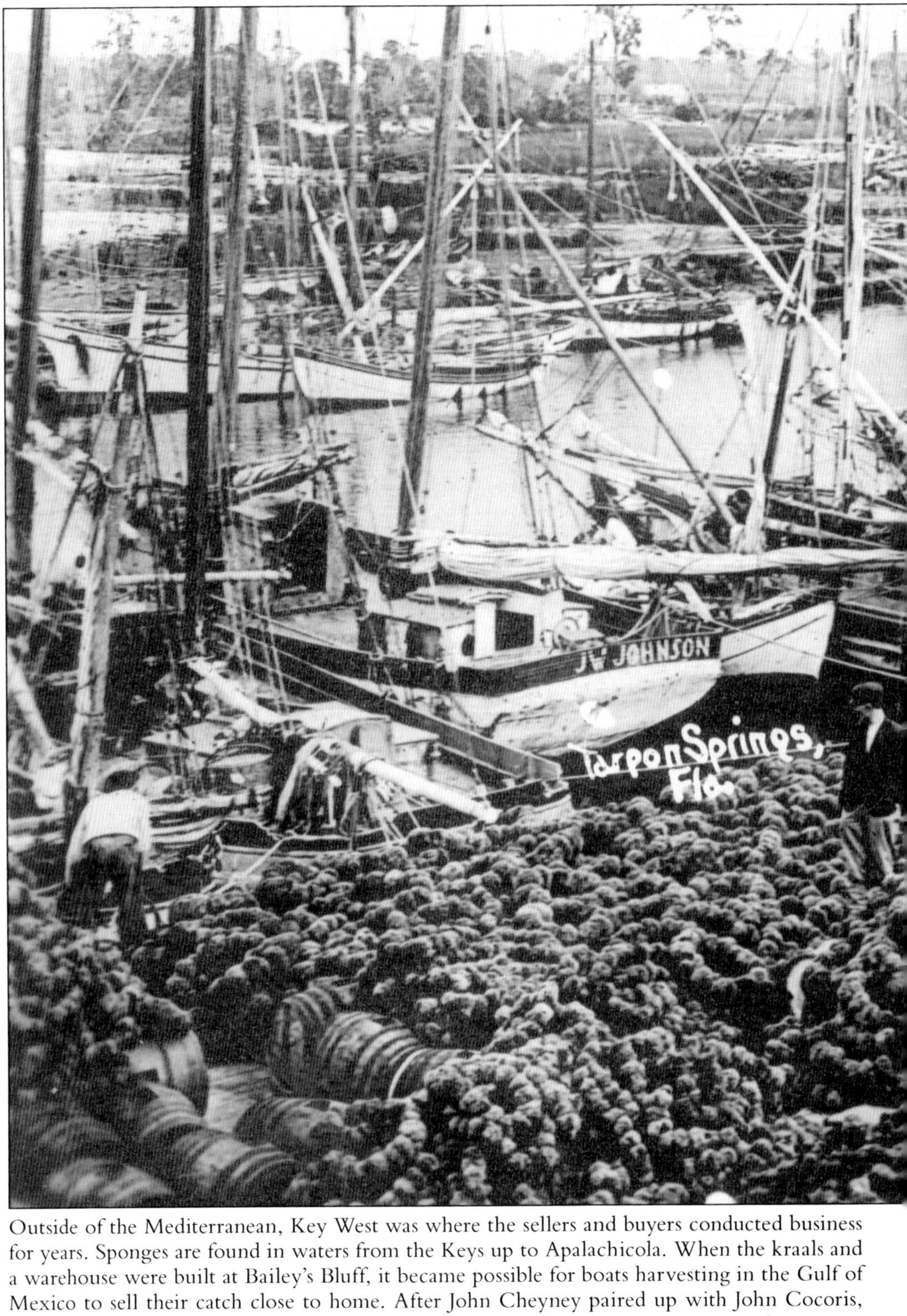

Outside of the Mediterranean, Key West was where the sellers and buyers conducted business for years. Sponges are found in waters from the Keys up to Apalachicola. When the kraals and a warehouse were built at Bailey's Bluff, it became possible for boats harvesting in the Gulf of Mexico to sell their catch close to home. After John Cheyney paired up with John Cocoris, who suggested the use of diving suits for sponging, the wheels were set in motion and 500 more

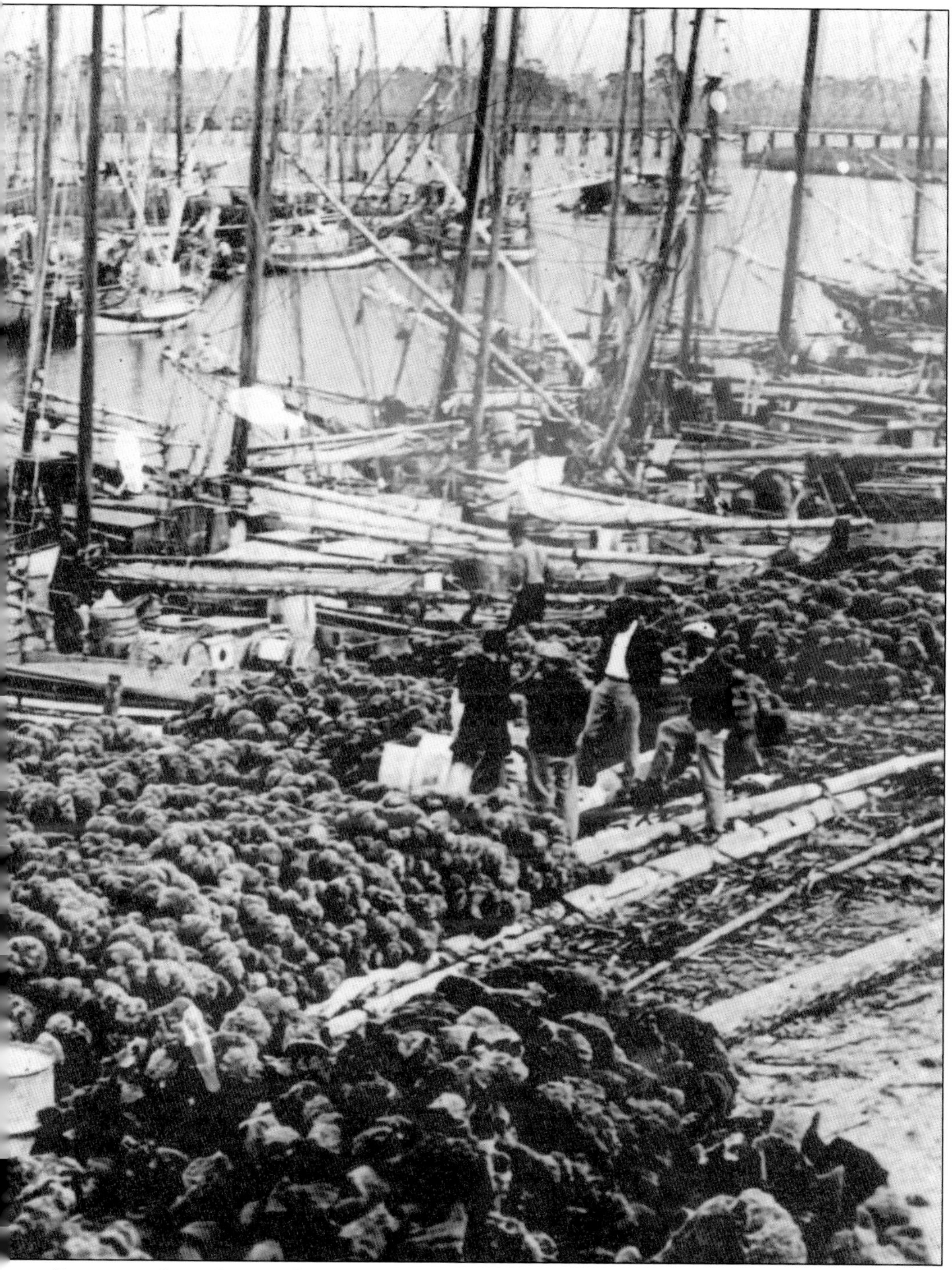

divers were brought over from the Greek islands of Halki, Kalymnos, Aegina, and Symi. There were 1,500 sponge industry workers in Tarpon Springs by the end of 1906. This photograph may look chaotic, but it indicates the volume and industrious ability of these men from a foreign land.

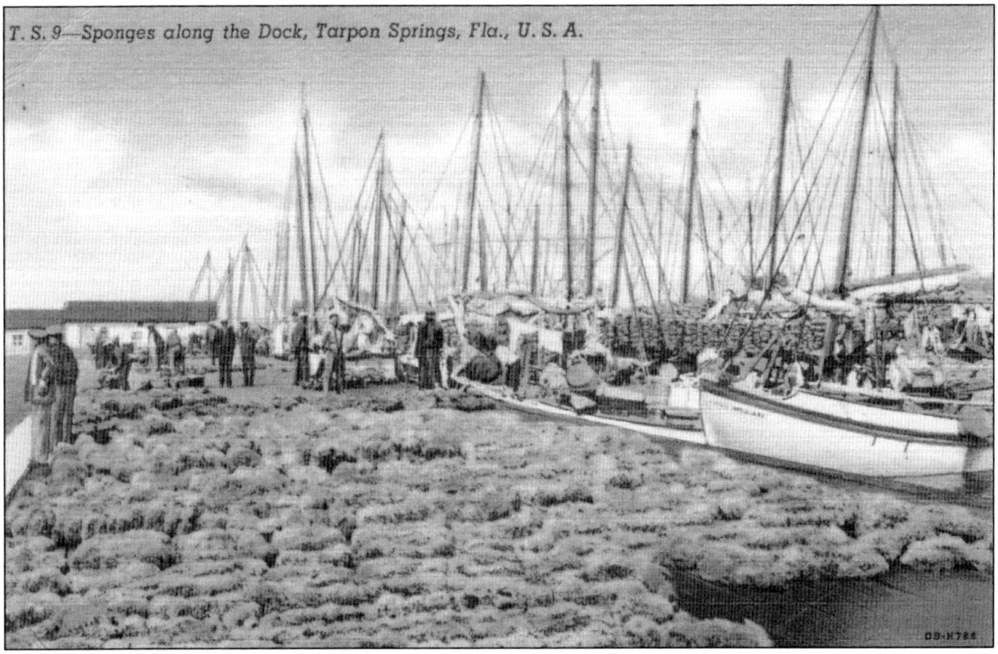

A successful haul of sponges is laid out on the docks. The sun has bleached them; however, some of the uses of sponge dictate that they be bleached by chemicals to sterilize them. They were immersed in sodium permanganate or hydrochloric acid. Although this process makes them softer, it can also damage them by making them weaker. (Courtesy of Tampa Bay History Center.)

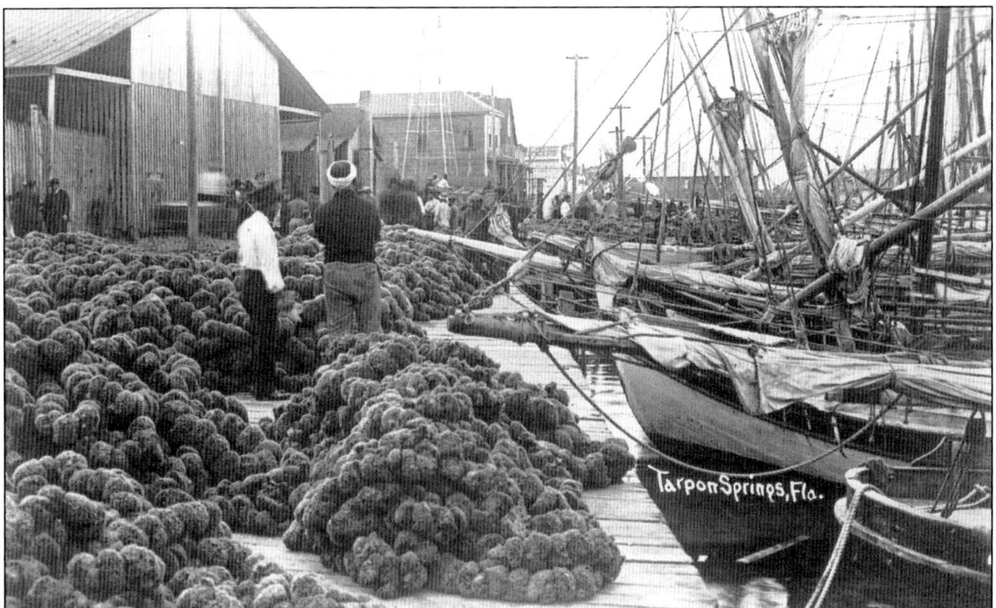

This postcard, dated January 19, 1918, shows a scene on the docks. These sponges are strung together and will be moved into the locked storage area of the Sponge Exchange, which can be seen past the warehouse on the left. A water tower is centered at the entrance. (Courtesy of Jackie Payne.)

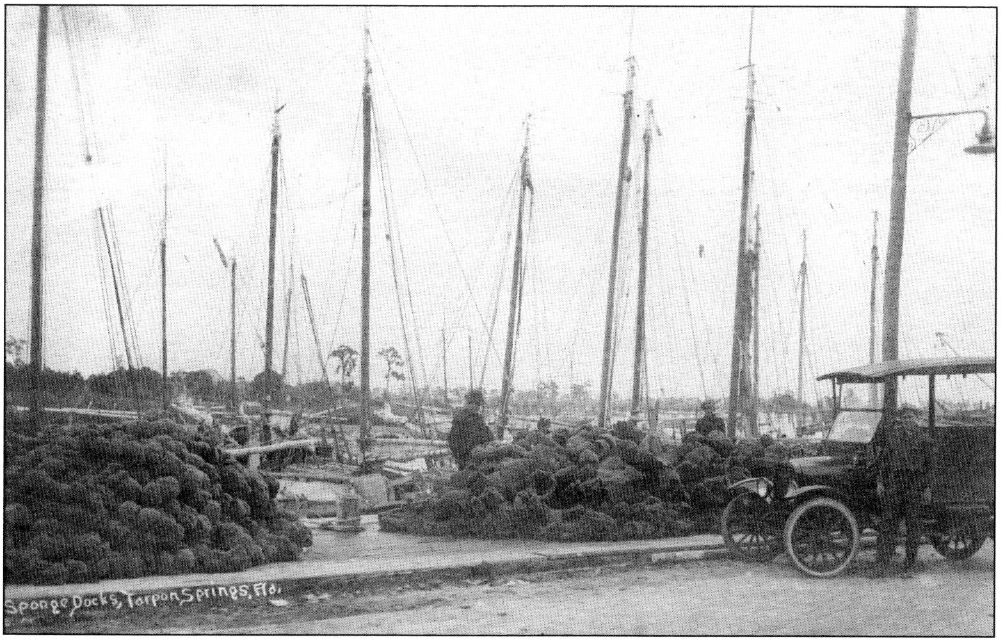

Here is another view of an extremely successful harvest of sponges, amassed almost four to six feet high on the wooden dock. Before the time of motors on boats, spongers went out twice a year, from Epiphany (January 6) to the end of June and from the beginning of August until Christmas. (Courtesy of Sam H. Mack.)

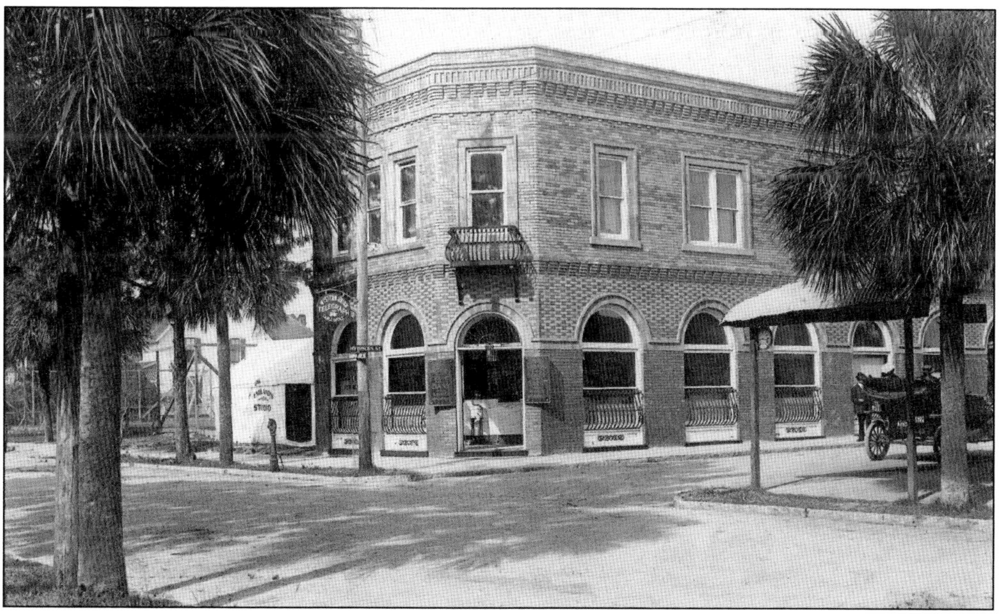

In 1906, the Sponge Exchange Bank was established as the first state-chartered bank, housed at the northwest corner of Tarpon Avenue and Hibiscus Street. Matching plaques flank the door, indicating the savings department. Safety deposit boxes were also available for rent. The bank remained open until the crash of 1929. Directly across Hibiscus Street, the Greek American Bank was founded in 1911 and went into receivership in 1933. (Courtesy of Irene Giannaras Garner.)

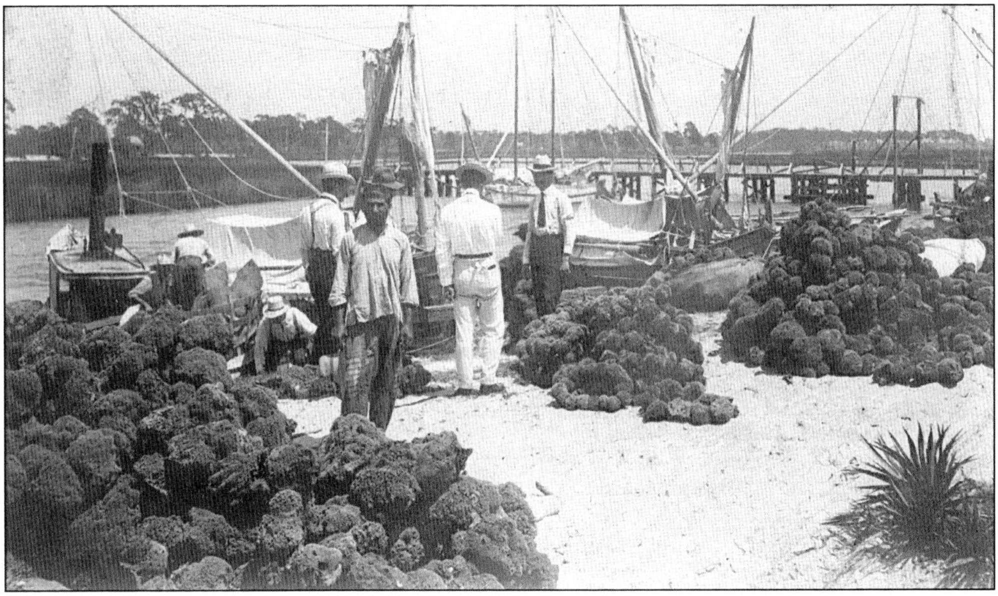

This very early postcard shows the sponges that have been offloaded from the boats onto the banks of the Anclote River before the Sponge Docks or Sponge Exchange existed. Seen in the background is the Athens Street Bridge. (Courtesy of Tarpon Springs Area Historical Society.)

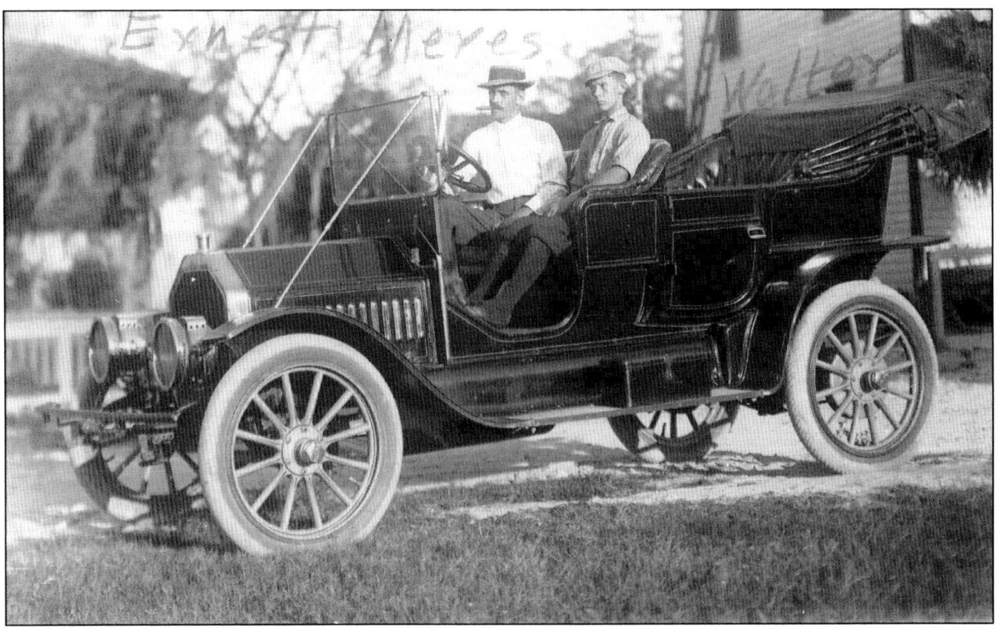

Ernest Robert Meres and John Cheyney were two of the major buyers at the Bailey's Bluff sponge auctions. Together, they founded the Sponge Exchange in 1907. Ernest is seen here at left with his son Walter Dudley Meres in 1911. (Courtesy of Hammond Salley.)

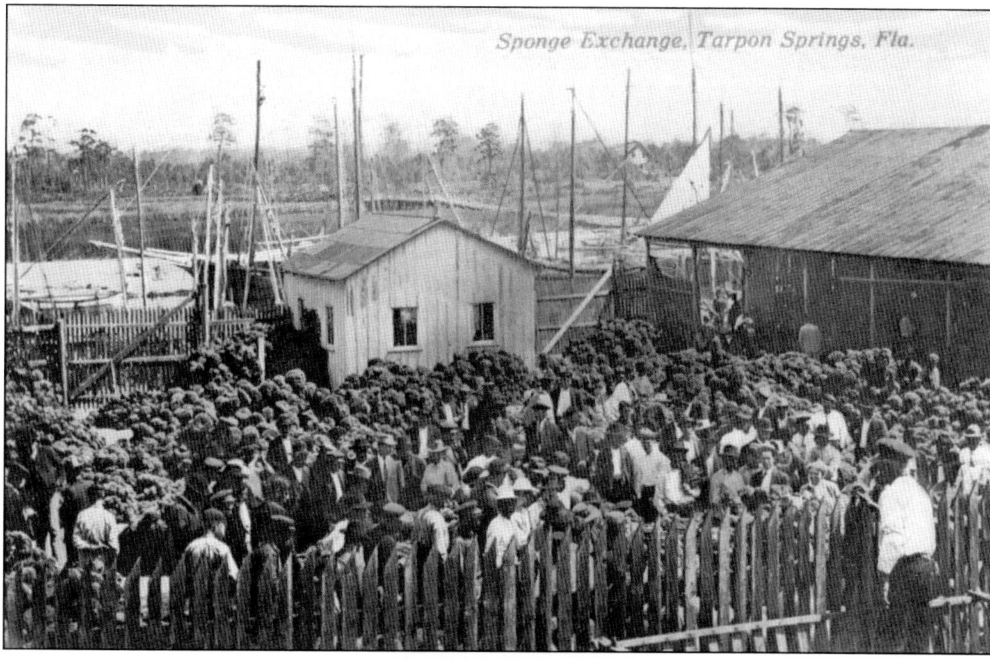

The Sponge Exchange was founded as a nonprofit shareholding entity to offer its members a place to dock their boats, unload, and securely store the sponges until auction. It also provided an area in the center where auctions were held. (Courtesy of Sam H. Mack.)

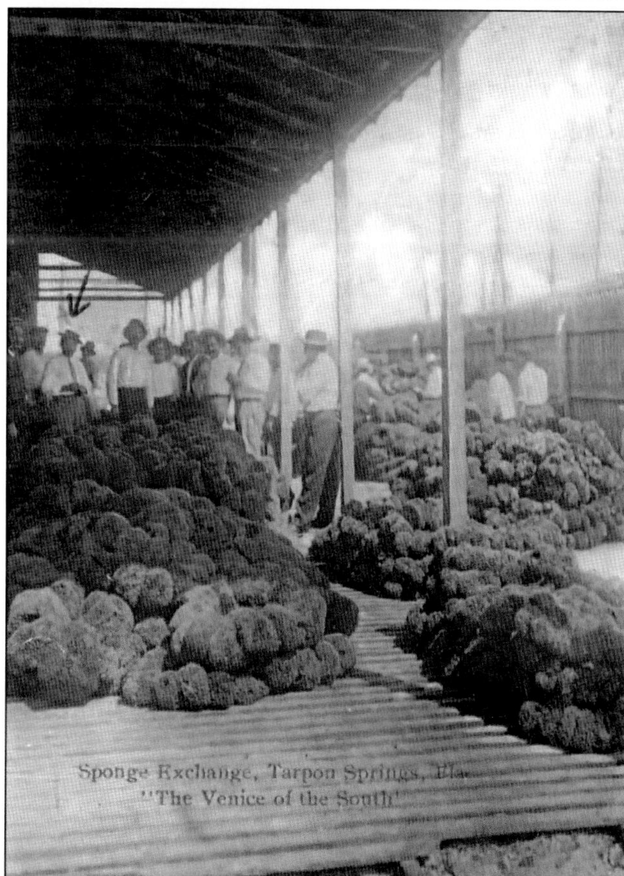

In this card, postmarked August 21, 1910, men are attending the auction at the Sponge Exchange. Submitting bids were made by Nick Nicholas and George Founduklis, indicated by the arrow. (Courtesy of Irene Giannaras Garner.)

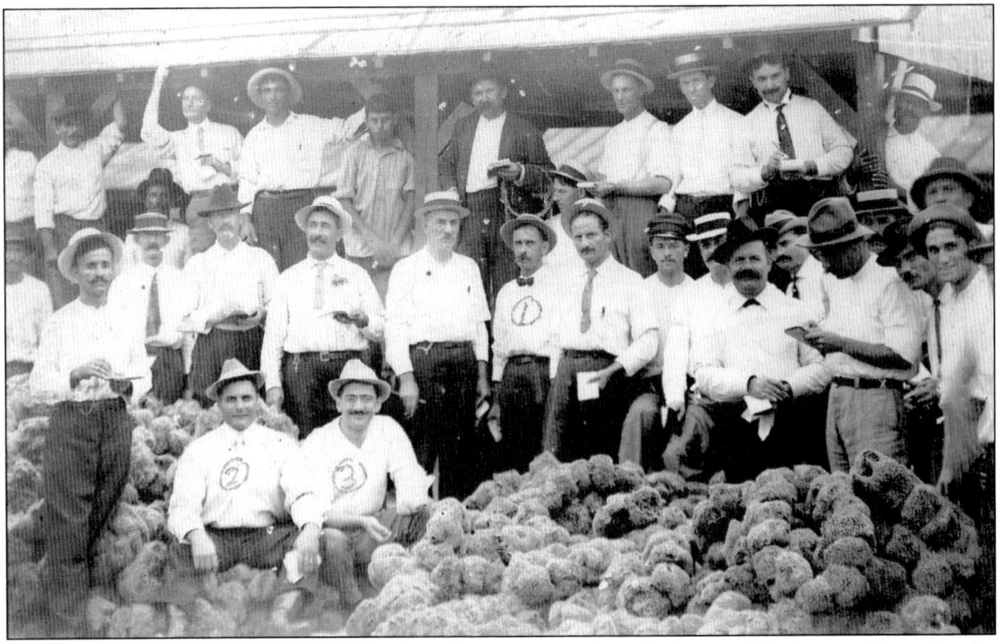

Buyers assembled for a group photograph to document a sale at the Sponge Exchange. Seated in the first row are Nick Arfaras (2) and George Emmanuel (3). Standing in the second row, fifth from the left, is Ernest Meres (1). The others are unidentified. (Courtesy of Hammond Salley.)

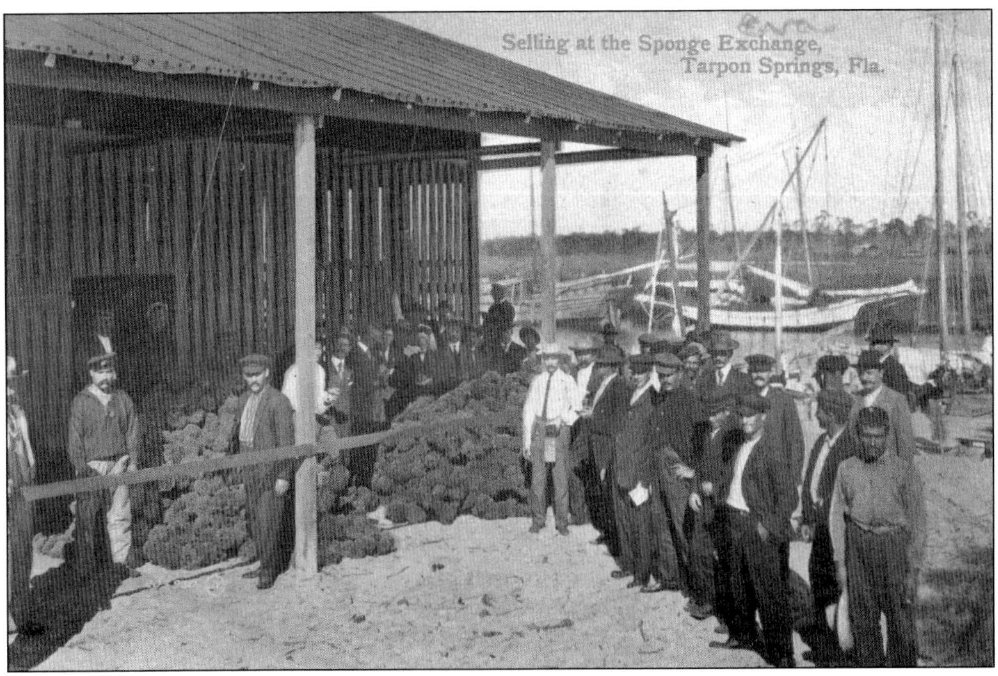

The Sponge Exchange consisted of a group of 50 local buyers who supported it by each paying one percent of each purchase. Sellers also were assessed one percent. One-half of a percent was given to the Greek Orthodox Church. (Courtesy of Sam H. Mack.)

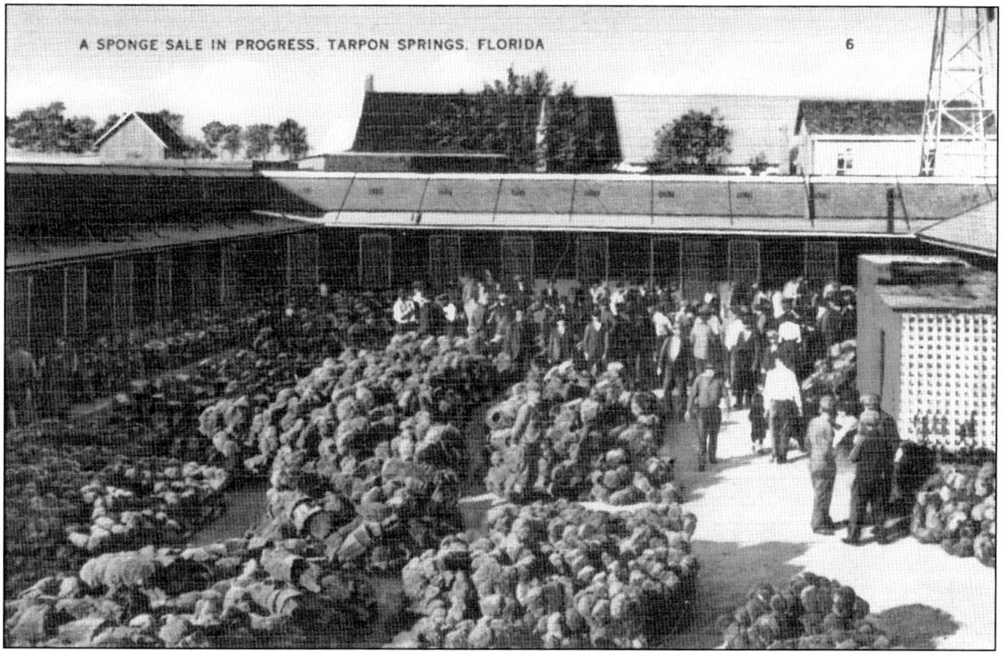

Surrounding the Sponge Exchange on three sides were 100 storage lockers. At the center was an area used for auctions, which happened twice a week on Tuesdays and Fridays at 9:30 a.m. It was a silent bid system, and sellers were not obligated to sell. (Courtesy of Sam H. Mack.)

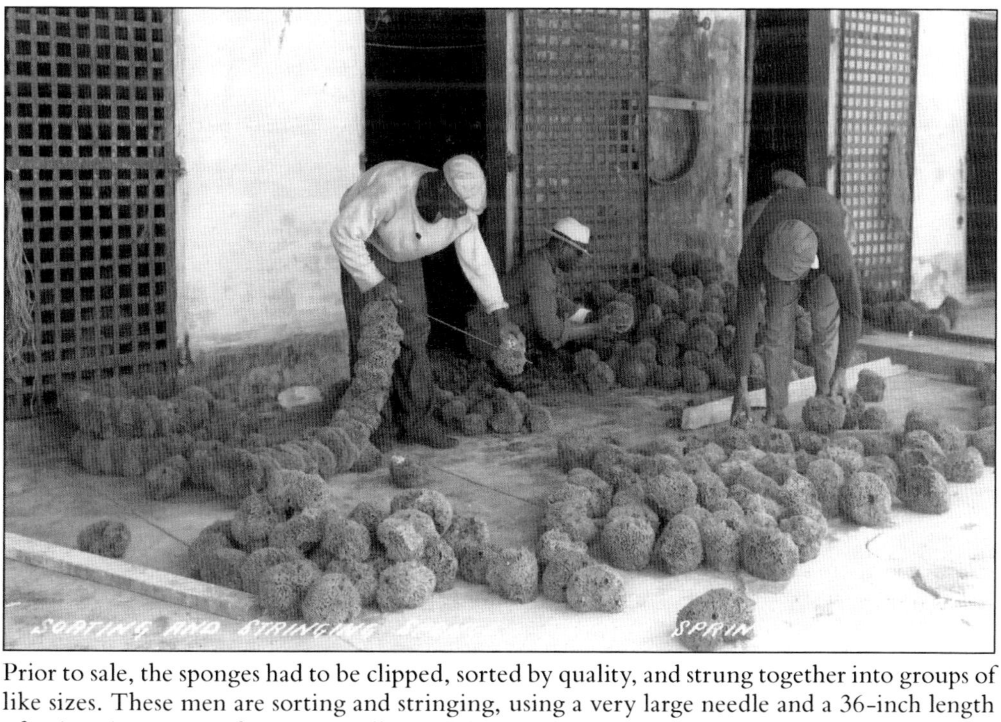

Prior to sale, the sponges had to be clipped, sorted by quality, and strung together into groups of like sizes. These men are sorting and stringing, using a very large needle and a 36-inch length of twine. (Courtesy of Heritage Village Archives and Library.)

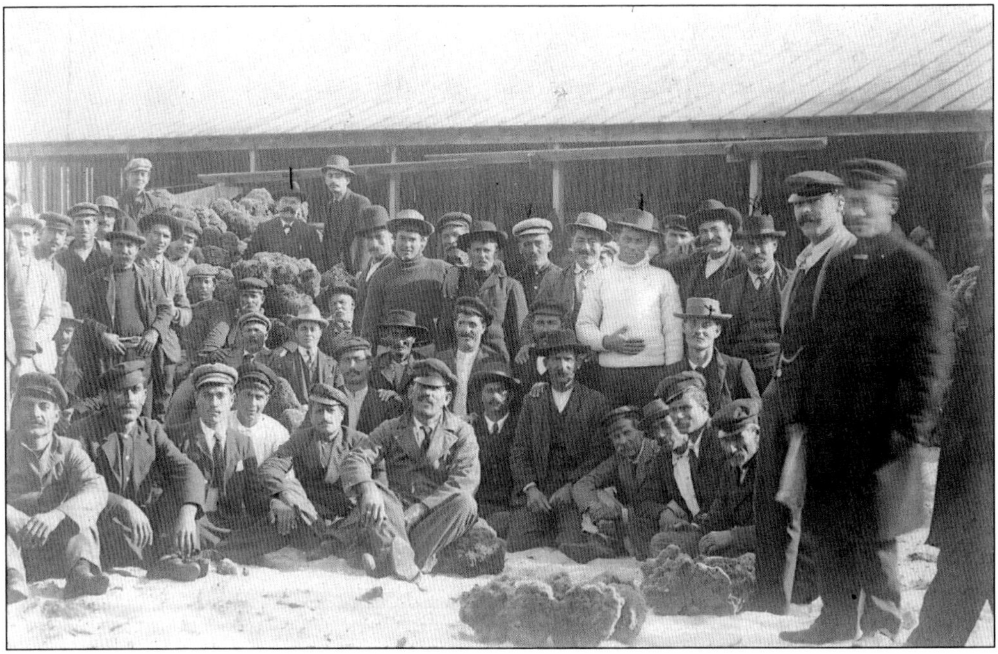

This is another posed photograph on auction day. A majority of the men seated are wearing the same style cap, that of the Greek captain's hat. They are traditionally made out of black wool and have been hand made in Greece since 1886. (Courtesy of Irene Giannaras Garner.)

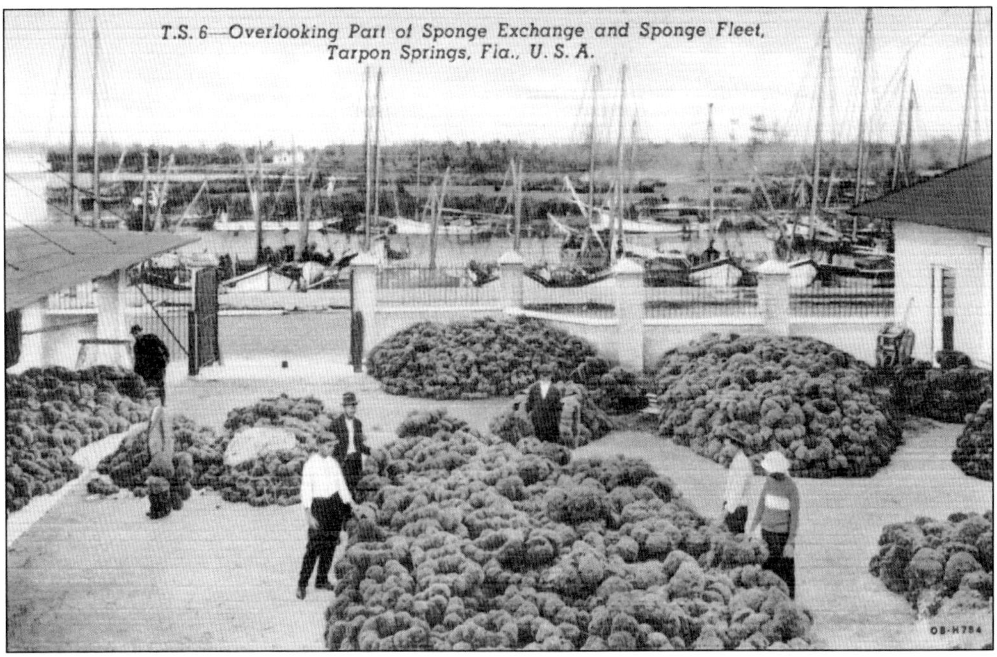

The sponges are stacked in bunches, known as couloures, prior to a sale. The artist who hand tinted this postcard chose to make the brick fence and walls of the exchange gray, though the walls were actually constructed of red brick. Postcard publishers sometimes took liberties with certain items, or the artists would make incorrect assumptions without having seen the actual locations. (Courtesy of Sam H. Mack.)

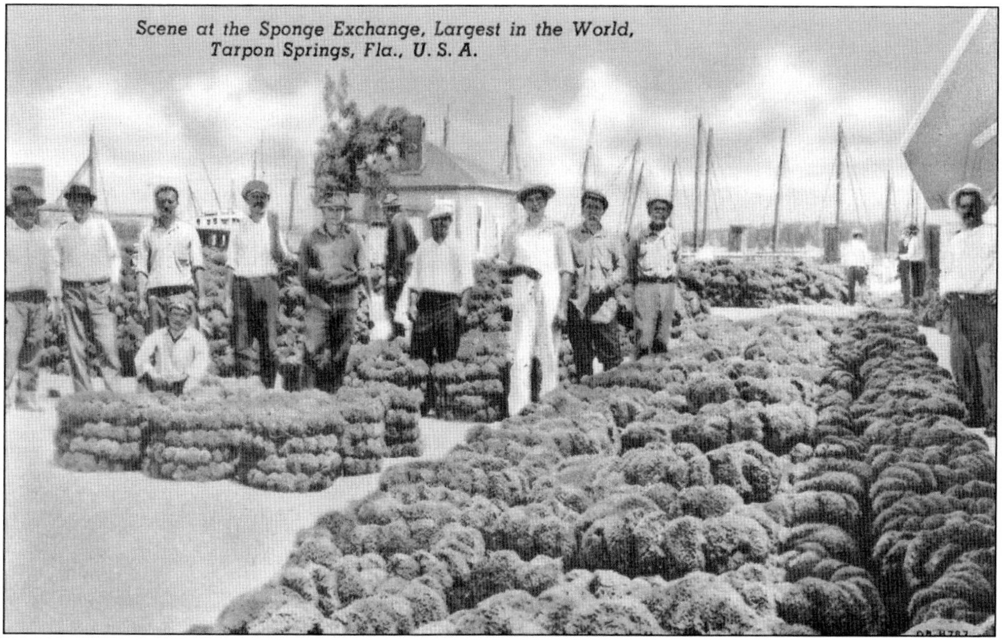

Tarpon Springs had two Odd Fellows chapters. Lodge No. 3116, formed in 1889, was for African Americans. One of the lodge's first members registered as a sponger was Robert Russell in 1895. The two most common professions listed among the lodge's members were laborers and spongers. (Courtesy of Sam H. Mack.)

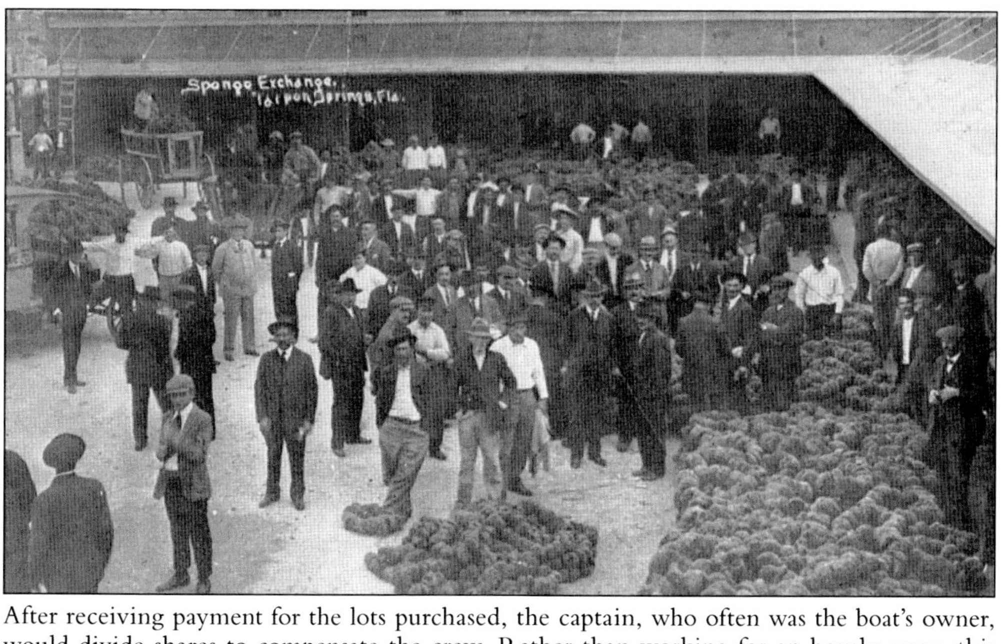

After receiving payment for the lots purchased, the captain, who often was the boat's owner, would divide shares to compensate the crew. Rather than working for an hourly wage, this system created a team whose income was based on the actual harvest. Divers were the highest paid, since they were the ones most at risk. (Courtesy of Sam H. Mack.)

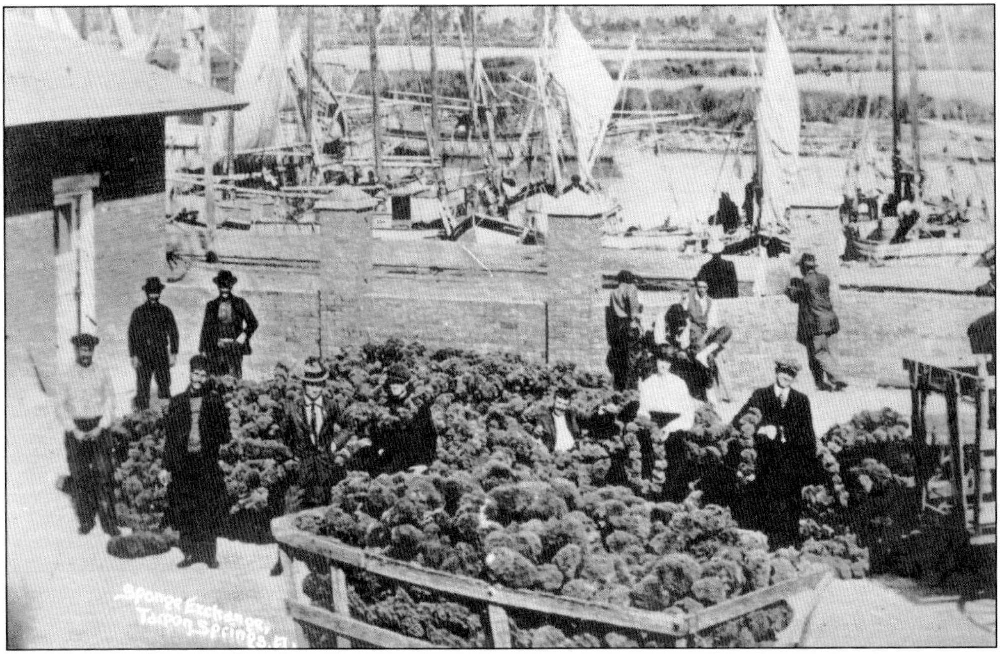

The image above shows a wagonload of sponges that probably just arrived and are waiting to be unloaded. The two people behind the wagon are holding sponges in bunches. Meanwhile, some of the buyers overlook the schooners moored close by in the Anclote River. This illustrates the close proximity of the Sponge Exchange to the Sponge Docks, which were built by the city in the 1920s. The docks can be seen in the postcard below. A magnificent mound of large basket sponges is the focal point of this postcard. Bunches of wool sponge are seen in the surrounding clusters, and a wagon driver stands behind the gathering of men. (Above, courtesy of Sam H. Mack; below, courtesy of Pauline Pavlis Phillips.)

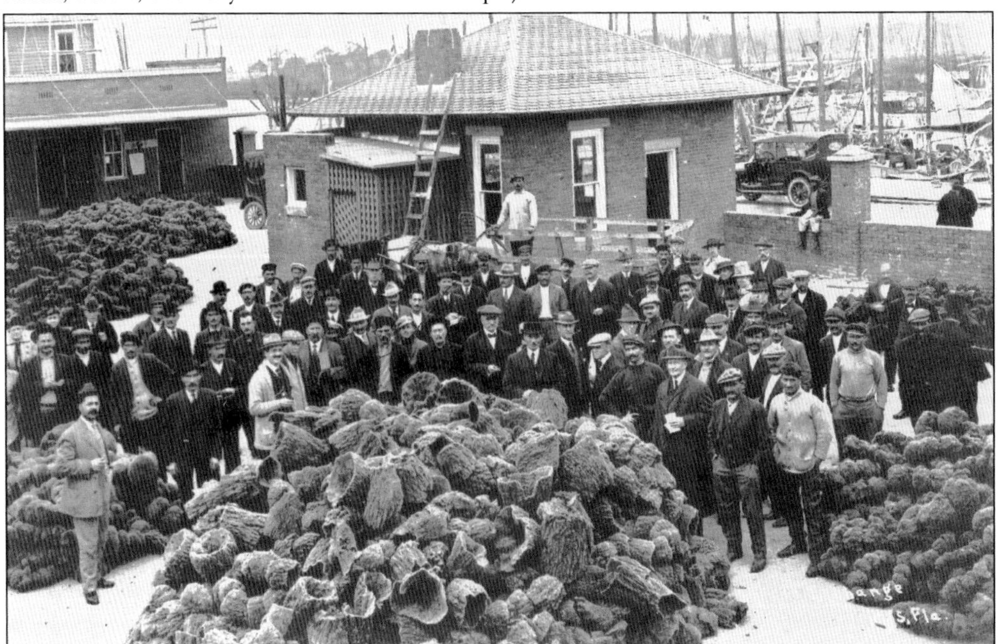

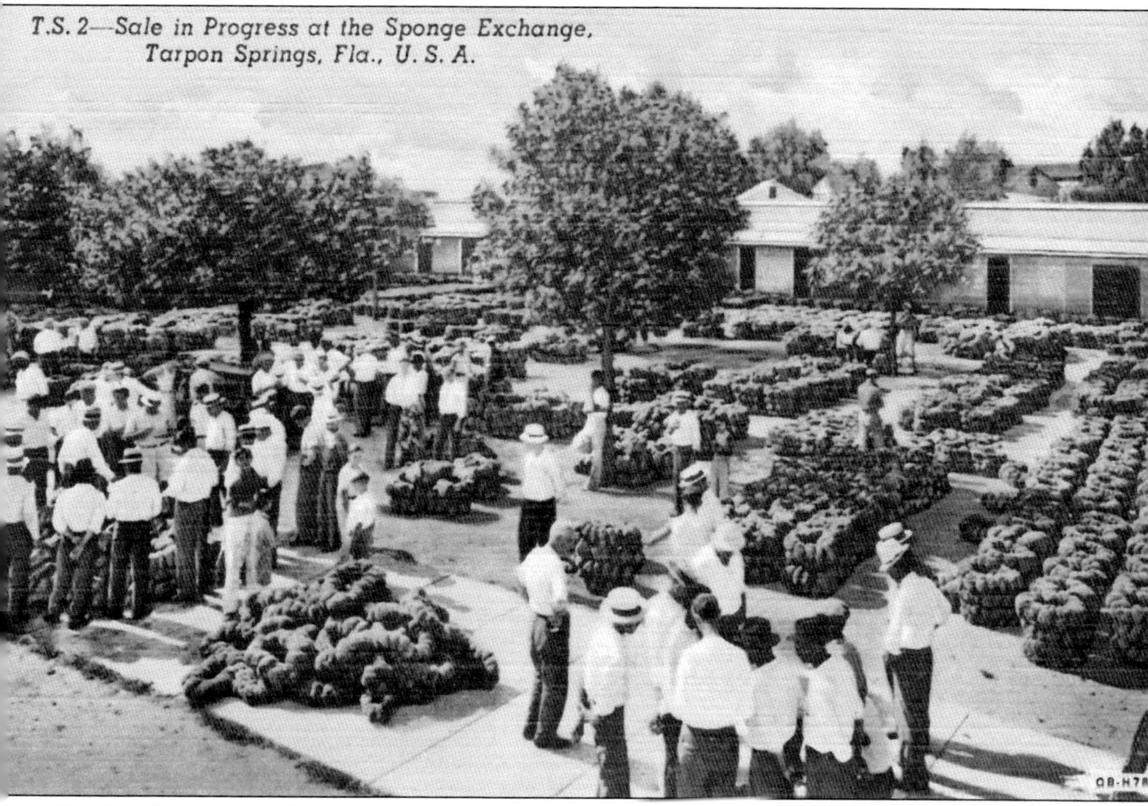

During this auction, the boat's crew stands near the lots, while buyers examine each catch for quality and prices. The auctioneer blows a whistle to silence the crowd. Each buyer writes his bid on paper and hands it to the auctioneer, who reviews the bids and divulges the highest offer. All other bids are destroyed, and a seller does not have to accept a bid if he believes it is not in his crew's best interest. When announced, the seller answers with "Sold!" or refuses the bid. If sold, the buyer then takes his possessions to his sponge-packing house. There, the sponges are graded, trimmed, and baled. It is estimated that for every sponge diver, there are 12 to 15 others in supporting roles in the industry. Boat builders and machine shops surround the area. Machine shops build and repair engines, as well as make dive helmets by hand and engineer any other parts a diver may need. (Courtesy of Sam H. Mack.)

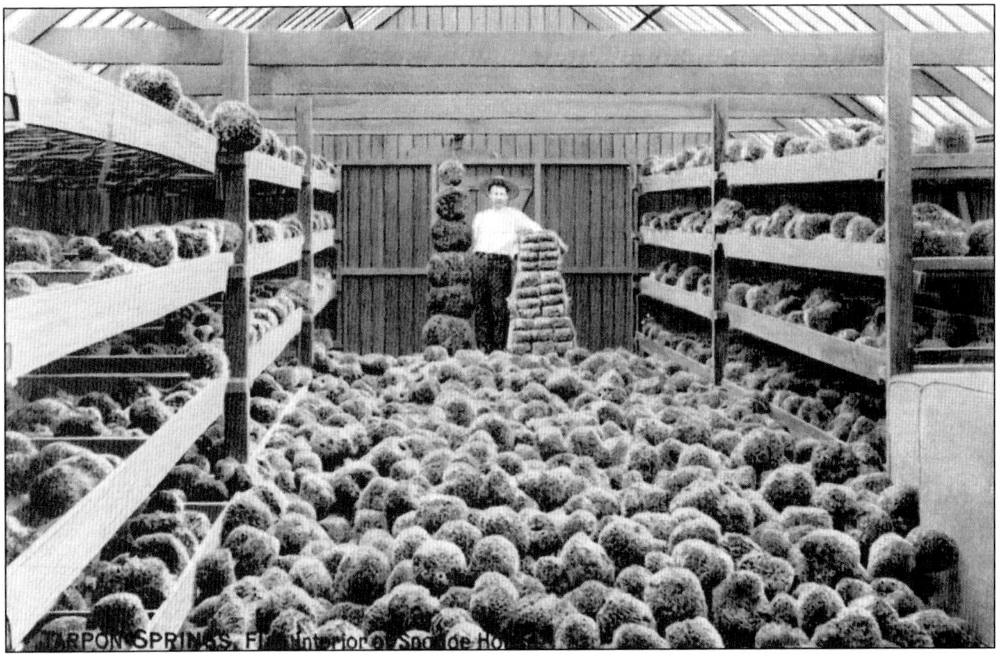

This image reveals the interior of a sponge-packing warehouse. After the auction, the bunches are opened and spread out to cool. Larger sponges are separated and cut into a size more in demand. If small, the sponge remains in its natural harvested size. Next, a shearing crew makes a final preparation of trimming before the sponges are once again sorted according to quality. (Courtesy of Heritage Village Archives and Library.)

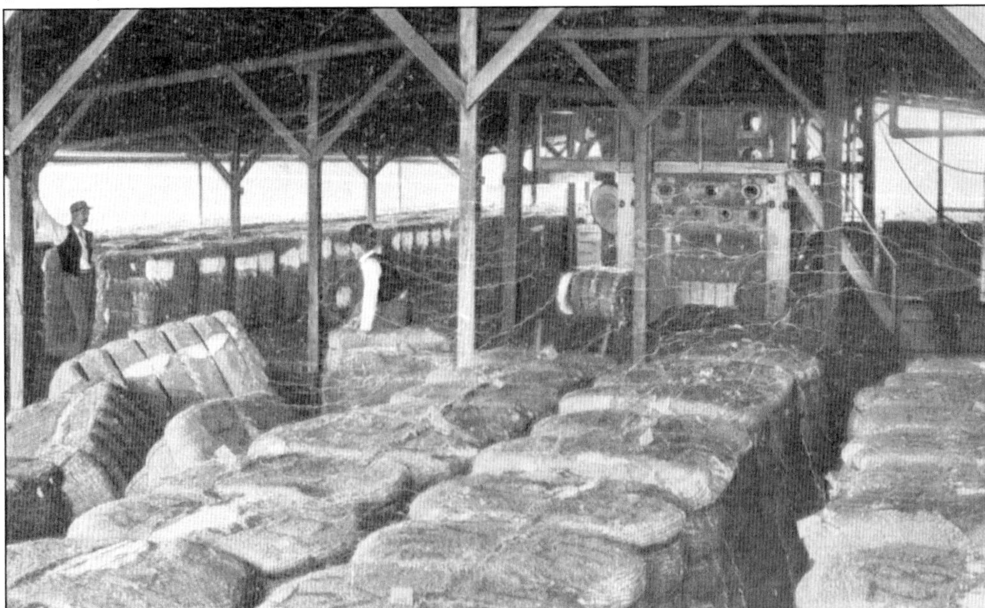

When the buyers are at auction, they may base their prices upon orders already placed. Getting the sponges ready for shipment requires them to be compressed and put into bales. A sponge press is used to reduce the volume into compressed, manageable bundles that are sent to wholesalers who resell them. (Courtesy of Tarpon Springs Area Historical Society.)

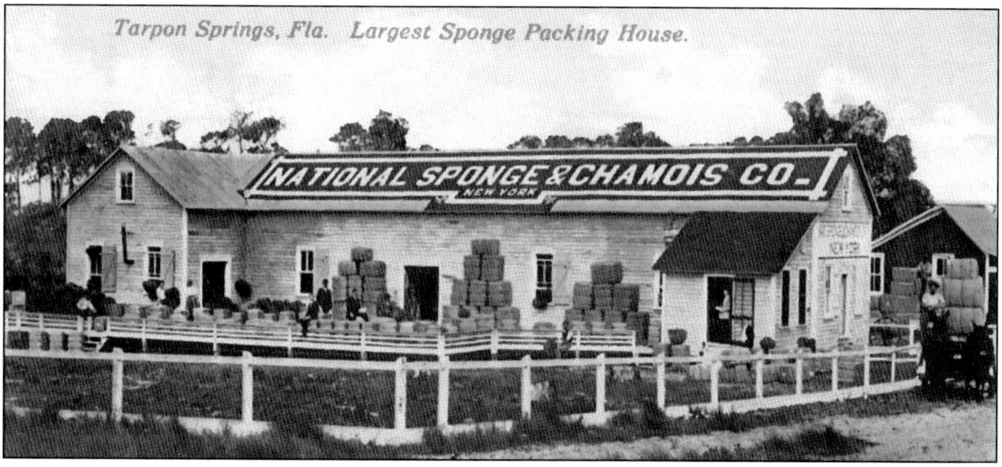

This is the National Sponge & Chamois Company. The card, dated January 24, 1913, claims that this is the largest sponge-packing house. The Ernest R. Meres Sponge Packing House at 106 Read Street is listed in the National Register of Historic Places. Another warehouse, built in 1930 by Drosos Alahouzos, later operated as the Gulf of Mexico Sponge Company. It was moved to Pinellas County's Heritage Village in 2004. (Courtesy of Sam H. Mack.)

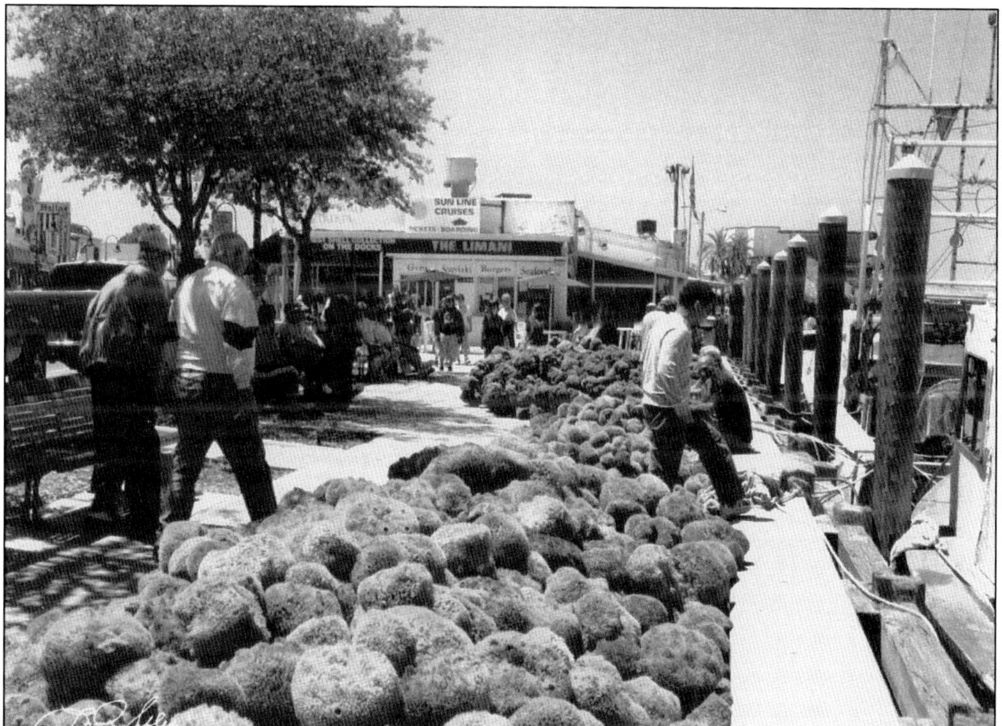

During the 1930s, Tarpon Springs earned the title of Sponge Capital of the World. Unfortunately, blight struck in 1939, almost destroying the Gulf of Mexico beds. In 1947, red tide hit, ruining beds. A third decline was the advent of the synthetic sponge. However, this 2007 postcard shows nearly 18,000 pieces of sponge that diver Jerry Kalouris harvested on his 40-day dive trip. Second from left is George Billiris, who was quoted by the *St. Petersburg Times* as saying, "It's one of the biggest catches we've had in decades." (Courtesy of Lisa Sibley, photographer.)

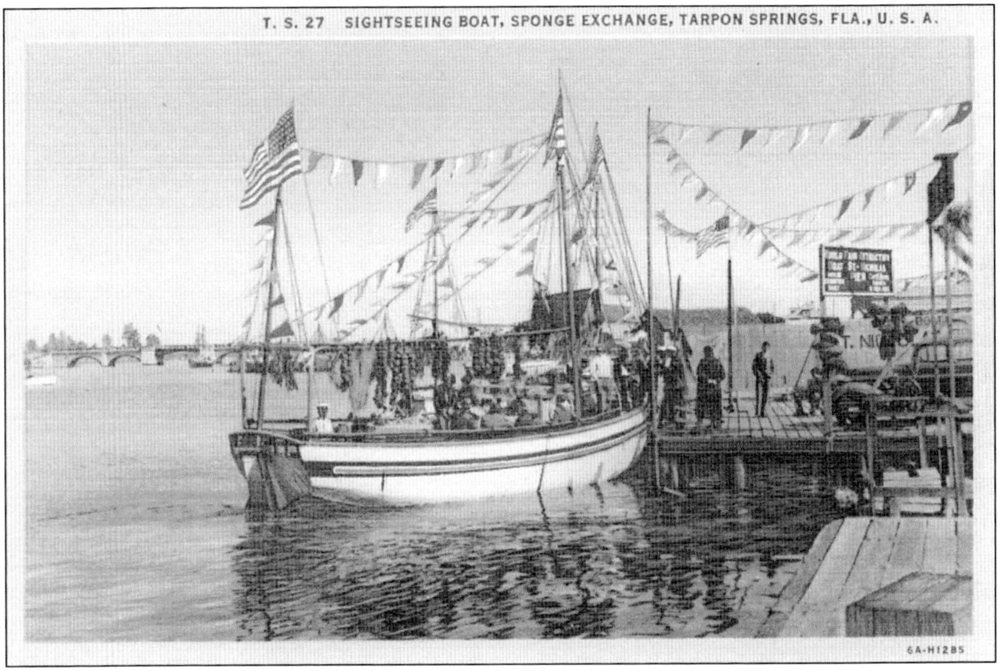

Tourists board an exhibition boat at the Sponge Exchange. Tourism has always been a major industry in Pinellas County, even dating back to the 1880s. Over the years, employment in the service industry has increased. It would replace sponging as the biggest revenue producer and employer in Tarpon Springs.

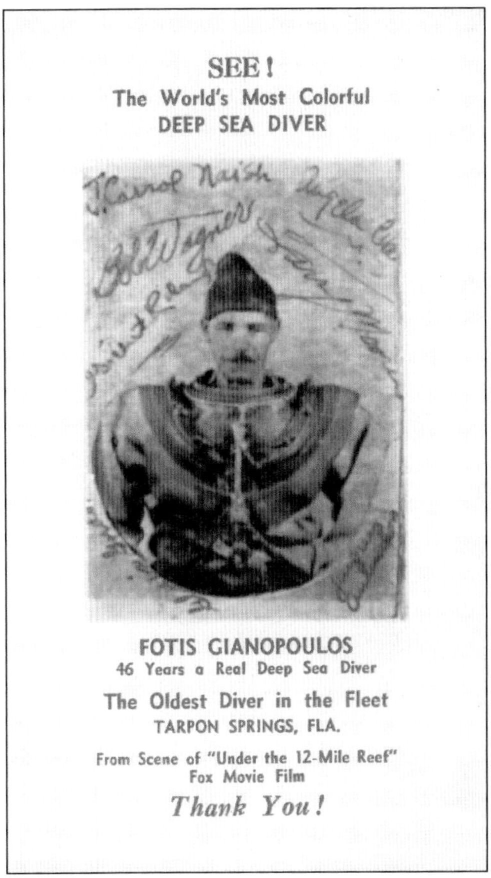

This promotional postcard advertises a deep-sea fishing tour with Capt. George Billiris. Surrounding the photograph of the sponge diver Fotis Gianopoulos are the signatures of the actors who starred in *Beneath the 12 Mile Reef*, including J. Carrol Naish, Bob Wagner, Gilbert Roland, Angela Clarke, Terry Moore, Gloria Gordon, and Jacques Aubuchon. (Courtesy of Sam H. Mack.)

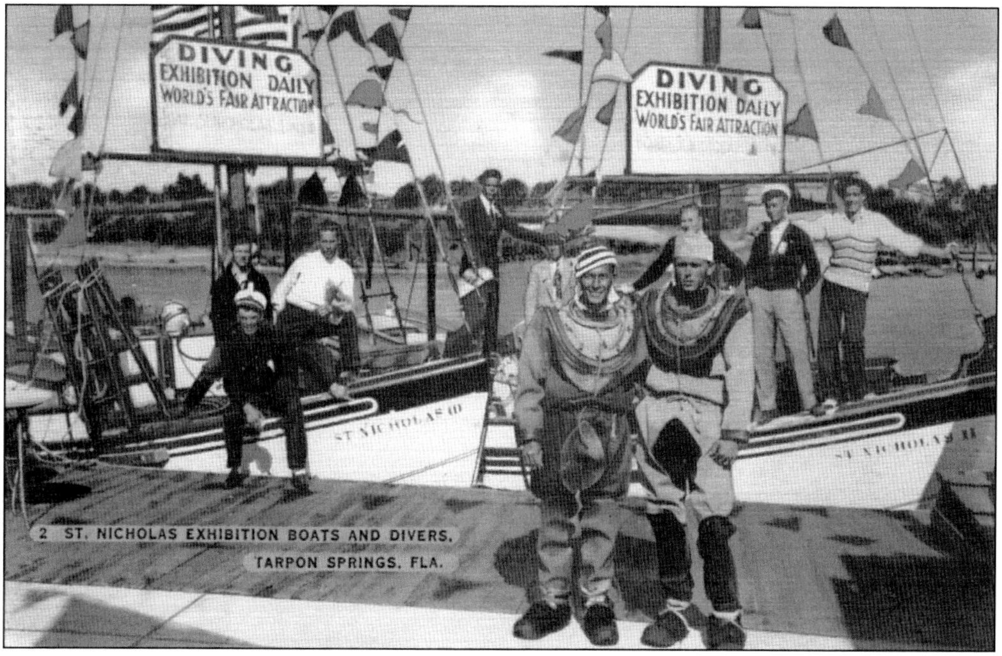

Two divers stand in front of the sponge-diving boats *St. Nicholas II* and *St. Nicholas III*, which promote their achievement. The State of Florida chose this boat line to represent sponging at A Century of Progress International Exposition, the 1933 Chicago World's Fair. The boat sailed across the Gulf of Mexico, up the Mississippi River to the Illinois River, and to a canal that connected to Lake Michigan. In the postcard below, the name of the boat is *A Century of Progress*. (Both images courtesy of Sam H. Mack.)

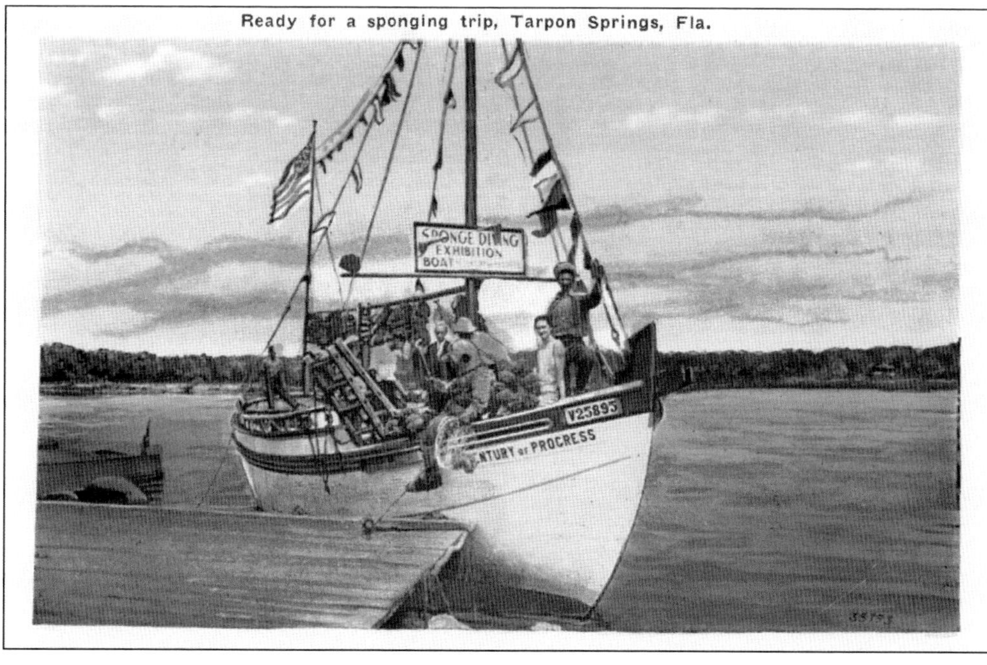

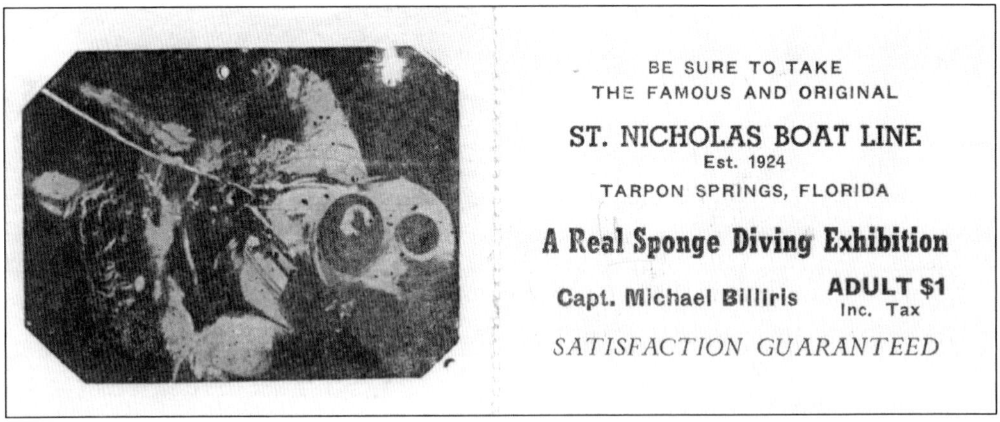

This is one of the separated tickets from the St. Nicholas Boat Line for a "Real Sponge Diving Exhibition." Established in 1924, the St. Nicholas Boat Line is still in operation today, offering sponge-diving exhibition cruises. One of the tickets has the image of this sponge diver on the back, and another ticket displays the photograph of the boat pictured below on the back. (Both images courtesy Sam H. Mack.)

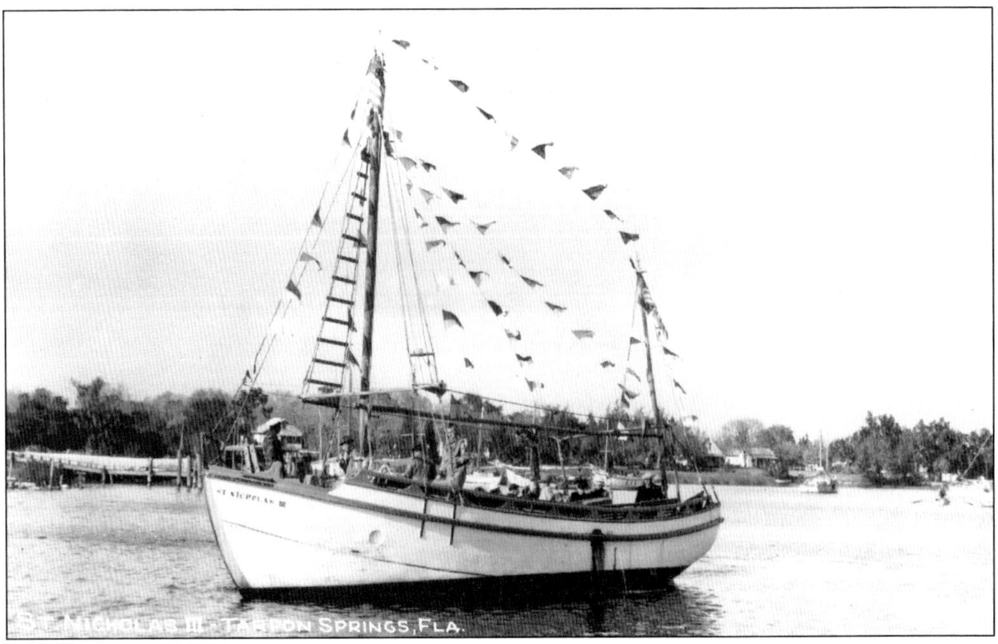

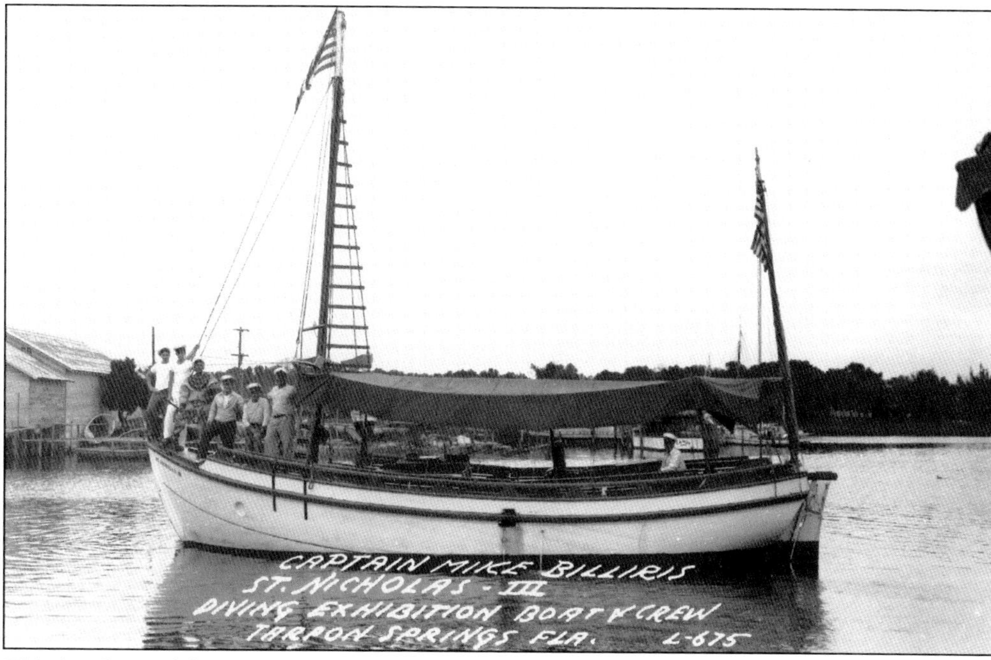

This is a beautiful example of a typical sponge-diving boat. They traditionally had the stern shaped similar to the bow, both curved, to ease the effects of waves breaking over either end. This boat, however, has been adapted as a tourist-cruising vessel; its canopy offers shade from the penetrating sun. (Courtesy of Sam H. Mack.)

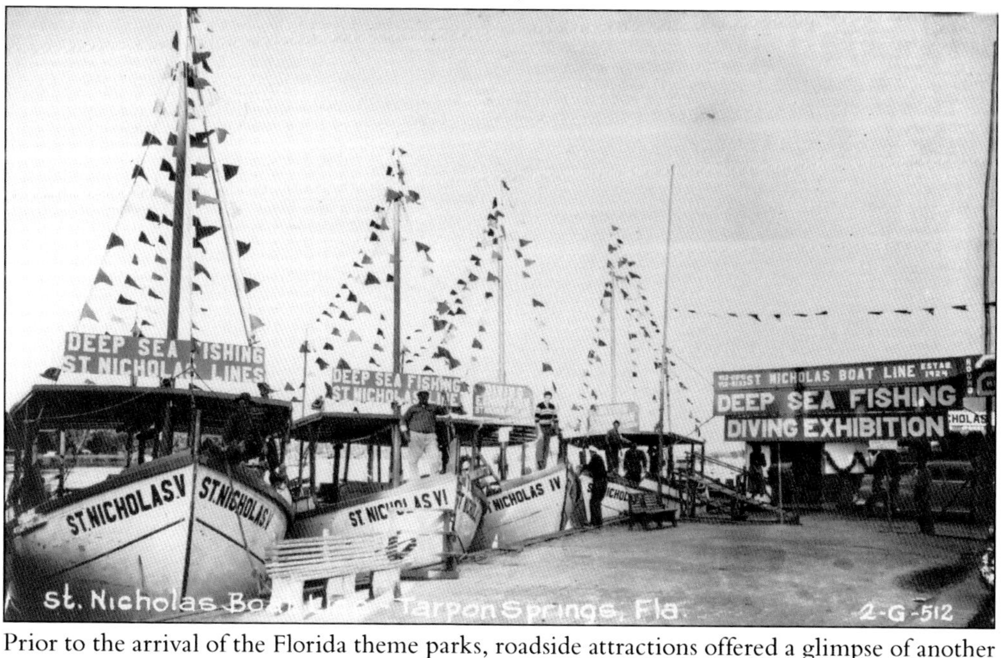

Prior to the arrival of the Florida theme parks, roadside attractions offered a glimpse of another way of life for tourists. Whether going out for deep-sea fishing or a sponge-diving exhibition, travelers delighted in the experience that the "Greek City" could afford them. Shown here are four of the five boats available for a ride—a testament to the popularity of such excursions. (Courtesy of Sam H. Mack.)

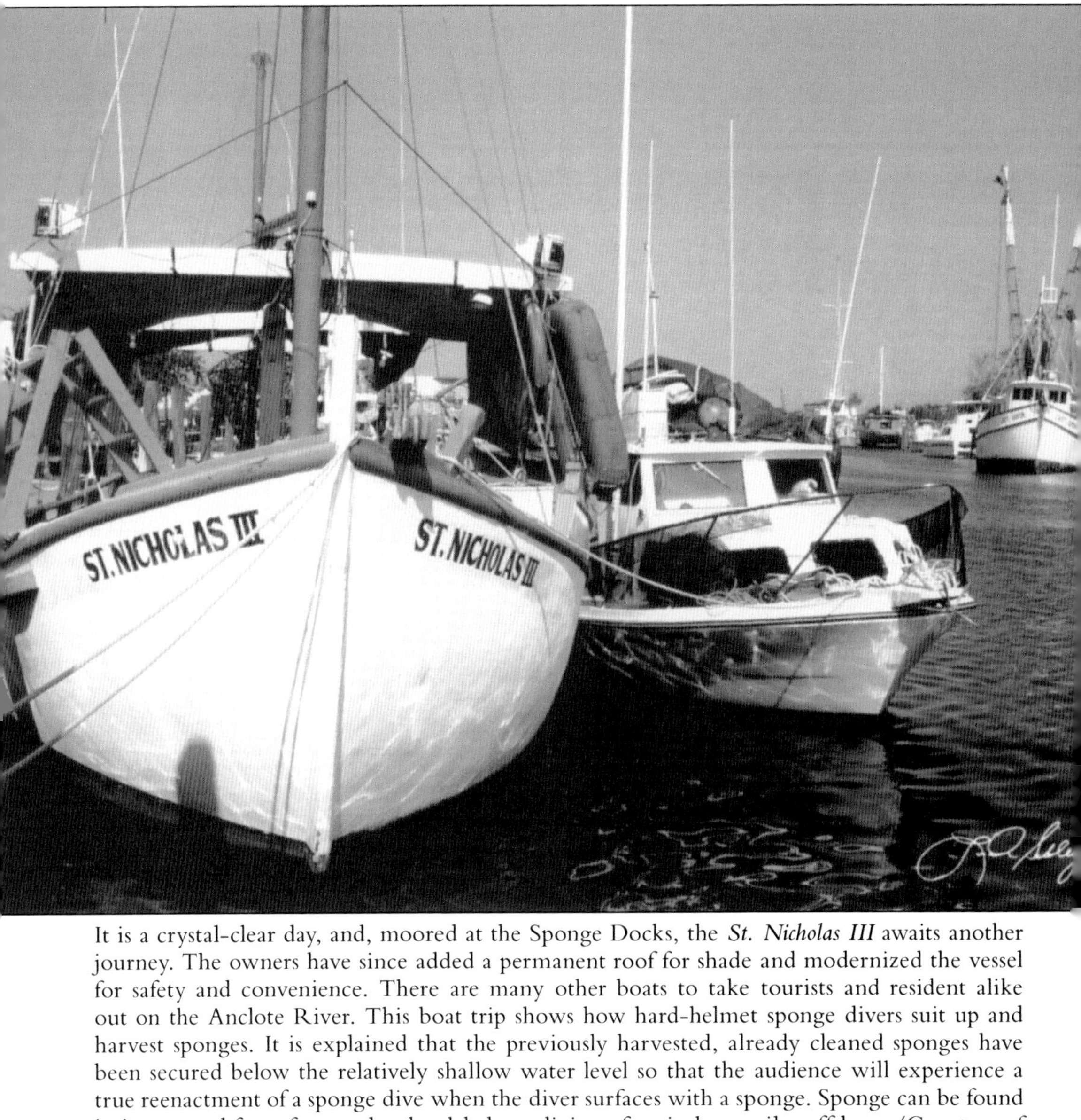

It is a crystal-clear day, and, moored at the Sponge Docks, the *St. Nicholas III* awaits another journey. The owners have since added a permanent roof for shade and modernized the vessel for safety and convenience. There are many other boats to take tourists and resident alike out on the Anclote River. This boat trip shows how hard-helmet sponge divers suit up and harvest sponges. It is explained that the previously harvested, already cleaned sponges have been secured below the relatively shallow water level so that the audience will experience a true reenactment of a sponge dive when the diver surfaces with a sponge. Sponge can be found in just several feet of water, but hard-helmet diving often is done miles offshore. (Courtesy of Lisa Sibley, photographer.)

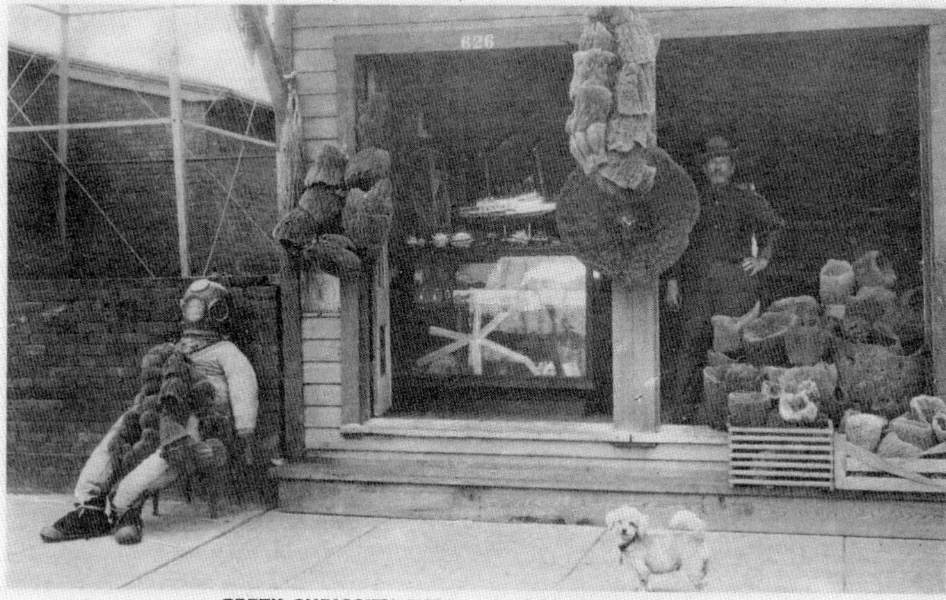

GREEK CURIOSITY SHOP. TARPON SPRINGS, FLA.

Another favorite activity that attracts tourists is visiting the curio stores. This very early postcard only identifies this as a Greek curiosity shop. It displays various types of sponge. (Courtesy of Sam H. Mack.)

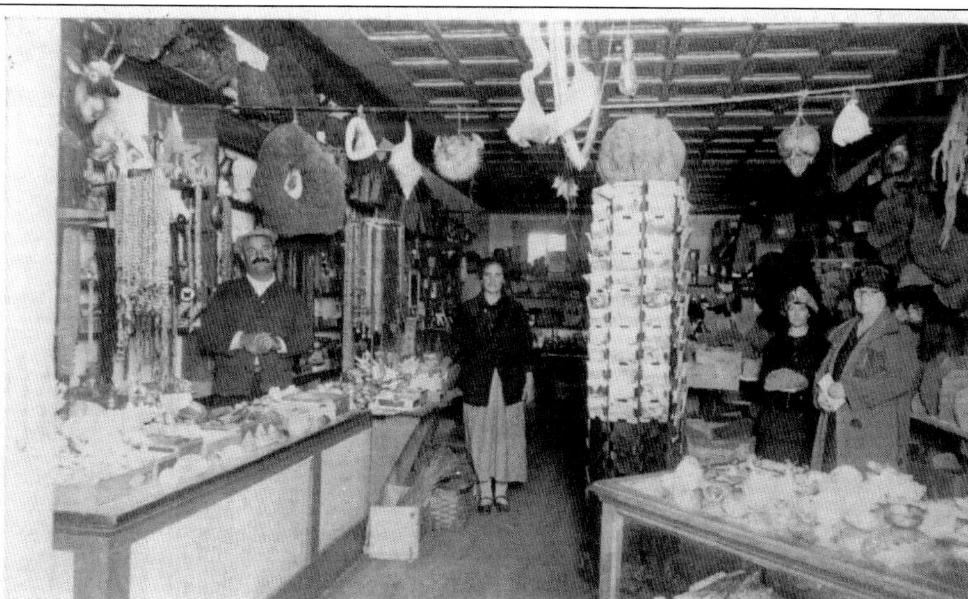

Interior View of Store of Costas Gianeskis, Tarpon Springs, Fla., U .S. A.

This postcard shows an interior view of Costas Gianeskis's curio store. Gianeskis was a trustee in the 1930 Symian Association Taxiarchis when it was first formed. Their mission was to help emigrating Greeks from the island of Symi to become familiar with the new customs and language. (Courtesy of Sam H. Mack.)

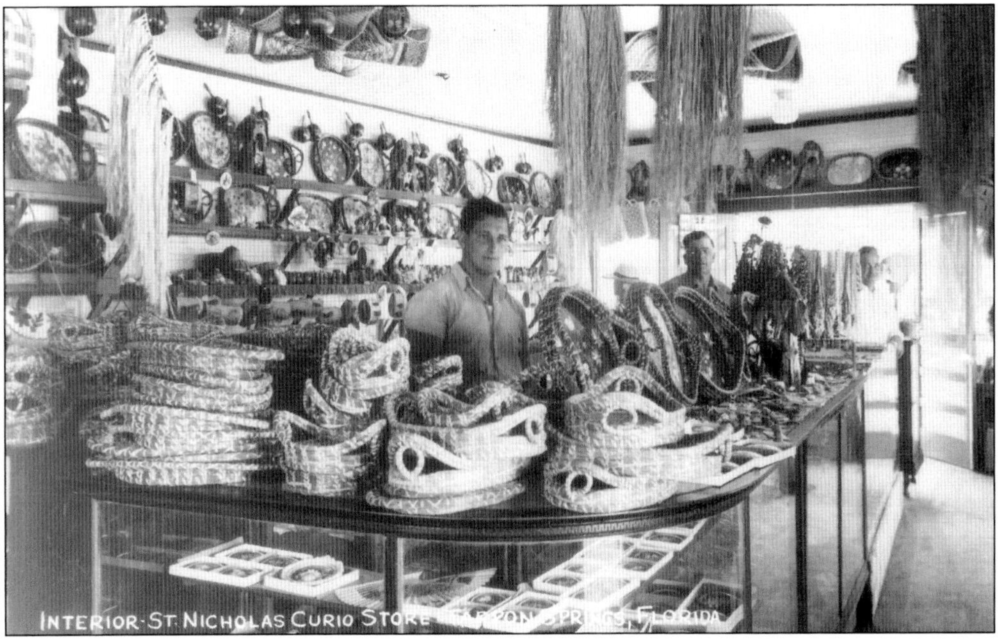

Peeking inside the St. Nicholas Curio Store, one can find exotic items of all kinds—handwoven baskets and trays, shells, shark teeth, and, of course, postcards. The first rate (to mail a postcard) varied by destination. In 1873, the United States issued its first official postcard, which cost 1¢ to mail. The first divided back postcard in this country debuted in 1907. (Courtesy of Sam H. Mack.)

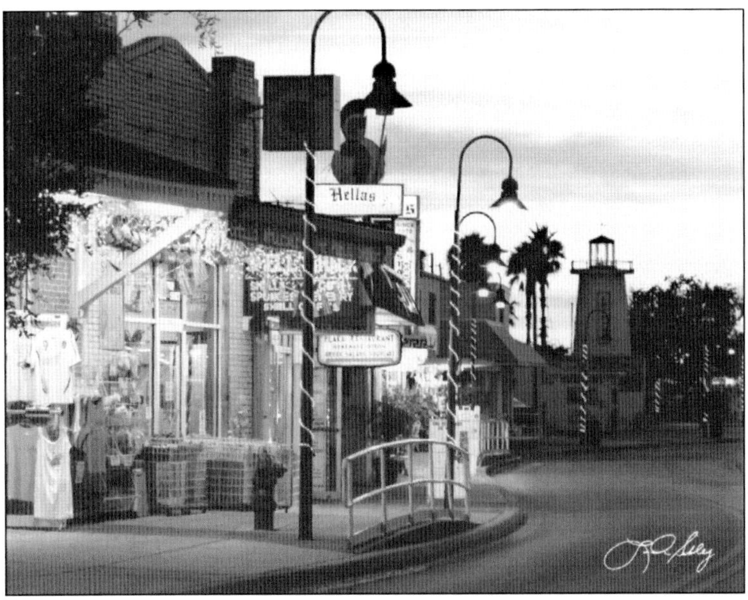

The items sold may change in popularity over time, but the curio stores remain. This 2009 nighttime view of Dodecanese Boulevard shows the stores with their wares. Also present are the restaurants serving Greek-style meals, pastries, and coffee, as well as Retsina wine, which has been made for at least 2000 years. (Courtesy of Lisa Sibley, photographer.)

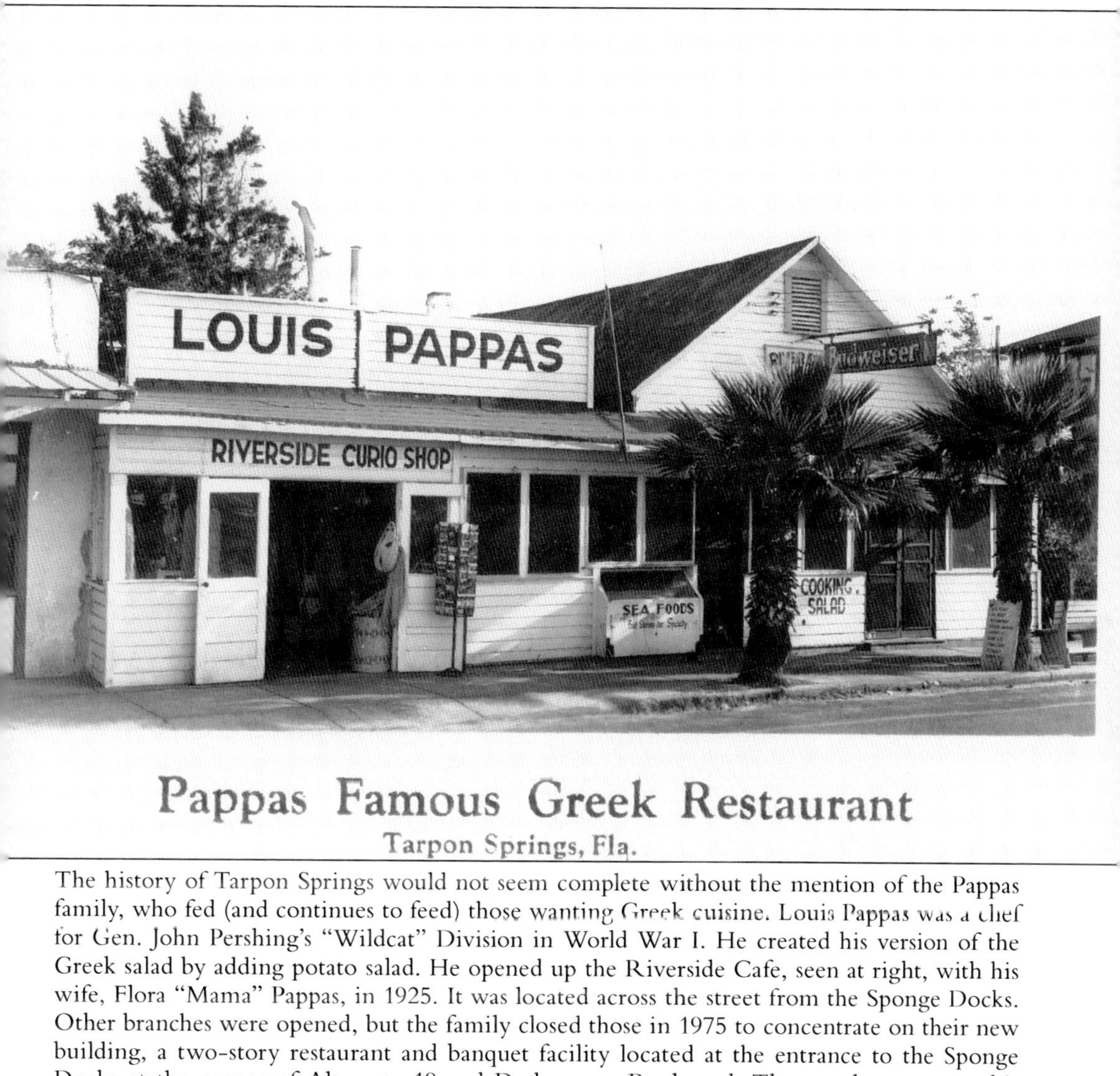

The history of Tarpon Springs would not seem complete without the mention of the Pappas family, who fed (and continues to feed) those wanting Greek cuisine. Louis Pappas was a chef for Gen. John Pershing's "Wildcat" Division in World War I. He created his version of the Greek salad by adding potato salad. He opened up the Riverside Cafe, seen at right, with his wife, Flora "Mama" Pappas, in 1925. It was located across the street from the Sponge Docks. Other branches were opened, but the family closed those in 1975 to concentrate on their new building, a two-story restaurant and banquet facility located at the entrance to the Sponge Docks at the corner of Alternate 19 and Dodecanese Boulevard. They no longer own this restaurant, but there are offshoots of the original that can be found in nearby cities. (Courtesy of Sam H. Mack.)

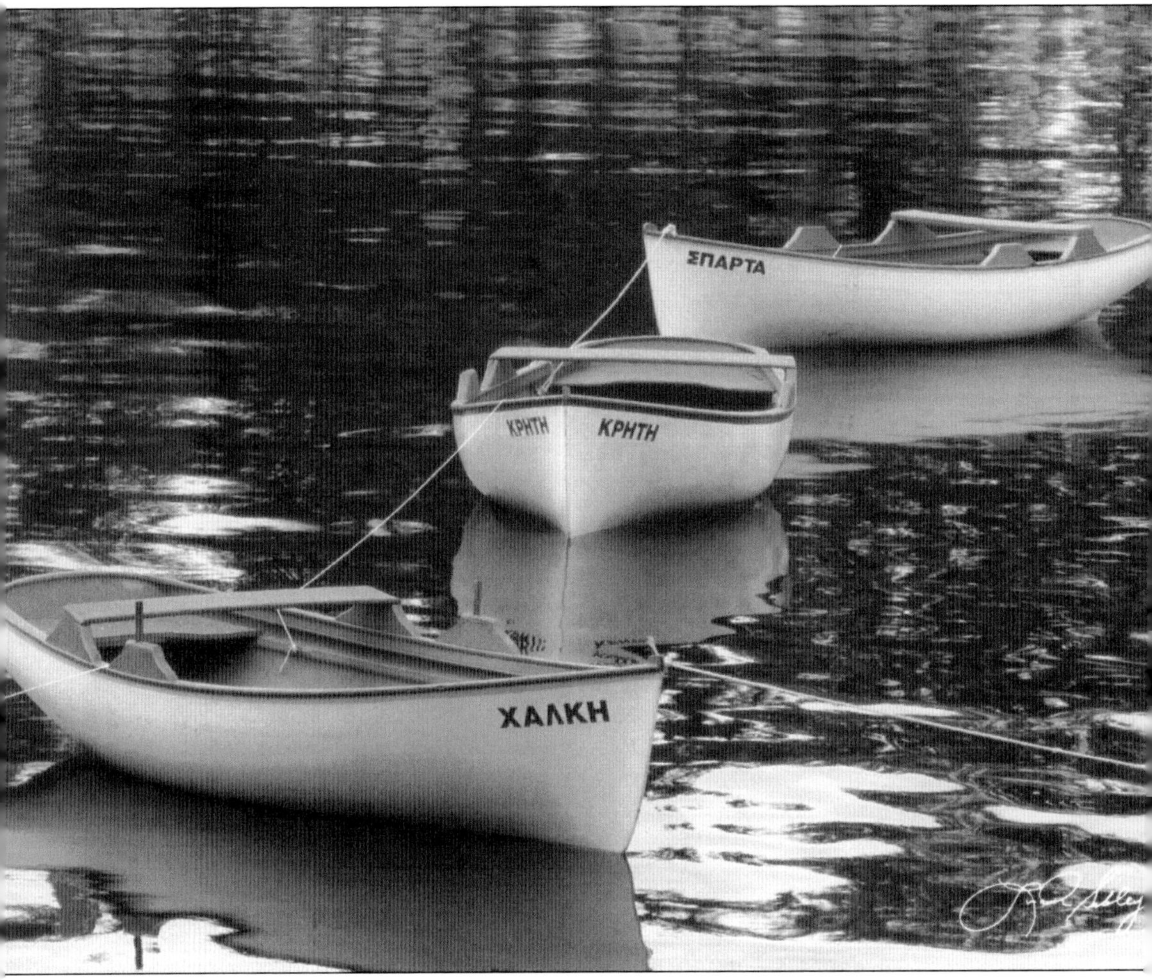

To those from this area, this simple, but elegant, shot of three Greek boats quietly bobbing in the reflective water speaks volumes. Show this image to any Tarponite, and they will proclaim, "Epiphany!" (Courtesy of Lisa Sibley, photographer.)

Central to the Greek's existence is their devout faith and support of their church and family. Epiphany is the celebration of the baptism of Jesus in the Jordan River. Nowhere else outside of Greece is it celebrated in a more jubilant and reverent fashion than here at St. Nicholas Cathedral where the day begins with Mass and a blessing of the holy water. (Courtesy of Shelly Rocktoff.)

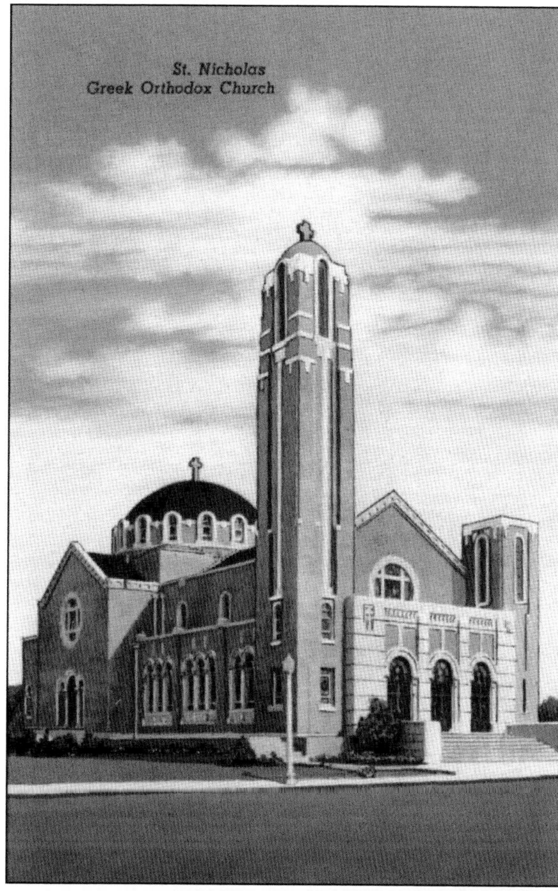

After Mass, a procession forms, consisting of church officials and choir, children in native dress, different representative Greek clubs and societies, officials, guests, and church dignitaries.

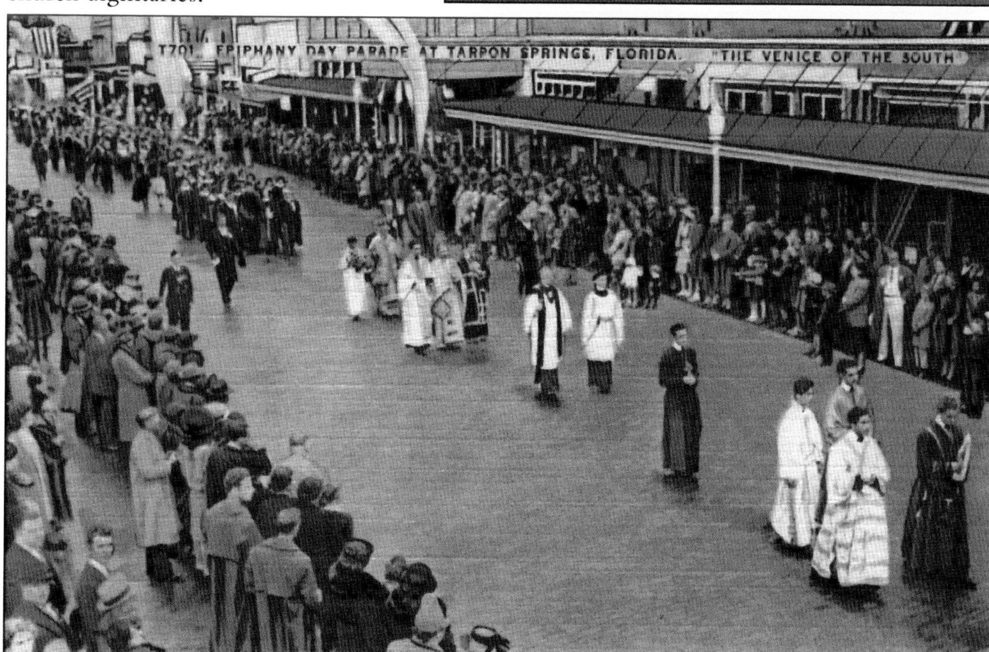

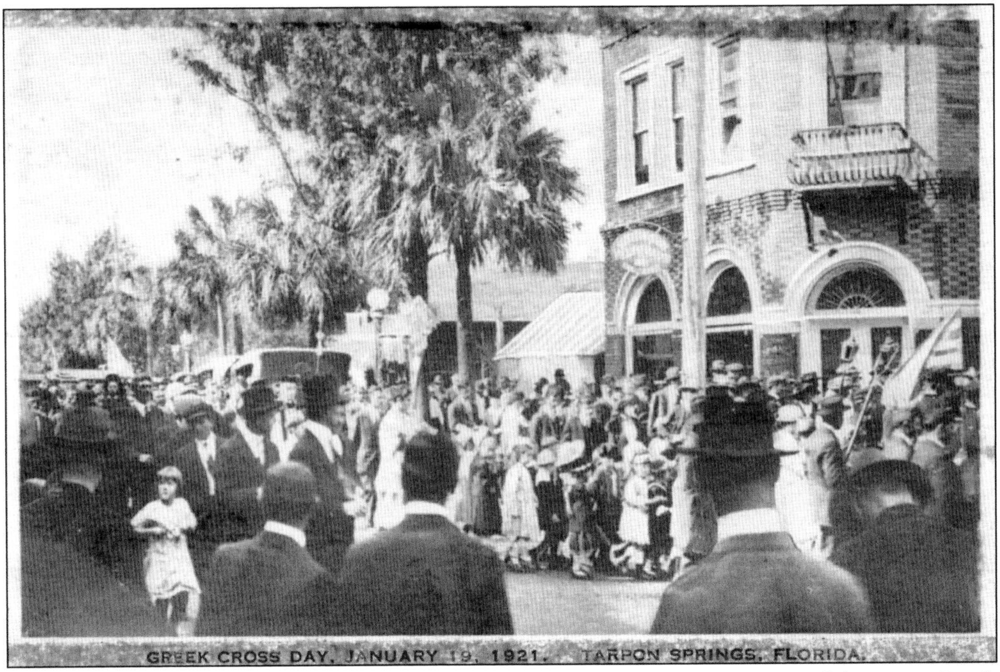

The streets are lined with crowds during the most important church event of the year, Greek Cross Day, held on January 6. The Gregorian calendar, used by Eastern churches, sets the date for Epiphany as January 6, while churches that use the Julian calendar celebrate Epiphany on January 19. (Courtesy of Irene Giannaras Garner.)

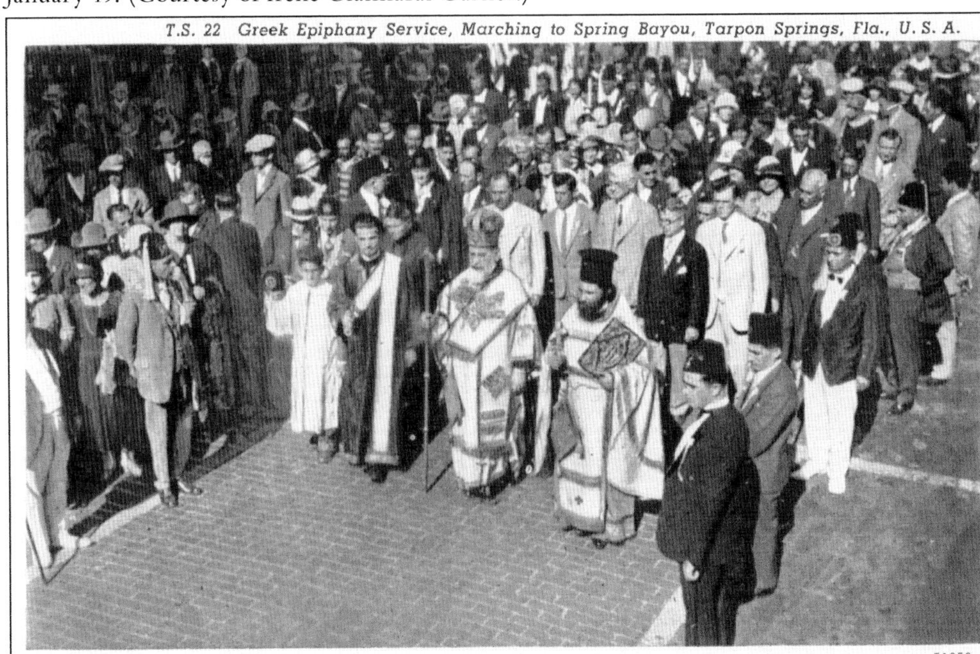

The procession continues moving through the streets. This event began as a local church celebration in 1903 and has grown in stature whereby now Tarpon Springs is known as "Epiphany City." (Courtesy of Sam H. Mack.)

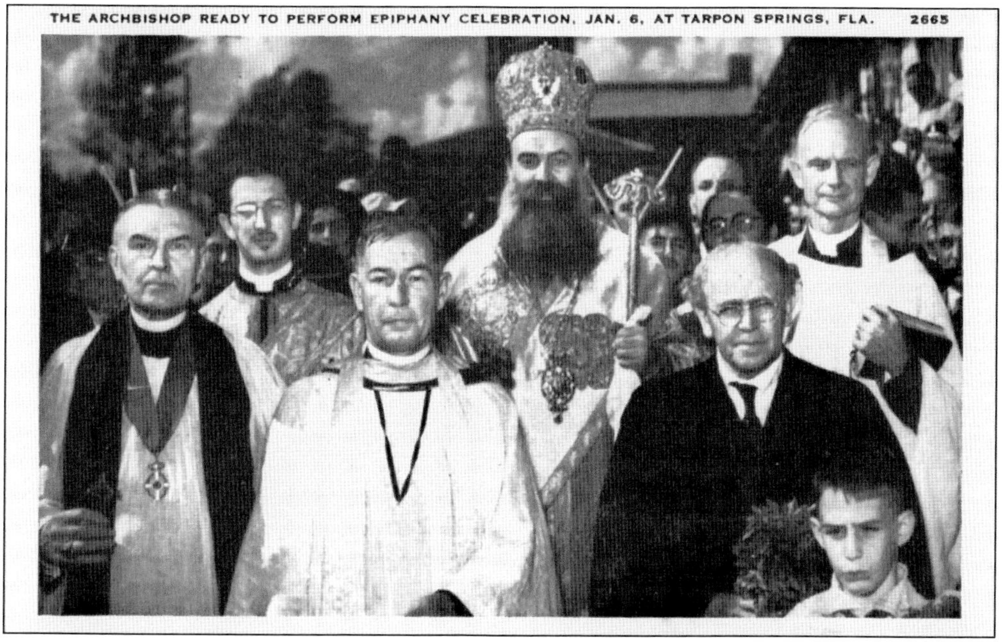

The ceremony is led by an archbishop or another elevated dignitary of the Greek Orthodox Church. During the centennial anniversary of St. Nicholas Cathedral in 2006, All Holiness Bartholomew, archbishop of Constantinople, New Rome, and Ecumenical Patriarch, blessed the waters of Spring Bayou. (Courtesy of Sam H. Mack.)

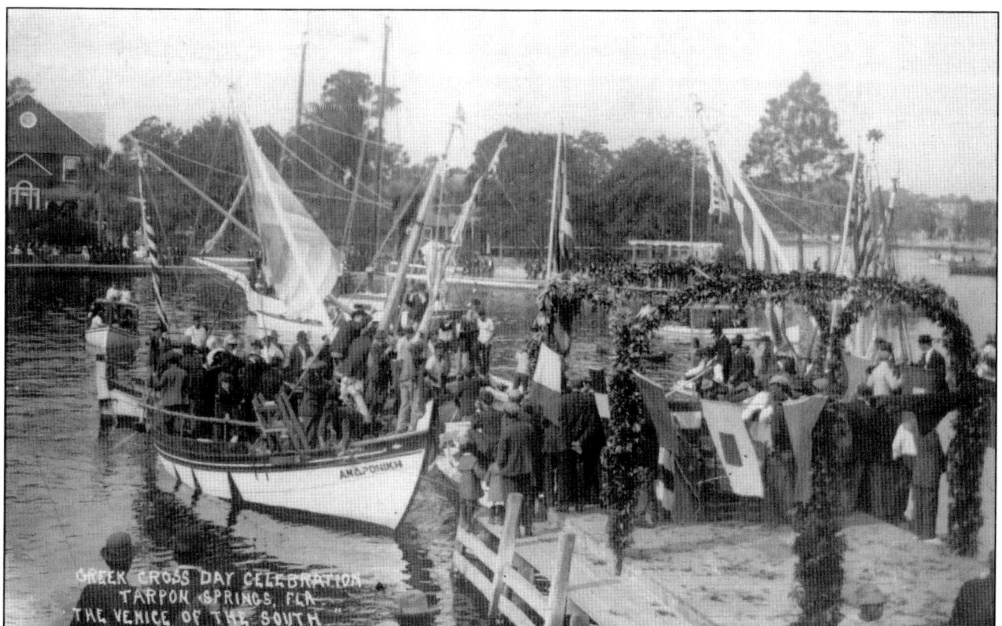

Upon his arrival at the dock, the archbishop blessed the waters and read St. Mark 1:9. Then, the dove bearer, a role filled by a young girl since 1935, released the white dove, symbolizing the Holy Spirit. (Courtesy of Sam H. Mack.)

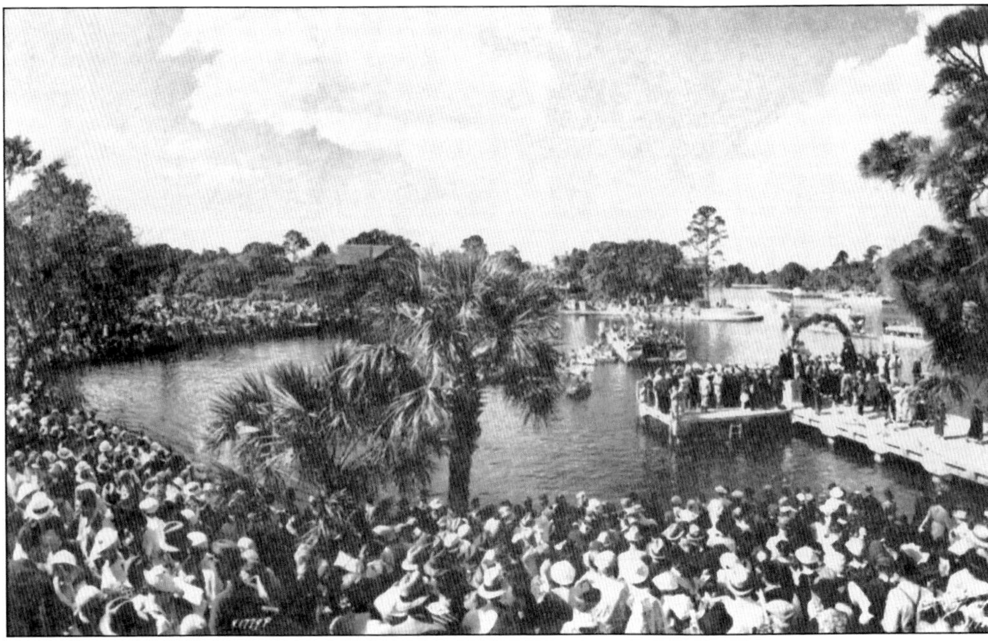

In both images, the crowd waits for the throwing of a golden cross into the bayou. The archbishop, priests, and deacons, and the choir formerly embarked on a barge so all could see. In 1956, a sponge boat was used, and in later years, the dignitaries remain on the dock. The image above shows the large numbers of spectators who attend this ceremony. (Both images courtesy of Sam H. Mack.)

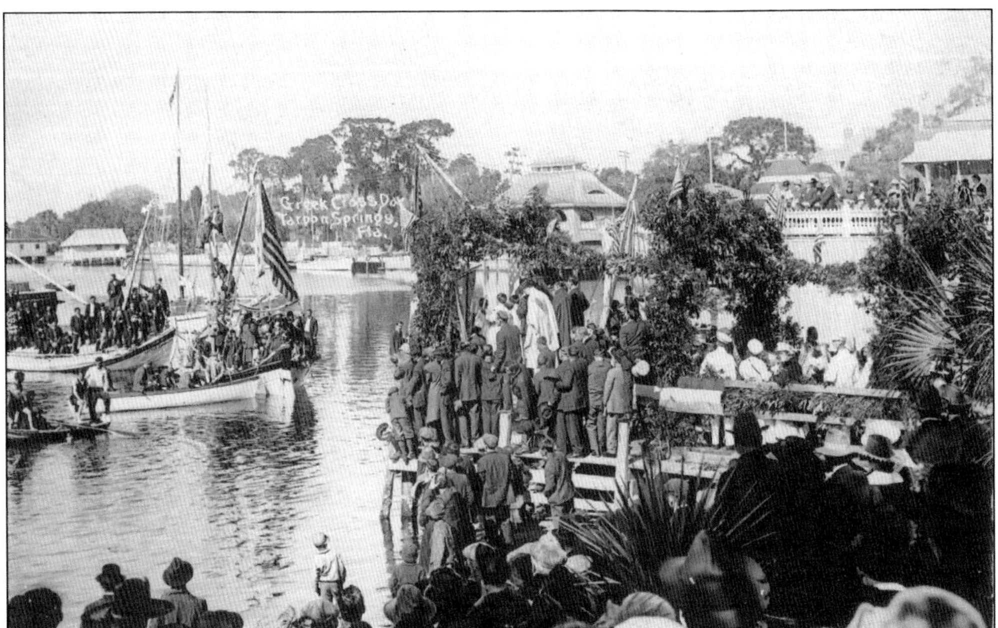

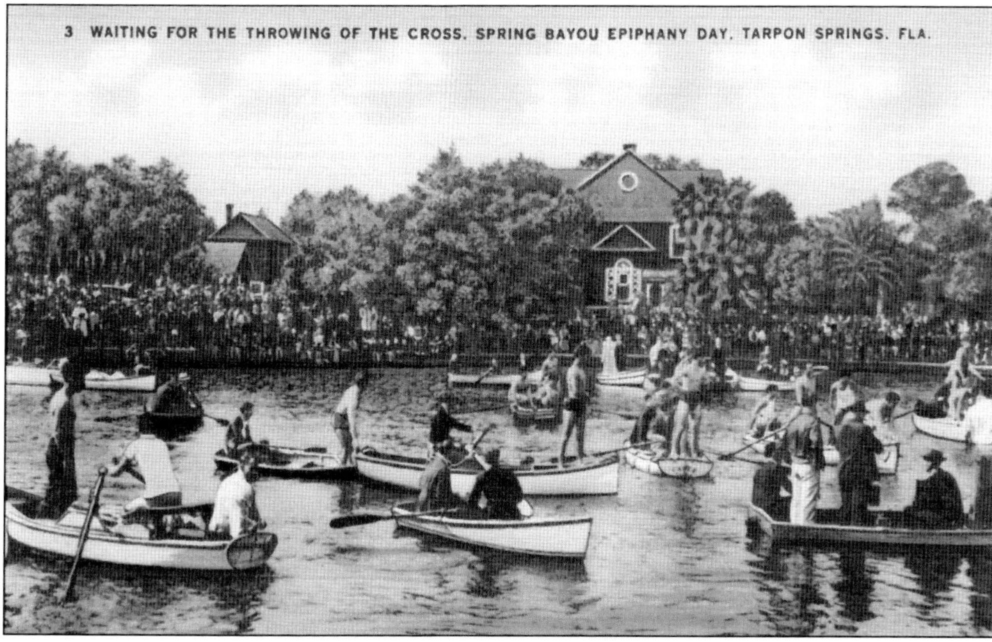

About 50 young men ready themselves to dive for the cross. Though fully aware that the water will be shockingly cold, they also know that retrieval of the cross will bless them with good fortune. (Above, courtesy of Jackie Payne; below, courtesy of Hammond Salley.)

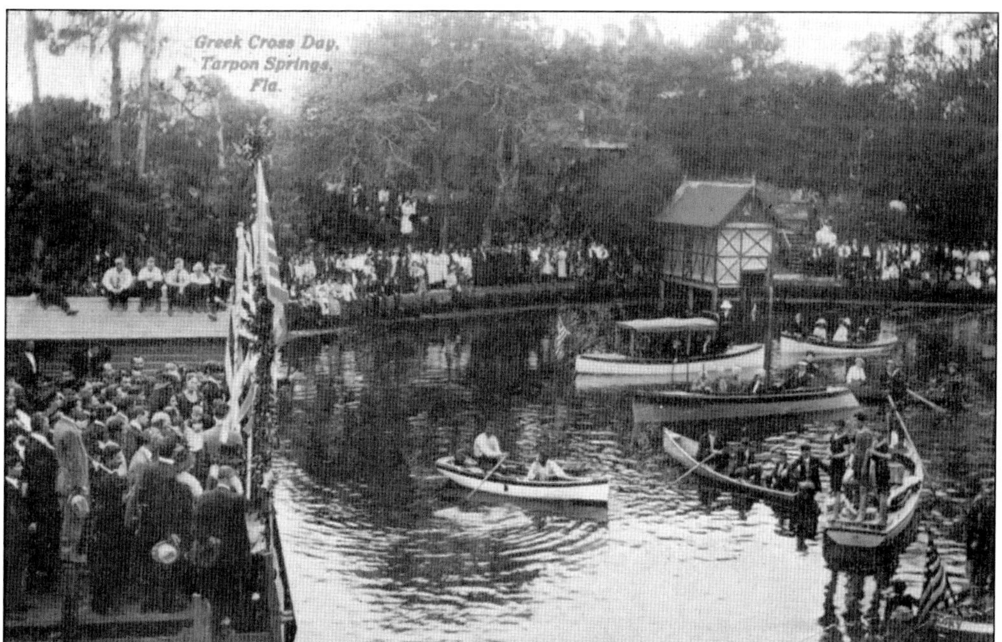

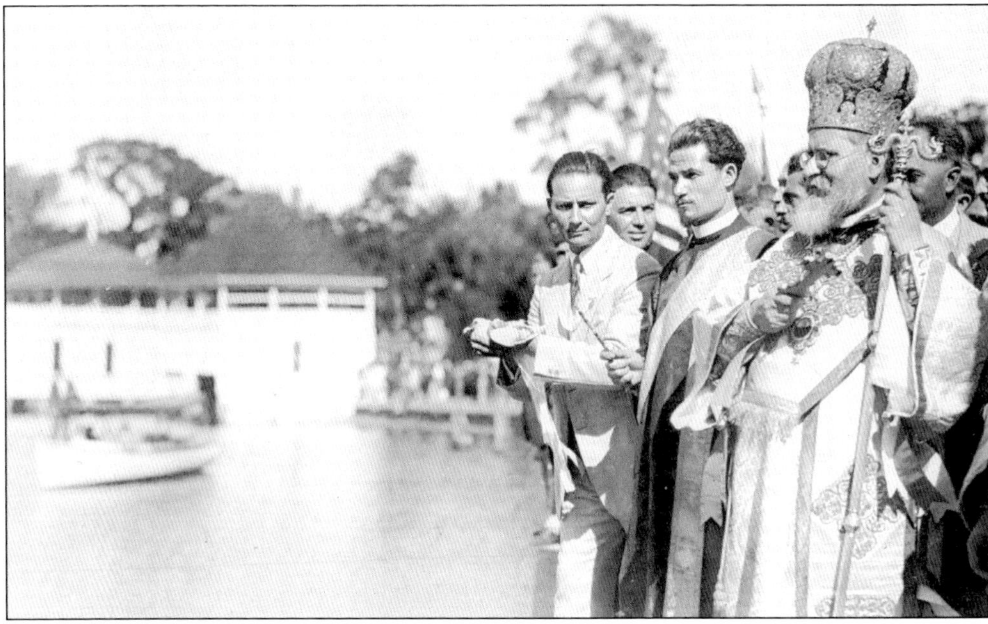

The archbishop throws the golden cross into Spring Bayou. Upon release of the cross, the young men who have been waiting in a semicircle of boats dive into the water and search for it. (Courtesy of Tarpon Springs Area Historical Society.)

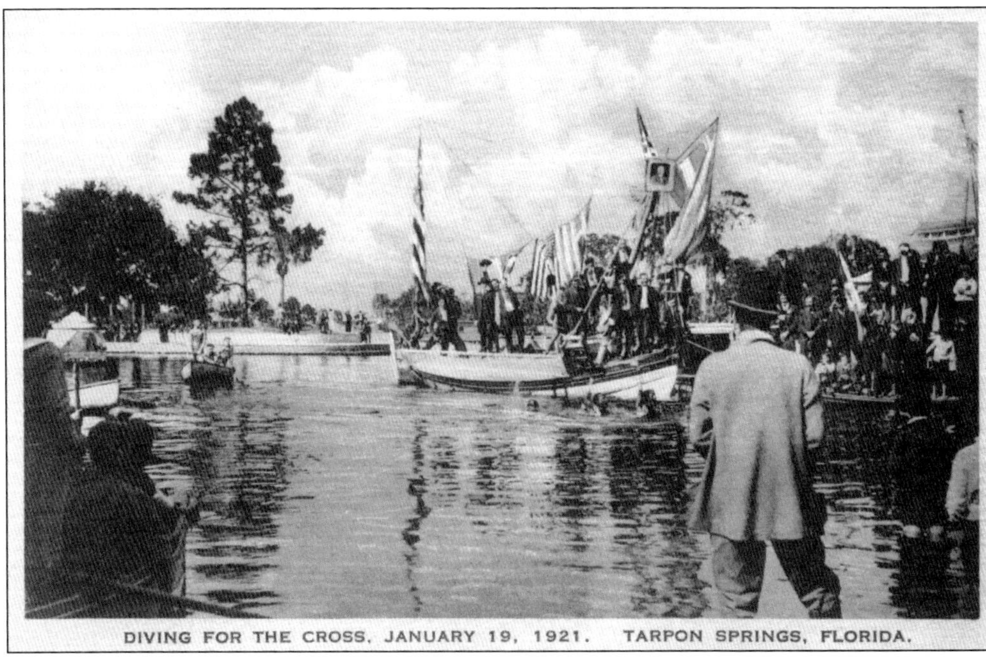

Although Epiphany is held on January 6, there may have been a time when it was held on January 19, as printed on this card. Here, the divers surface in the water. (Courtesy of Sam H. Mack.)

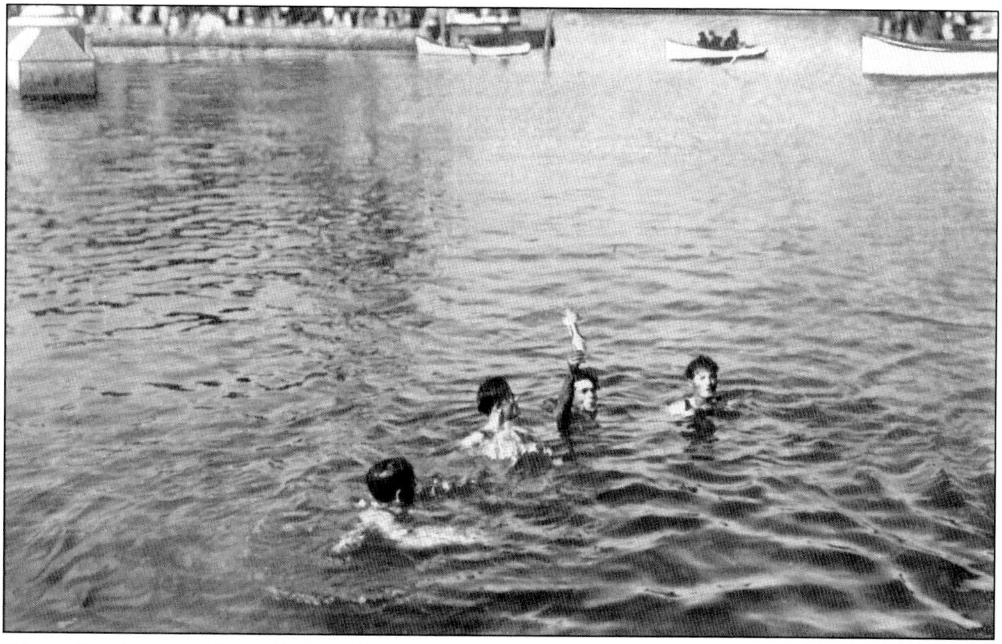

Throwing the cross is symbolic of the casting of the bread of truth upon the troubled world. The fortunate retriever of the cross holds it high above his head, signaling to all that the search is over. (Courtesy of Tarpon Springs Area Historical Society.)

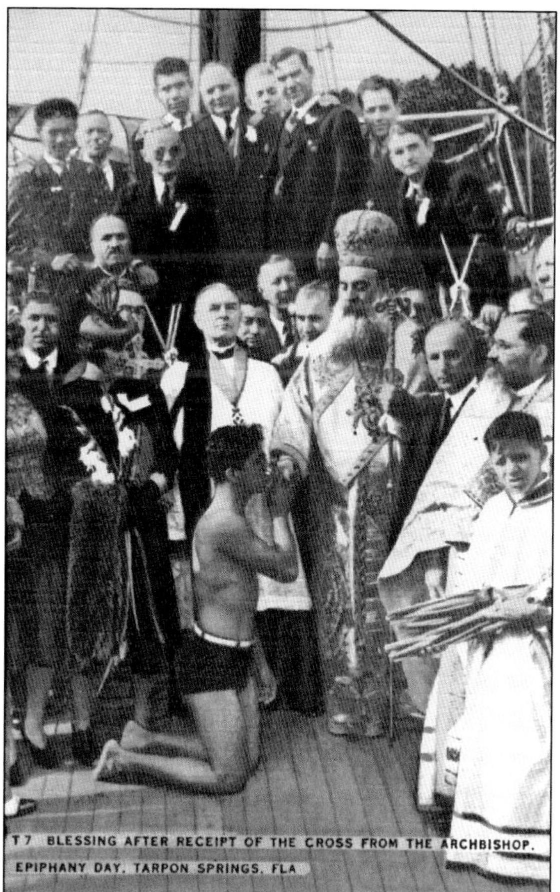

Kneeling before the archbishop, the diver hands the cross to him. The young diver is now blessed and congratulated. He will receive a favorable future with divine blessings. (Courtesy of Sam H. Mack.)

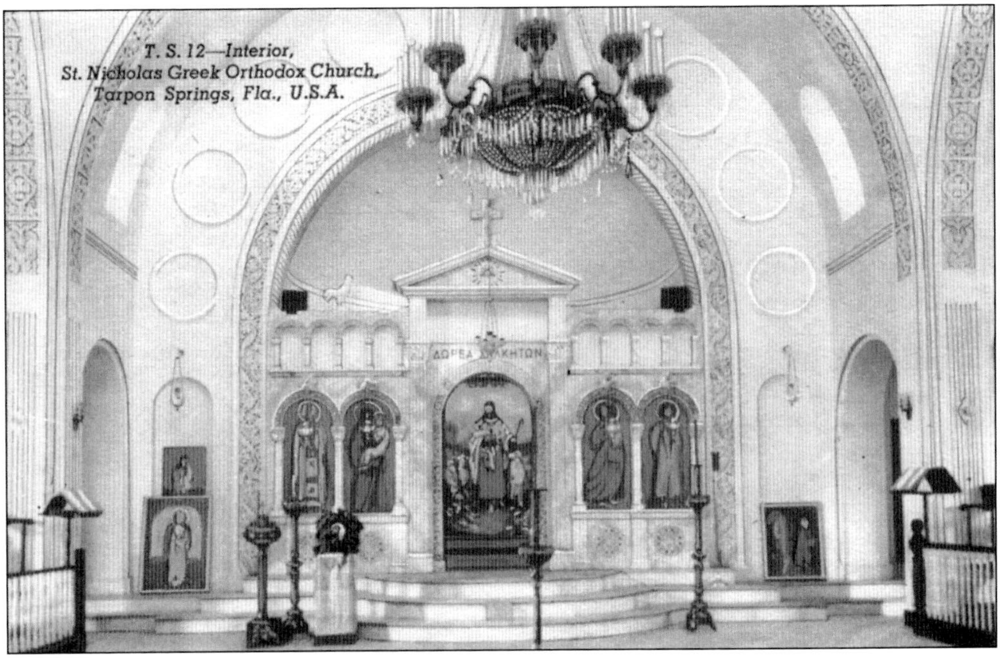

This is the interior of St. Nicholas Cathedral. The divers all return to church to be blessed, and the bottled water, which was blessed earlier in the day, is handed out to the faithful. The archbishop and priest then return to the bayou to bless the water and the boats. A great celebration at the Glendi festival follows, where young and old alike enjoy food, music, and dance. (Above, courtesy of Shelly Rocktoff; below, courtesy of Lisa Sibley, photographer.)

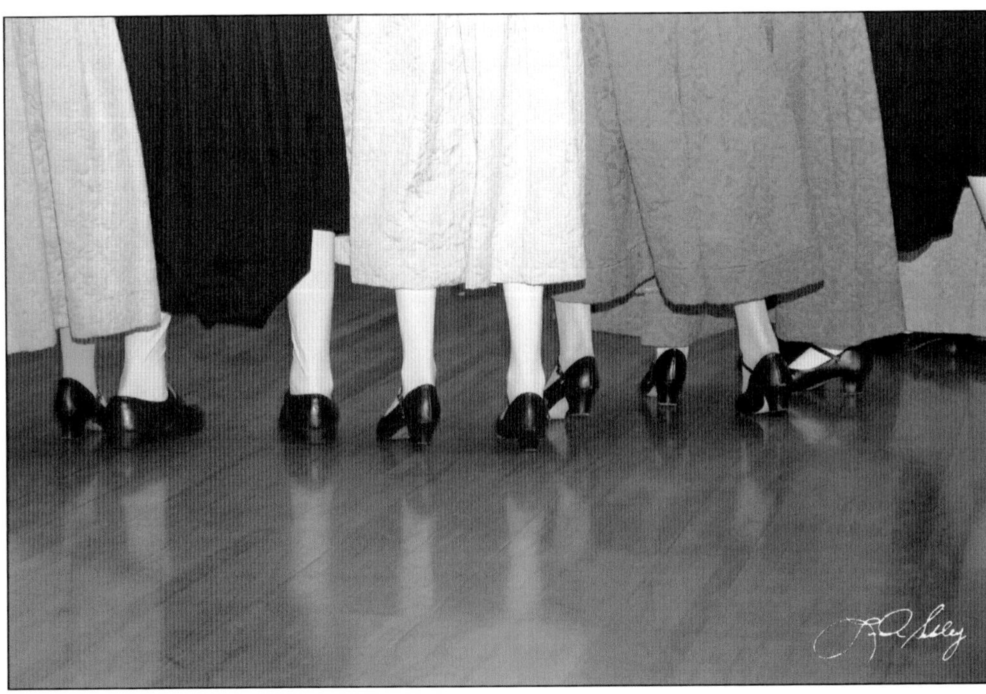

Five

Wish You Were Here

The first pioneers out at the settlement of Anclote formed a tightly knit culture, similar in structure to the society formed by the first homesteaders, in what would become Tarpon Springs. They both appreciated the scenic waterways, boundless forests, gentle breezes, and abundant hunting and fishing, all in the surrounding beauty of an artist's chosen palette of the green-blue Gulf of Mexico. All the best that Florida has to offer is found in Tarpon Springs. In an era without the instant contact available to people today, time moved a bit slower. The written word was a common link between places, people, and the events of their lives.

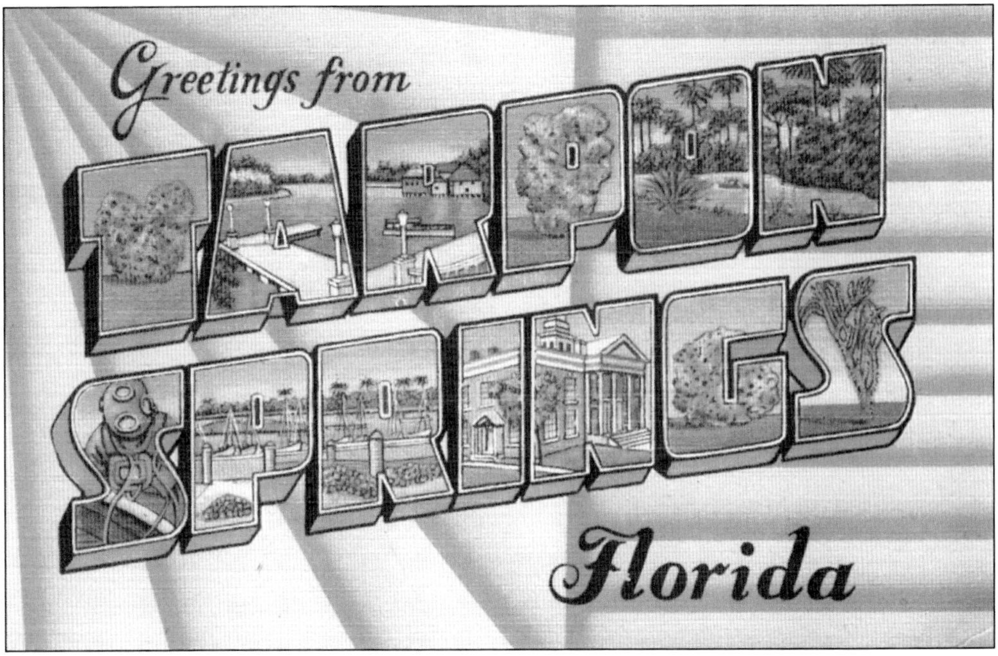

Everyone is familiar with this type of postcard, as almost every tourist destination in every state has one. The cutout letters spelling the city's name have little vignettes of the area, giving recipients a quick glimpse into the sender's delightful vacation.

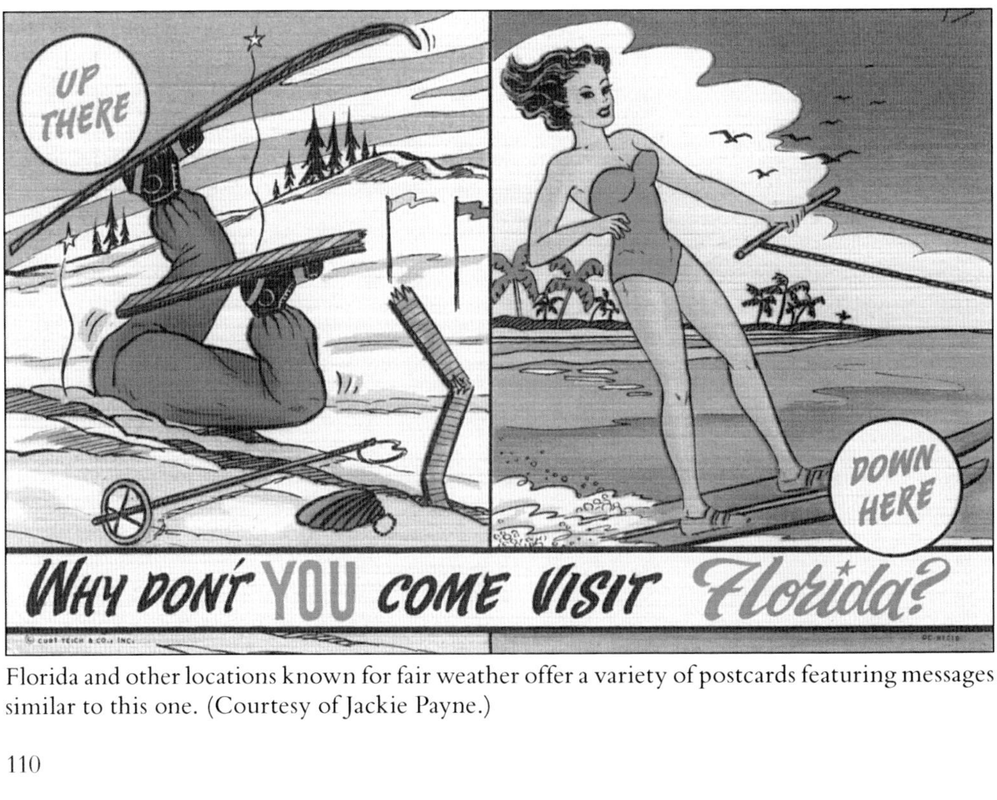

Florida and other locations known for fair weather offer a variety of postcards featuring messages similar to this one. (Courtesy of Jackie Payne.)

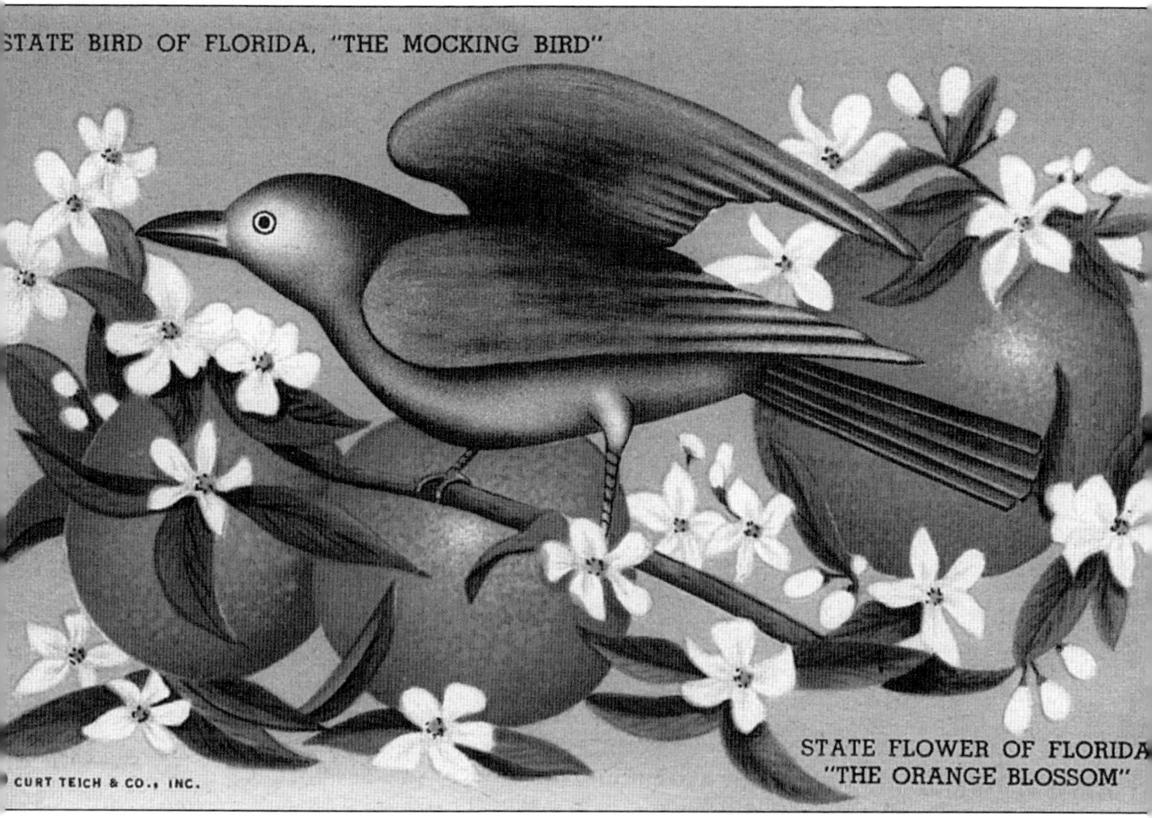

Several state symbols were adopted by Florida. In 1927, Florida designated the mockingbird as its state bird. The state flower, an orange blossom, one of the more fragrant flowers in the state, was adopted by the legislature in 1909. In 1991, the coreopsis became Florida's official wildflower. The largemouth bass represents Florida's game fish, and the sailfish, one of Ernest Hemingway's favorites, is the state saltwater fish. Florida's saltwater mammal is the porpoise (commonly known as dolphin), and the state marine mammal is the manatee. The Florida State animal is the Florida panther, and the sabal palm is the state tree.

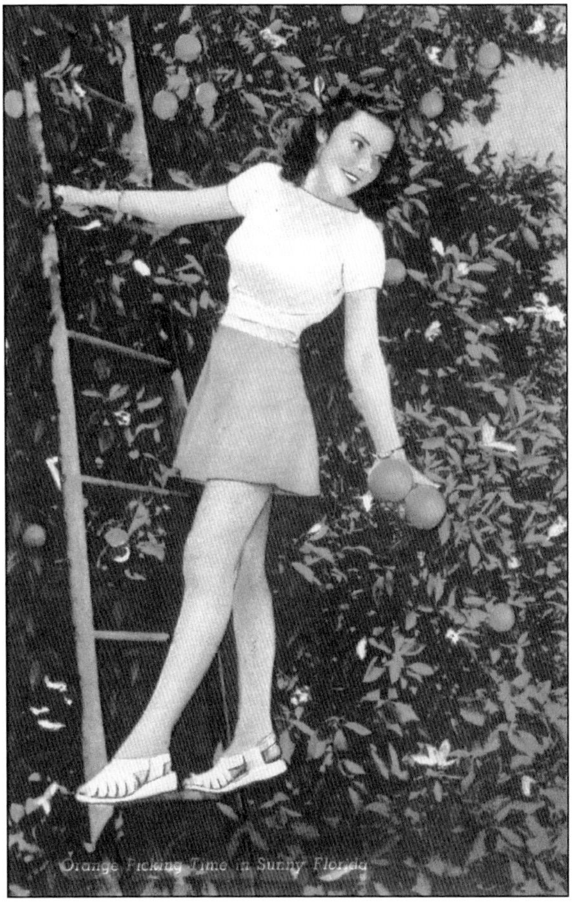

Nothing says Florida like a glass of fresh-squeezed orange juice, the official state beverage. The Florida Welcome Stations would attract many travelers entering the state with its offer of free juice. The Florida Citrus Commission hired Anita Bryant as its spokesperson in 1969, where she tagged the commercials with "Breakfast without orange juice is like a day without sunshine." Her contract was not renewed in 1979 due to her outspoken views against homosexuals.

Amelia Meres, at left holding a basket of citrus, also had a citrus grove in addition to planting palms downtown, cycads at the cemetery and many varieties of plants at the Ferns Hotel and in her yard. It was said that Meres Boulevard ran through her grove, although the exact location is unknown. (Courtesy of Hammond Salley.)

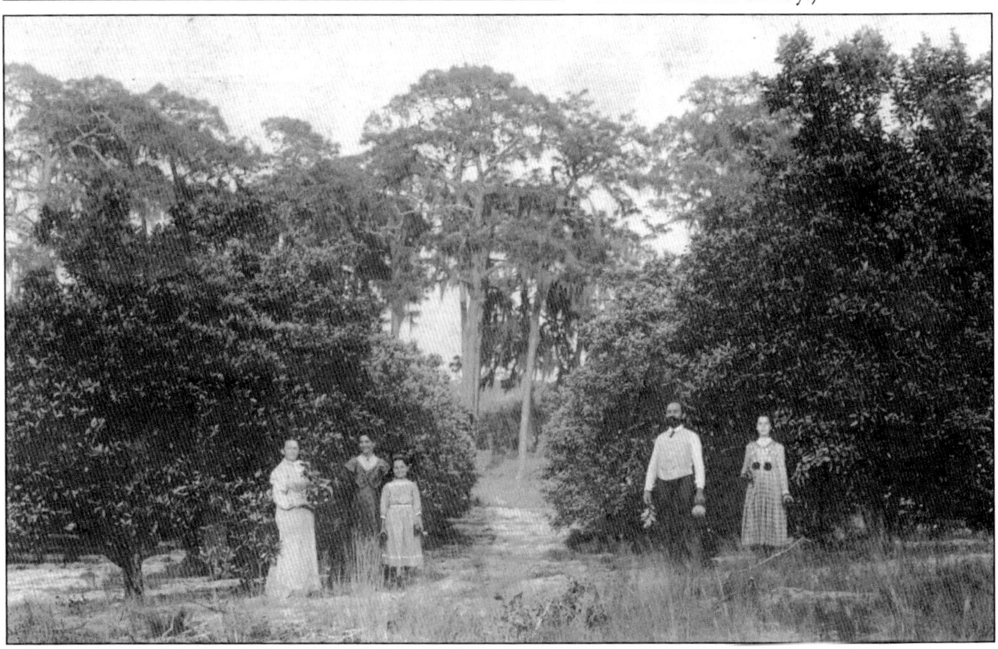

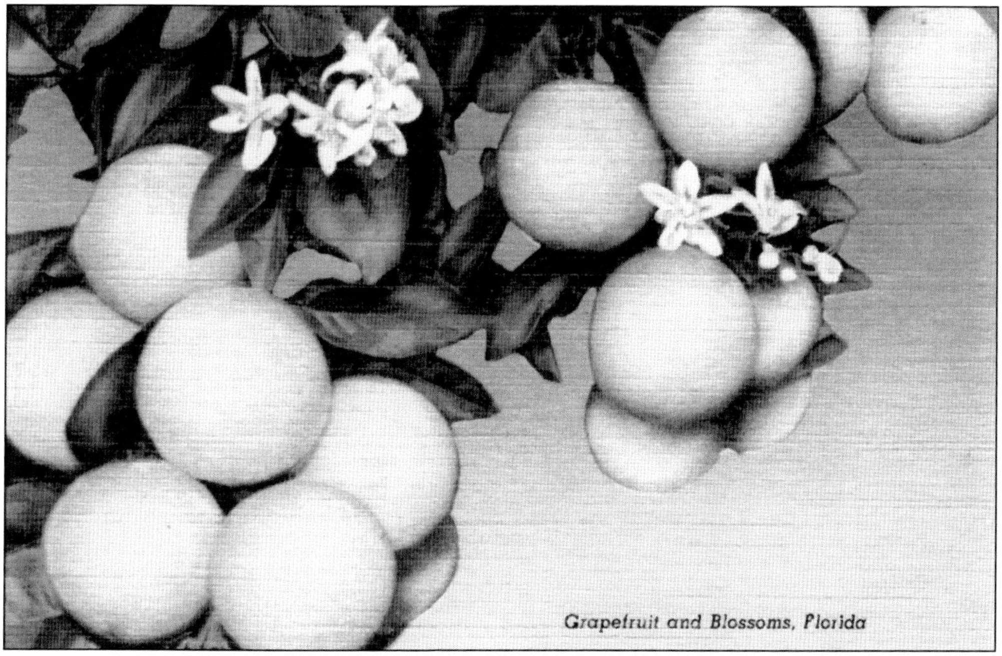

Grapefruit has been popular since the late 19th century. In 1823, Count Odette Philippe brought it to Florida when he planted citrus groves in Safety Harbor. Pink grapefruit was first discovered at the groves of Kimball Chase Atwood, a pioneer in America's citrus industry.

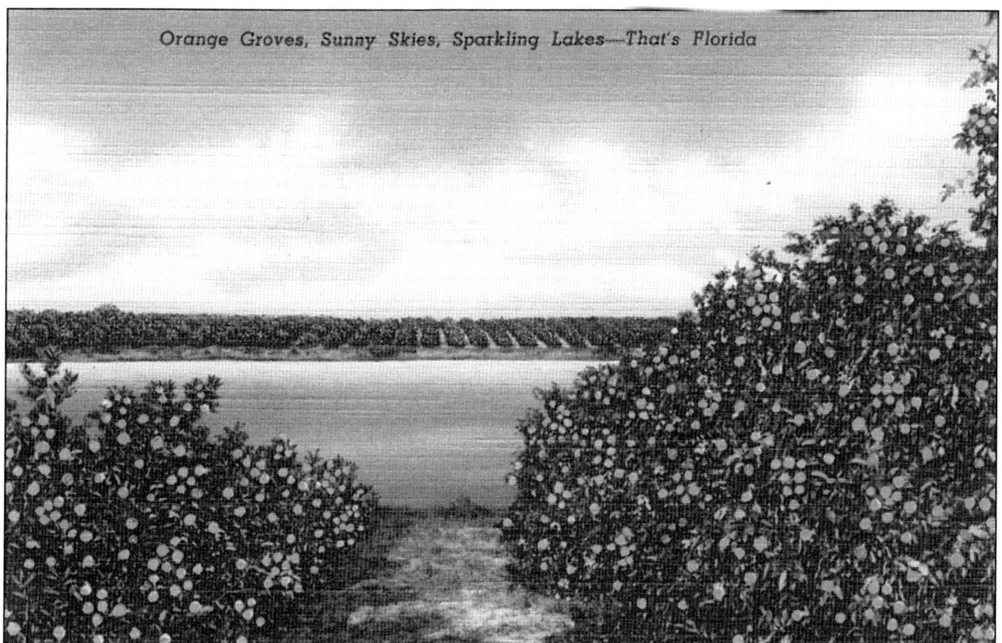

"Orange Groves, Sunny Skies, Sparkling Lakes—That's Florida" is the title on this card. At one time, citrus was a major agricultural crop in Pinellas County. After several freezes and the increase of land value for housing, many grove owners sold out. As of 2004, only .3 percent of the land area in Pinellas County is agricultural.

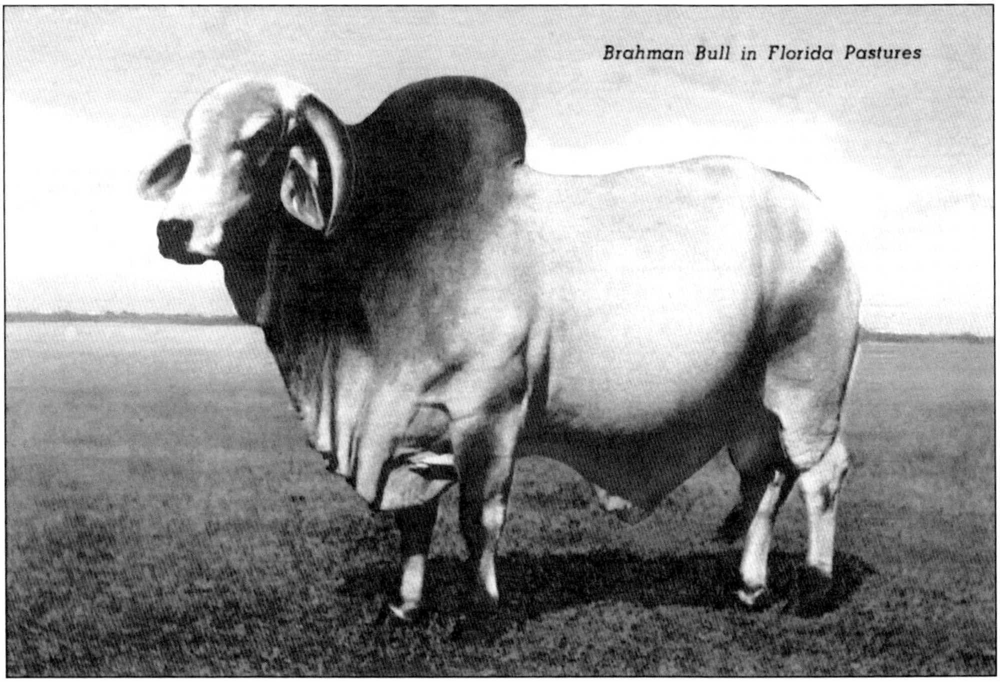

In the early 1900s, the American Brahman cattle were the first beef cattle developed in the United States. They do well in Florida due to their ability to withstand heat and their resistance to insects and parasites. Characteristic of the breed is the large hump at the top of their shoulder and neck, as well as a have a large dewlap. There were many free-range areas in the early 1900s.

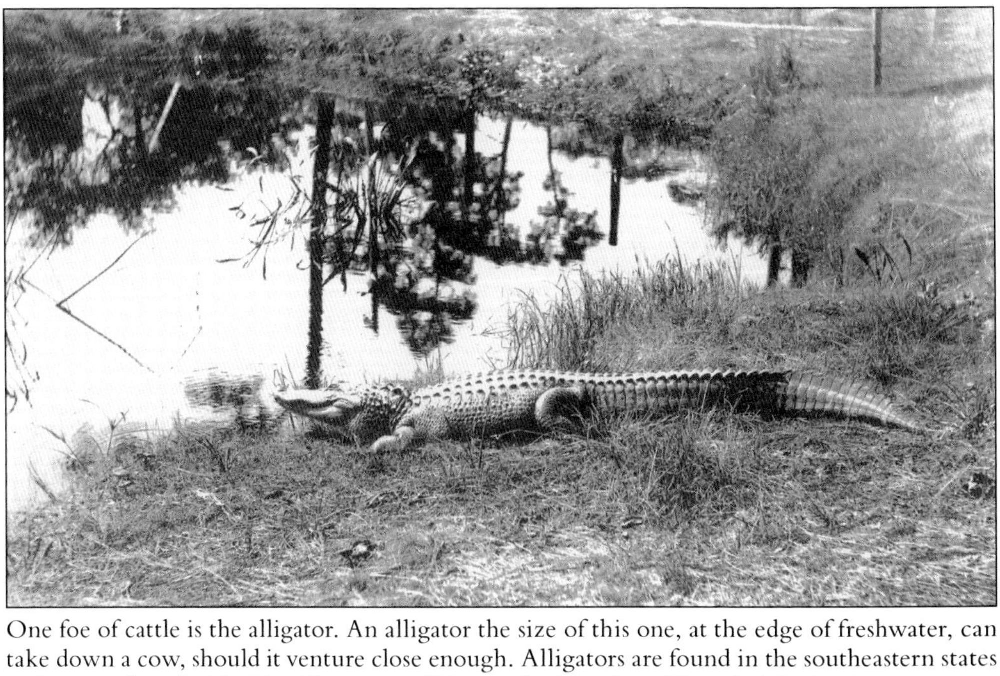

One foe of cattle is the alligator. An alligator the size of this one, at the edge of freshwater, can take down a cow, should it venture close enough. Alligators are found in the southeastern states and everywhere in Florida. (Courtesy of Tarpon Springs Area Historical Society.)

The sign posted on this palm tree leaning over the Anclote River reads, "The people should make it unpleasant for any man that kills an alligator." The person who felt kindly toward alligators probably felt that they were here before the people were. Note the tall pine trees in the far background. (Courtesy of Tarpon Springs Area Historical Society.)

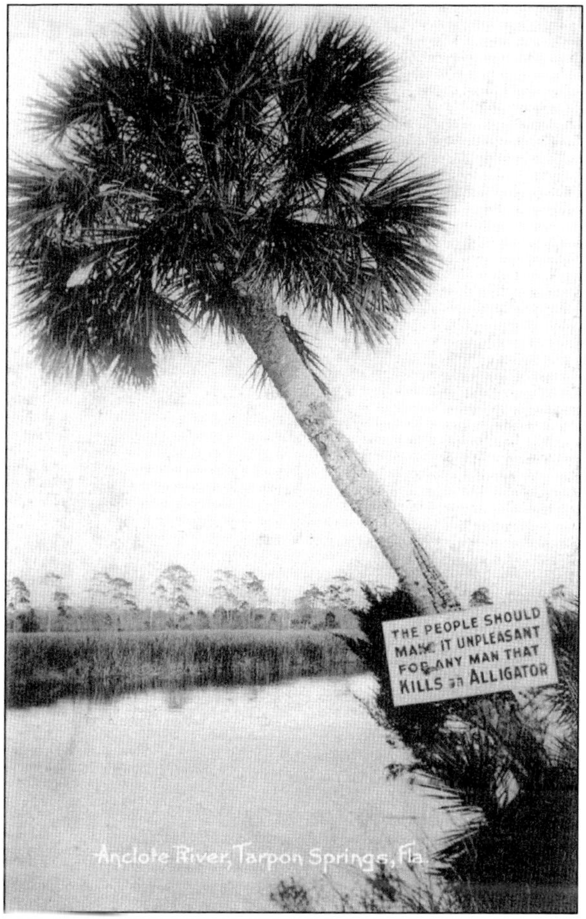

Alligators prefer freshwater but will venture into saltwater. This very large alligator proves that they can be found in any type of water, even brackish. This image was captured on the Anclote River, and this alligator must frequent this shore area because the typical vegetation growth seen along the banks of the river is absent where the gator is entering the water. (Courtesy of Tarpon Springs Area Historical Society.)

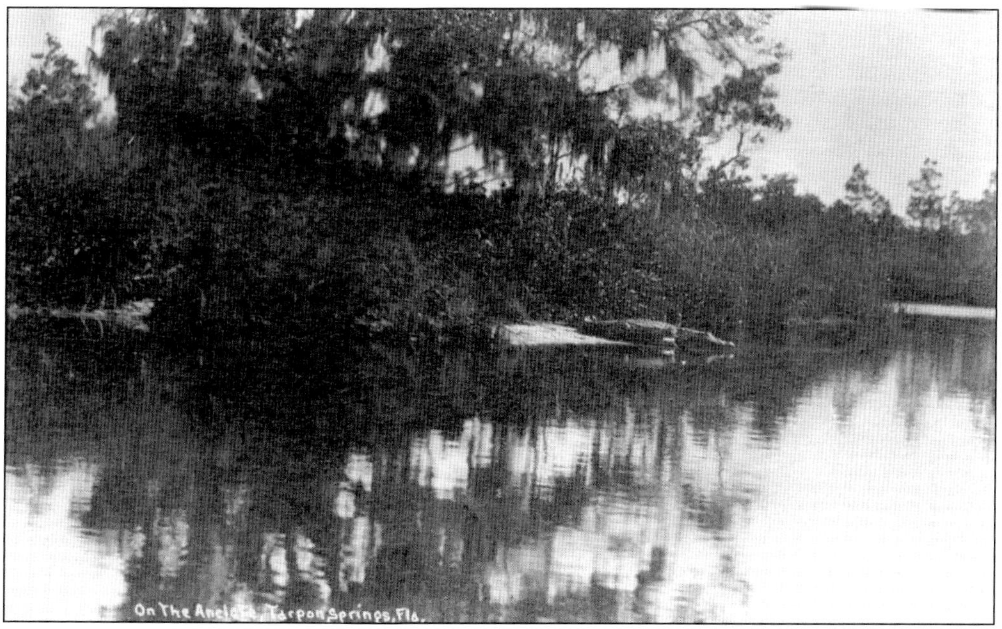

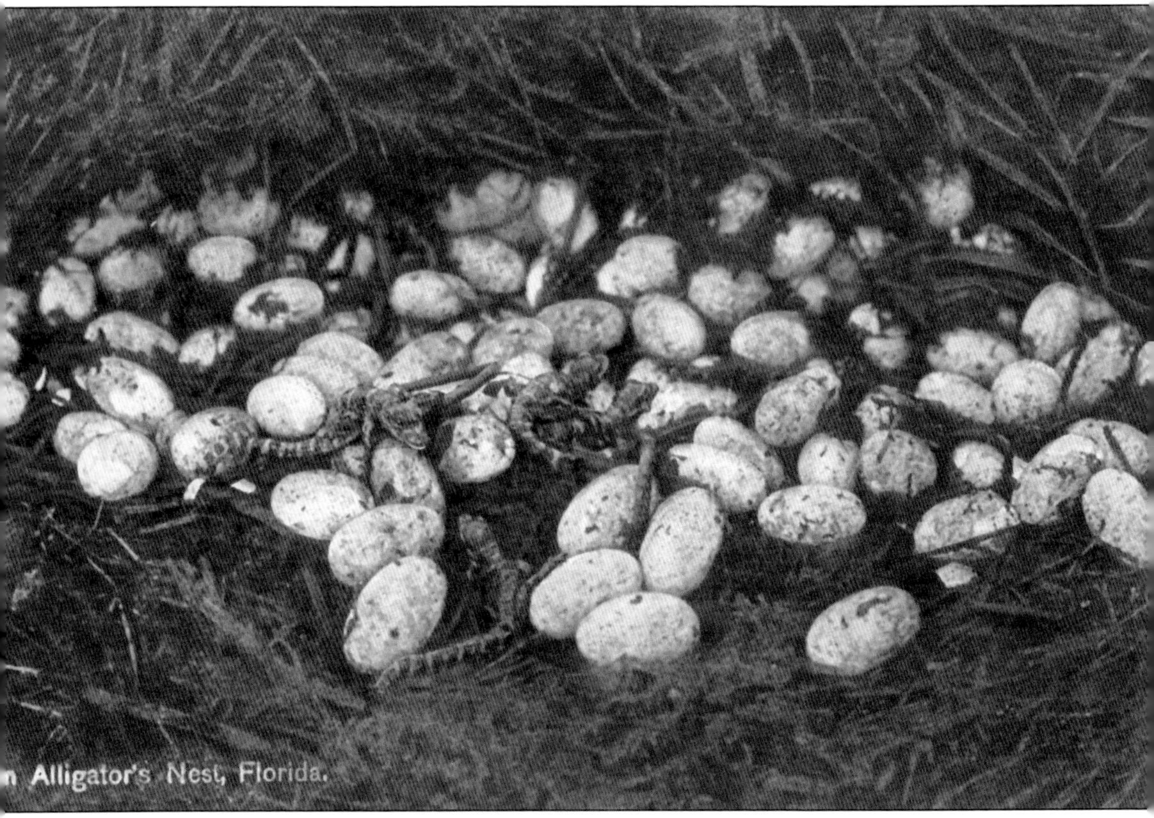

This is a rare shot of alligator eggs as they hatch. Taking this photograph was particularly risky for the photographer because mother alligators are highly protective of their young. A female alligator will lay 25 to 60 hard-shelled eggs, three inches in length, in a five-to-seven-foot-diameter mound-shaped nest of vegetation and mud. After incubating for around two months, the eggs will hatch. At the first calls of the hatchlings, the mother will return and stay in the same area with them for a while. They are vulnerable when young, as everything wants to eat them; they are only about 8 to 10 inches long. Alligators, the state reptiles, eat fish, turtles, snakes, frogs, small mammals, birds, and invertebrates; grow up to 800 pounds and 13 feet long; and hibernate in dens during winter. The word "alligator" is derived from the Spanish words *el lagarto*. (Courtesy of R.R. Mountain)

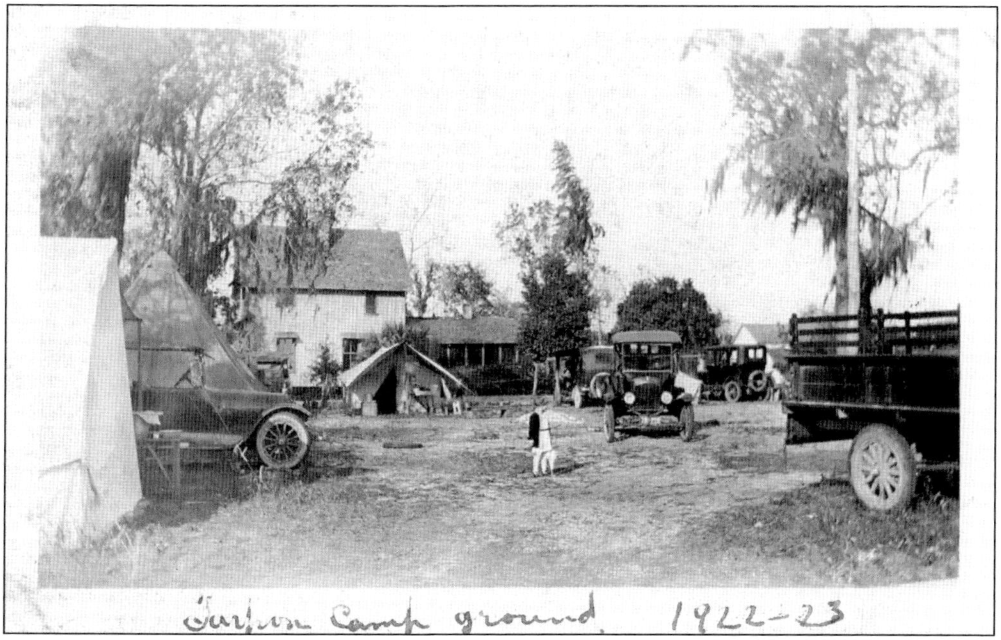

Post World War I saw an increase in travel as Americans took to the road. Vacation travel was no longer a luxury for only the wealthy. People packed their belongings, grabbed a tent, gassed up the automobile, and went on road trips. Florida was building good roads quickly during the 1920s to entice tourists and their dollars. Tarpon Springs afforded many beautiful natural settings in which to camp, especially the area surrounding Lake Tarpon. There also was a diverse culture, attractive and interesting to vacationers. Florida welcomed the Tin Can Tourists of the World, an association of tent and vehicle travelers, who established themselves in DeSota [*sic*] Park in nearby Tampa in 1919. This c. 1922 Tarpon campground is identified on the back of the postcard as a free campground, although its location is unknown. (Courtesy of Tarpon Springs Area Historical Society.)

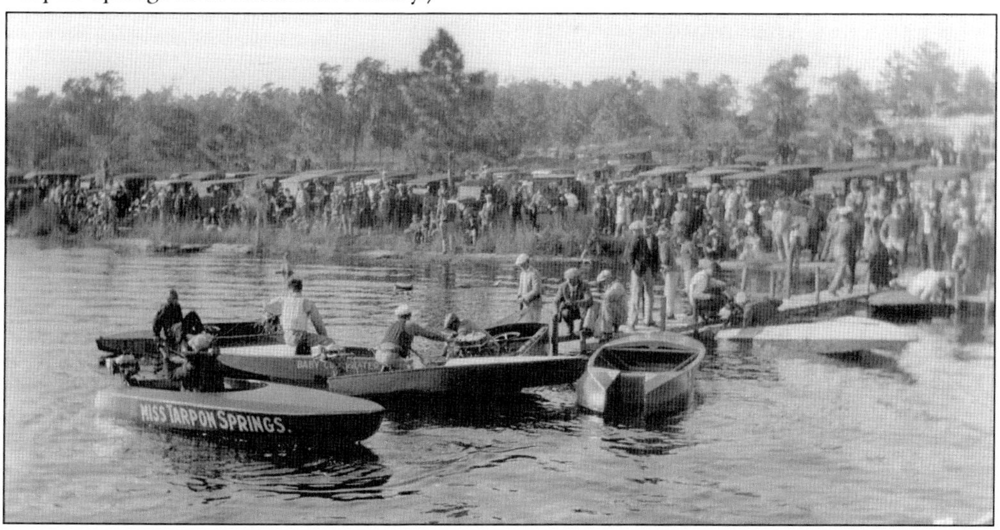

In the late 19th century, a favorite pastime of those first settling Tarpon Springs was sailboat races. In the 1920s, small powerboat races would take place in the bayous. (Courtesy of Tarpon Springs Area Historical Society.)

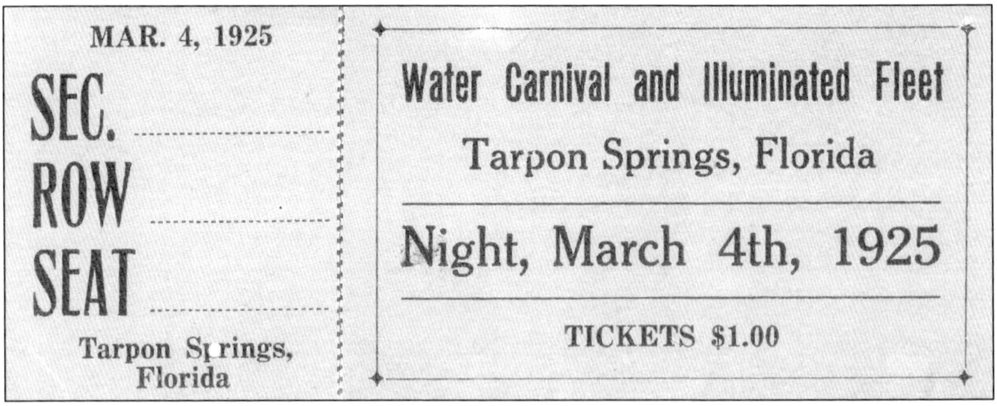

Tarpon Springs put on a water carnival in the winters of 1924, 1925, and 1926. There were many activities to participate in and equal fun for spectators. This is a ticket from the 1925 evening event. (Courtesy of Tarpon Springs Area Historical Society.)

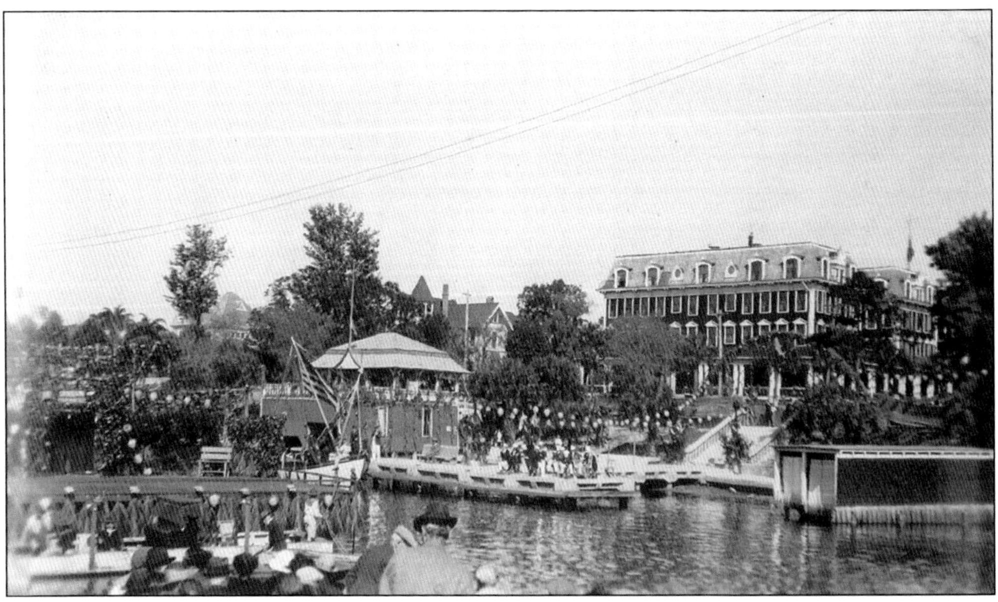

This postcard from the first Tarpon Springs Water Carnival shows the city dock decorated with hanging Japanese lanterns. A sponge-diving exhibition boat is seen just beyond the dock. They offered a demonstration of their hard-helmet diving. (Courtesy of Tarpon Springs Area Historical Society.)

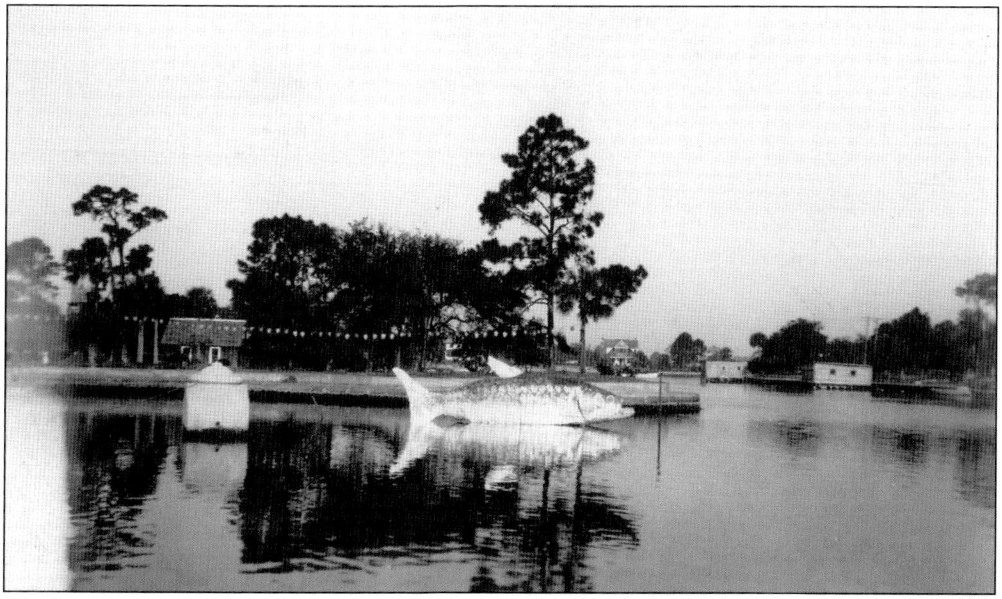

The largest catch of all, this tarpon float, built by Arthur R. Kaminis at the Anclote Shipbuilding Company, dazzled everyone in the Illuminated Fleet Parade. A 1926 accounting report showed receipts and payouts of over $19,000 for the event. (Courtesy of Tarpon Springs Area Historical Society.)

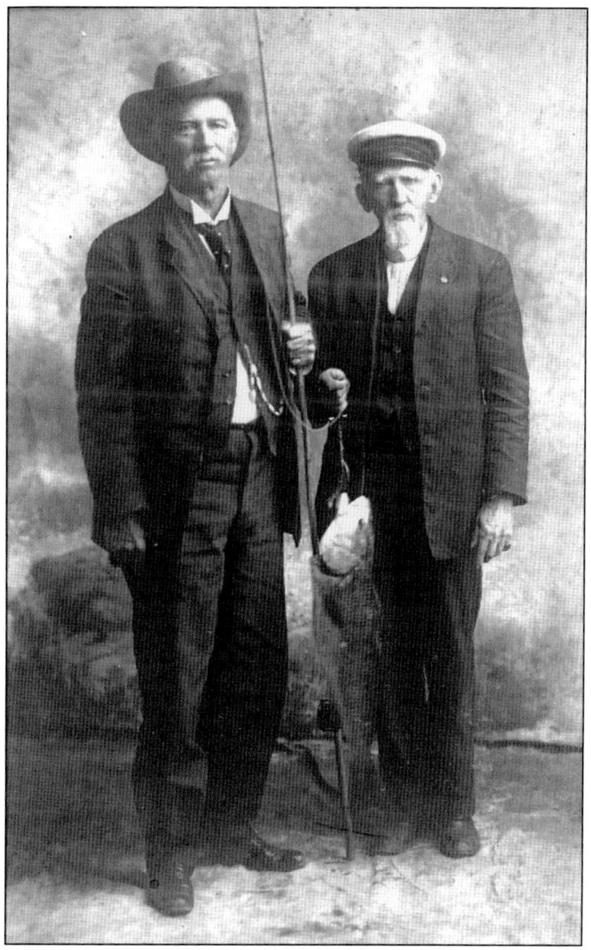

Brothers Ira and Nathan Cadwallader had their picture taken to document a successful dinner catch. Ira, who fought in the Civil War for one year in 1865, had a winter home in Tarpon Springs. (Courtesy of Tarpon Springs Area Historical Society.)

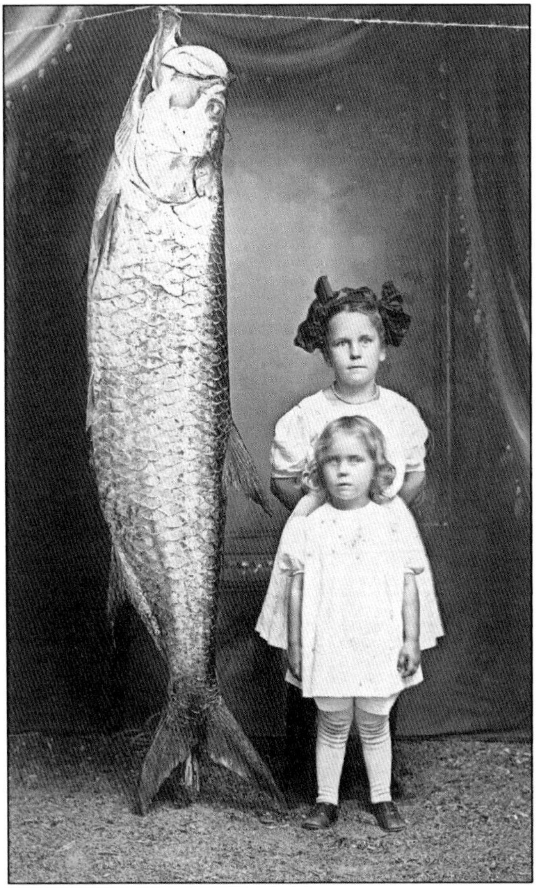

Emily and Ernestine Meres are dwarfed by what must be a six-foot tarpon. This real-photo postcard was probably taken outside by the bayou with a backdrop hung behind the young girls. (Courtesy of Hammond Salley.)

The girls' basketball team poses with their coaches. From left to right are (first row) Helen Hunt, unidentified, America ?, and Ruby Noblit; (second row) Margaret Thompson, Katherine Meres, Eva Whitcomb, Bessie Goodwin, and Florence ?; (third row) unidentified, Leola Boyette, Martha Fernald, and unidentified. (Courtesy of Tarpon Springs Area Historical Society.)

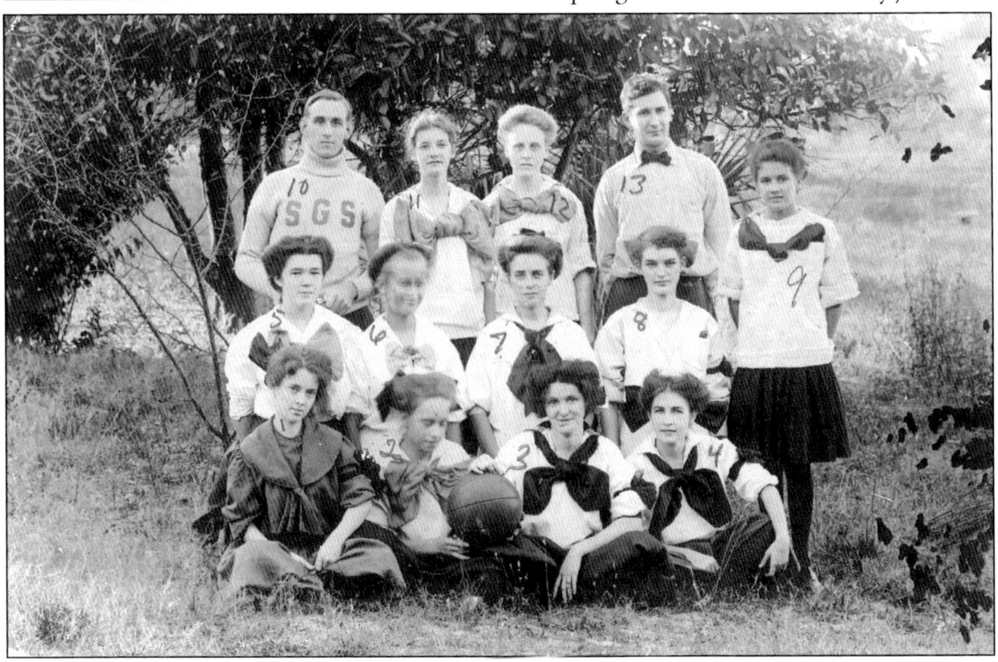

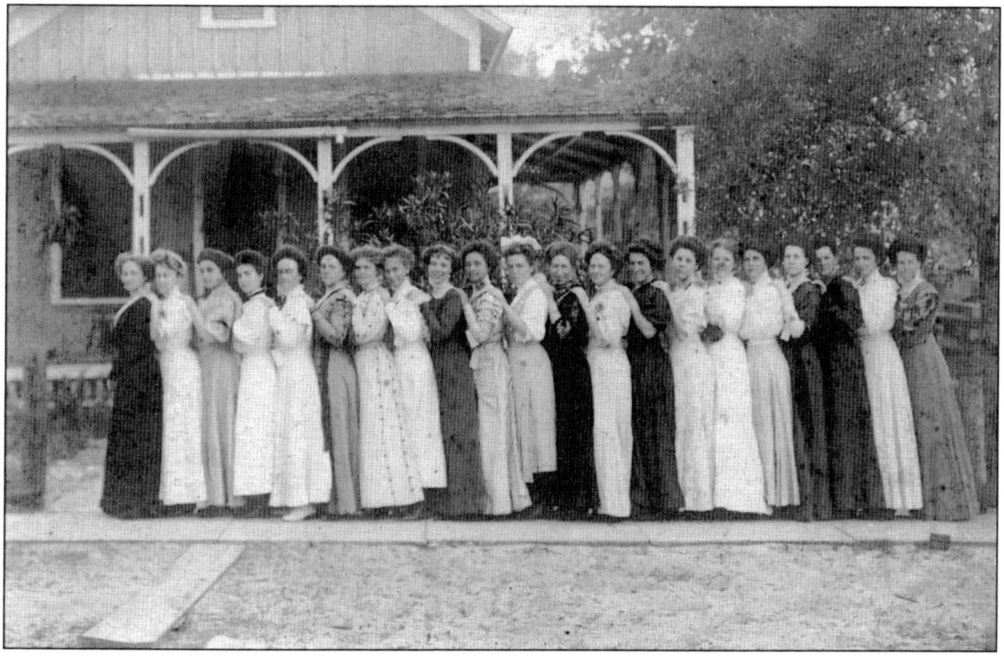

Clubs formed a backbone to the community. Outside of the Ferns Hotel owned by Walter and Amelia Meres, members of the Garden Club gather for a group portrait. (Courtesy of Hammond Salley.)

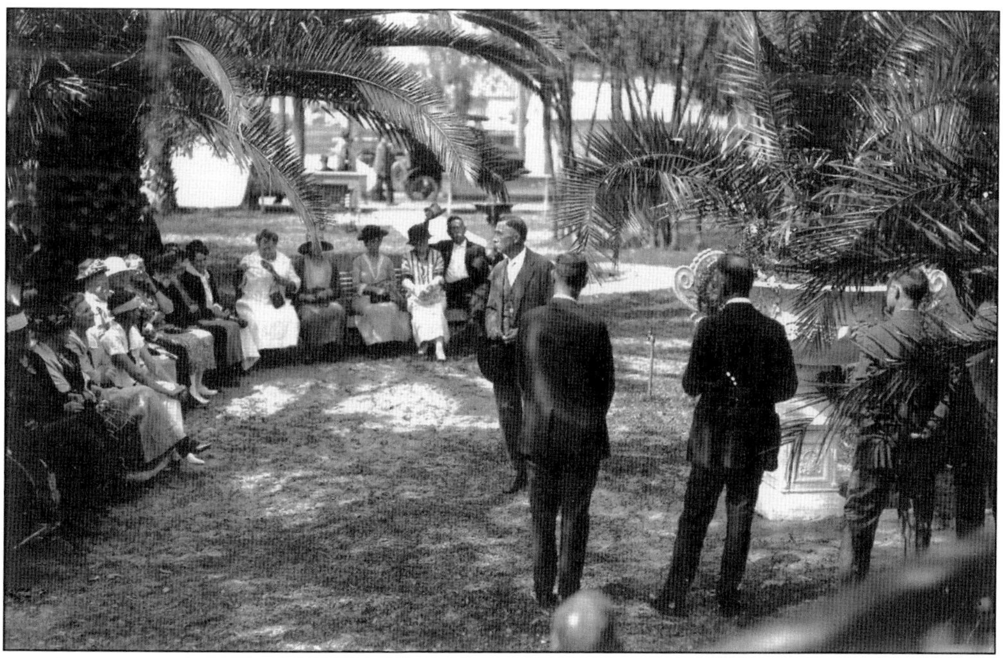

Amelia Mother Meres was memorialized with a presentation of an urn in her honor at the city park where she once lived and gardened, now located at the southeast corner of Tarpon and Pinellas Avenues. (Courtesy of Tarpon Springs Area Historical Society.)

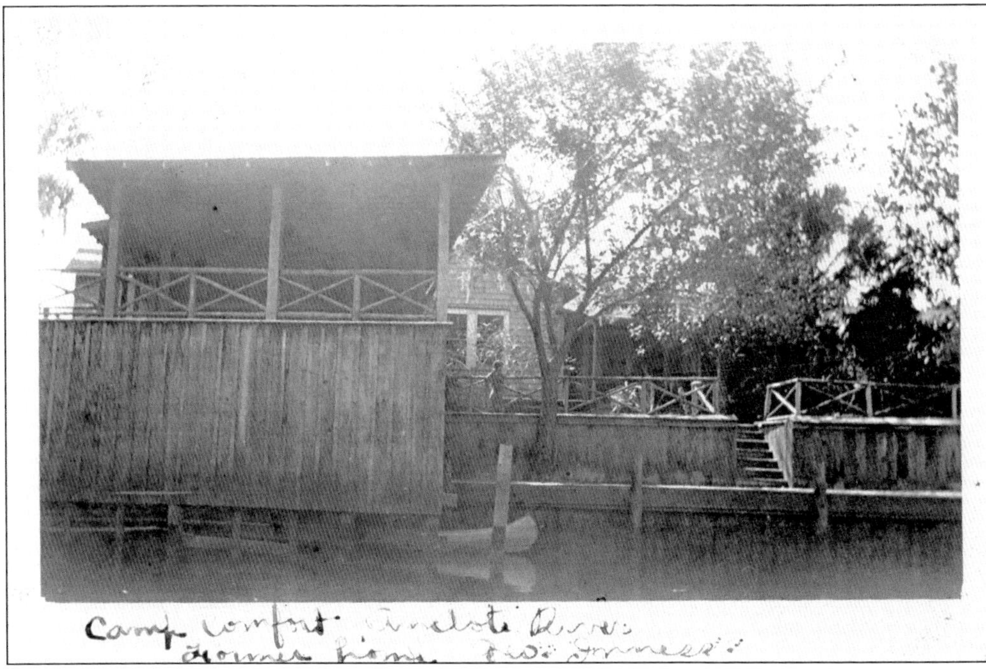

Camp Comfort, located on the Anclote River, was the artist studio of George Inness Jr. He and his father, George Inness Sr., were both renowned landscape artists. George Jr. painted a triptych to replace windows blown out of the Unitarian Universalist Church of Tarpon Springs on Grand Boulevard and Read Street by a hurricane in 1918. Tarpon Springs is still considered an artists' mecca today. (Courtesy of Tarpon Springs Area Historical Society.)

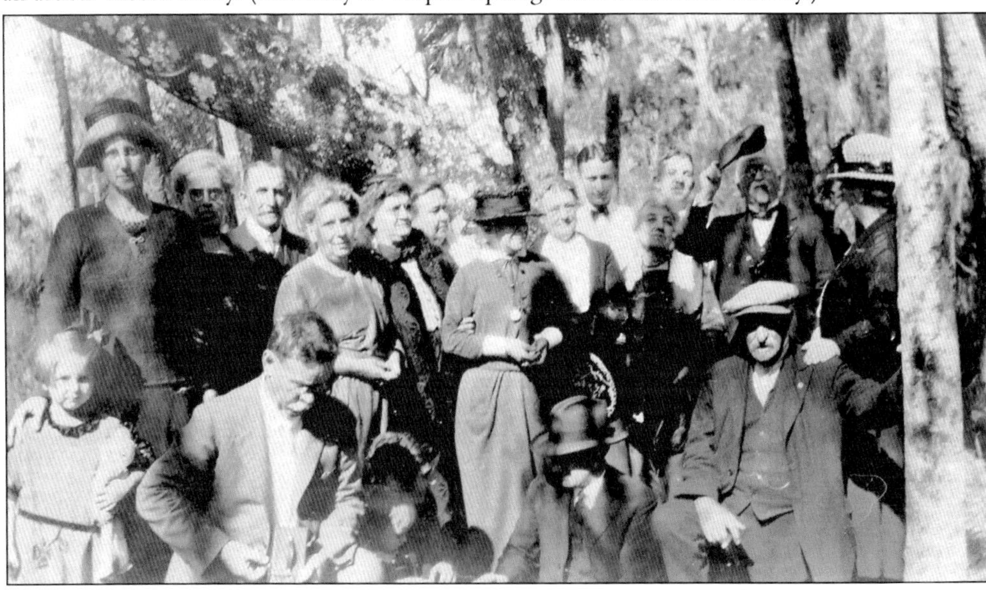

Outings into the natural world were a part of social life. Boats could bring passengers into areas inaccessible by land. This group went up the Anclote River to Pinder's Landing, located about 12 miles upriver in 1923 for a picnic under one his several thatched-roof pavilions. They saw lots of turtles and strange birds and one large alligator. (Courtesy of Tarpon Springs Area Historical Society.)

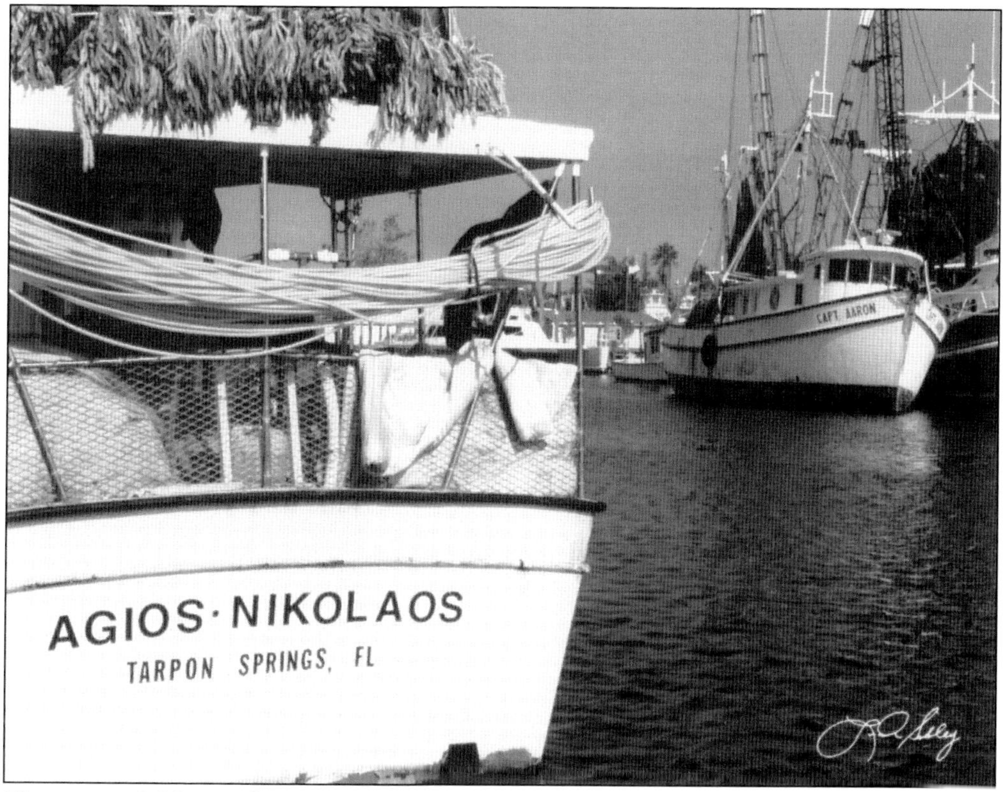

The name of this Greek sponging boat, the *Agios Nikolaos,* translates into "St. Nicholas." In the top left, finger sponges can be seen hanging upside down. The channel in the river can accommodate large vessels. The *Miss Suzanne, Charlee Girl,* and *Nancy Joe*, seen below, comprise three of the shrimp fleet. The nets used to catch the shrimp are seen in their upright position. (Both, courtesy of Lisa Sibley, photographer.)

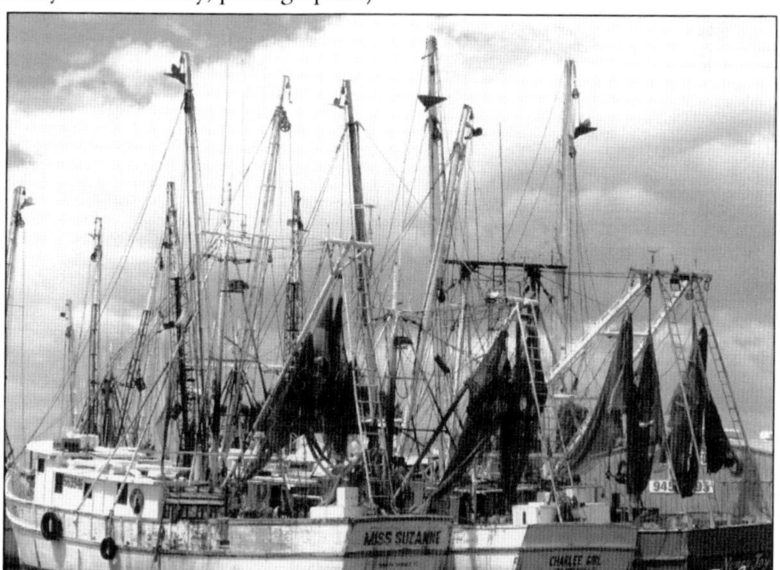

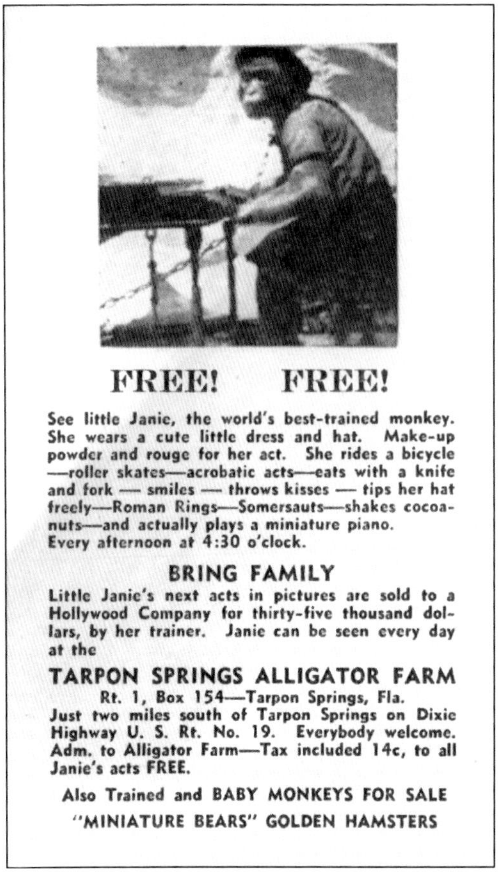

At one time, Tarpon Springs had an exotic animal zoo located close to where Anderson Park is now on Highway 19. There, one could see many animals including monkeys, wild cats, and alligators. Located on Alternate Highway 19 was the Tarpon Springs Alligator Farm, as promoted in this postcard featuring a monkey. The alligator farm's former location is now home to the Suncoast Primate Sanctuary. The original organization was established in 1954 by Robert and Mae Noell. (Courtesy of Sam H. Mack.)

The Gasparilla Pirate Festival enjoyed its first celebration in May 1904. The city of Tampa attempted to defend itself against a mock invasion of pirates led by Capt. Jose Gaspar. This vehicle took part in the Gasparilla Day parade. (Courtesy of Tampa Bay History Center.)

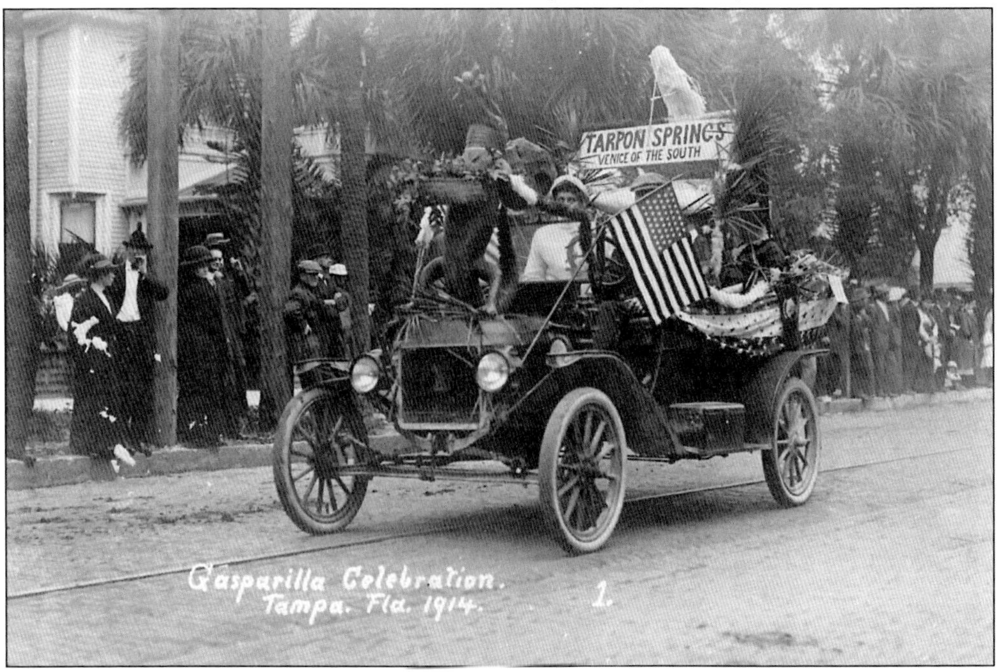

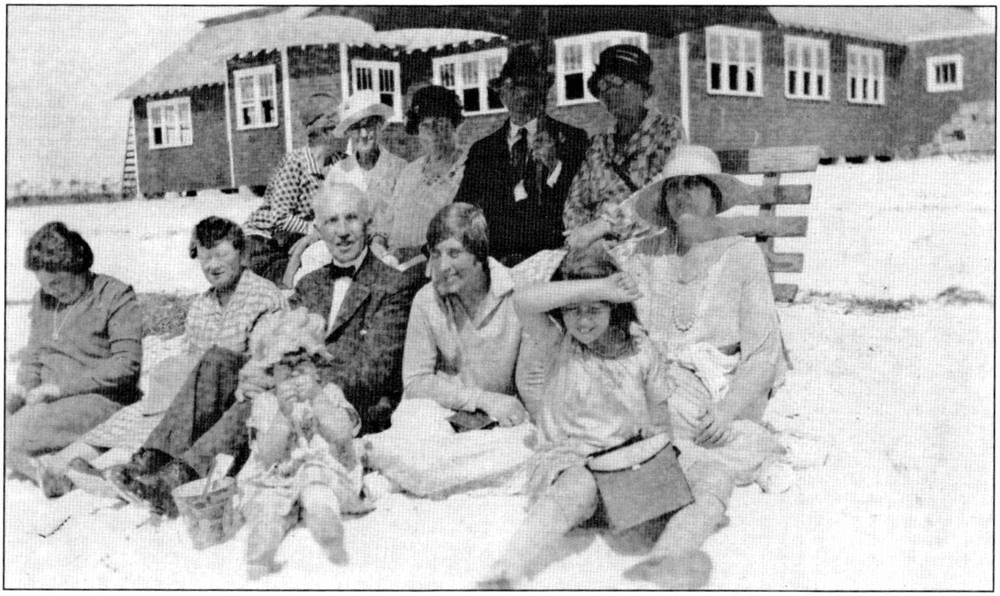

Enjoying the beach and sunshine at Sunset Beach is the H.G. Arnold family, as identified on the back of this postcard. Nick and Irene Nicholas donated land to the City of Tarpon Springs in the 1920s to be used as a free public beach in perpetuity. (Courtesy of Tarpon Springs Area Historical Society.)

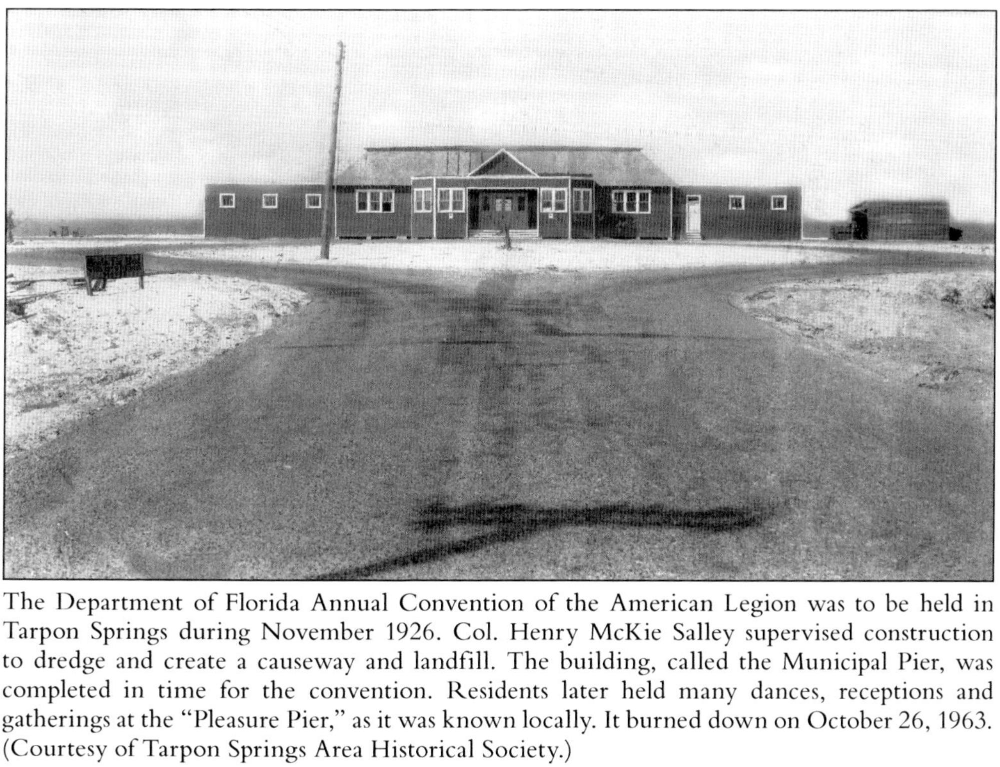

The Department of Florida Annual Convention of the American Legion was to be held in Tarpon Springs during November 1926. Col. Henry McKie Salley supervised construction to dredge and create a causeway and landfill. The building, called the Municipal Pier, was completed in time for the convention. Residents later held many dances, receptions and gatherings at the "Pleasure Pier," as it was known locally. It burned down on October 26, 1963. (Courtesy of Tarpon Springs Area Historical Society.)

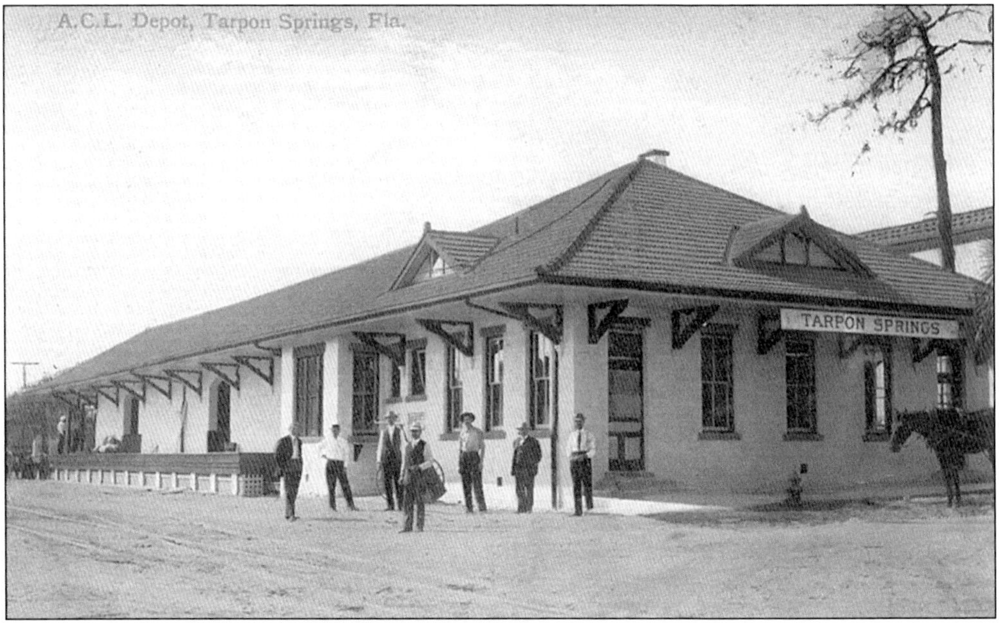

After a 1908 fire that destroyed the first wooden depot, a new depot was built one block north and became operational in 1909. Passenger service was discontinued in the 1970s, and freight service was discontinued in 1985. Arrangements were made for a special passenger trip during the centennial celebration of Tarpon Springs. (Courtesy of Tarpon Springs Area Historical Society.)

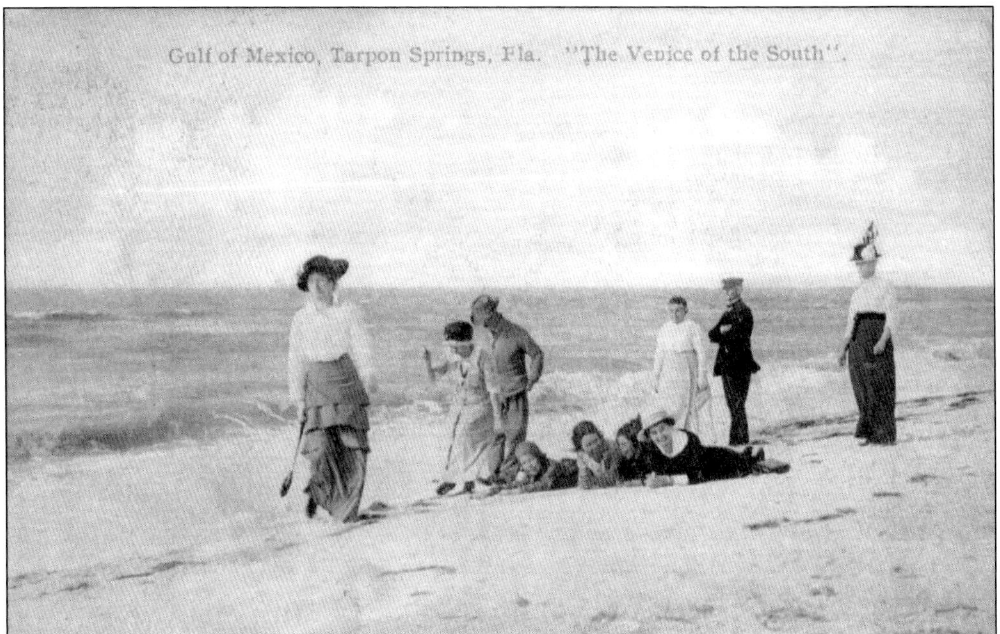

The people in this c. 1915 postcard enjoy a day at the beach on the Gulf of Mexico. It appears that there is a lighthouse keeper in uniform, second from right, who is escorting them around. Pale-skinned people during the Victorian era preferred to remain covered. It was not until the 1920s that sunbathing became vogue. (Courtesy of Sam H. Mack.)

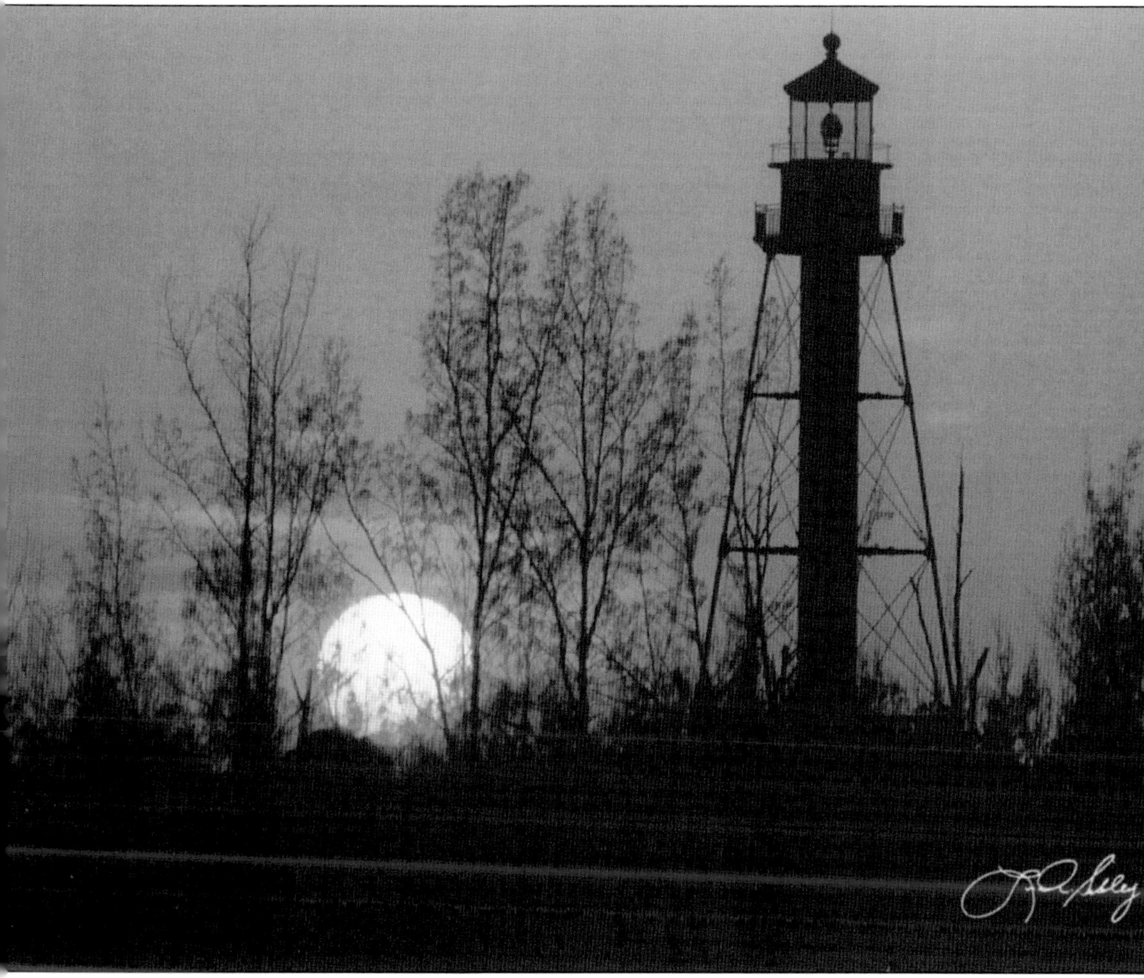

The sun quietly sets past the Anclote Key Lighthouse and island. This 2009 serene perspective serves to remind that all are protected and watched over by those above. The beacon has been relit and will show all safely home. (Courtesy of Lisa Sibley, photographer.)